W9-AZG-920

First Impressions

First Impressions

175 Memorable Appetizers and First Courses

Betty Rosbottom

William Morrow and Company, Inc.
New York

Library of Congress Cataloging-in-Publication Data

Rosbottom, Betty.
    First impressions : 175 memorable appetizers and first courses / Betty Rosbottom.
      p.   cm.
    Includes index.
    ISBN 0-688-10142-9
    1. Appetizers.   I. Title.
    TX740.R59   1992   91-42489
    641.8′12—dc20   CIP

Printed in the United States of America

First Edition

1 2 3 4 5 6 7 8 9 10

BOOK DESIGN BY PETER A. DAVIS

For my family, Ronny and Michael,
for their patience and understanding
and
for my friends, Tom and Nancy, Sheri,
Emily, Bob, and Merribell,
for being a second family to me
while I worked on this book

Acknowledgments

A cookbook is rarely the work of one person, and this one certainly reflects the collective efforts of many people. Emily Bell, Sheri Lisak, and June McCarthy worked countless days to help create the recipes. Donna White meticulously transcribed hard-to-read, handwritten recipes to the computer. And Elly Persing and Cindy Katz mailed completed recipes to testers all over the country and later promptly reported their evaluations. More than thirty volunteers tested 175 recipes for this collection. I would like to thank all of them, but especially Claire Farina, Sara Evans, Wendy Kersker, Ruth McNeal, Alice Ford, Sue Wilmoth, and Shirley Rubinstein.

Judith Weber, my agent, believed in this book from the first time I mentioned the idea and found a wonderful home for it at William Morrow. Harriet Bell, editor *extraordinaire*, has looked at page after page of the manuscript with an incredibly sensitive and astute eye and has guided me through every step. And Lisa Ekus, talented publicist, has spent many hours helping me chart the course for this book. My appreciation also goes to editorial assistant Valerie Cimino and to talented photographer Jerry Simpson.

To Karin Welzel and Sue Dawson at the *Columbus Dispatch* and to Russ Parsons, Food Editor at the Los Angeles Times Syndicate, I offer thanks for carefully editing my weekly columns, where many of these recipes first appeared. I would also like to thank the editors at *Bon Appétit* magazine for publishing some of these recipes over the past few years.

I am very grateful to Lazarus Department Stores for providing me with a beautiful teaching and testing kitchen, where many of these recipes and ideas were developed. And, to the students at

La Belle Pomme Cooking School I offer my warmest thanks for your support and enthusiasm—you are the ones who first suggested the idea for a book of appetizers and encouraged me to write it.

My close friends, Nancy and Tom Lurie, Merribell Parsons, Martha and Bob Davis, and Bob Corea, have been willing tasters, sampling both the memorable dishes as well as those best forgotten; they have invited me out to dinner often after my long days in the kitchen and, most important of all, have never been more than a phone call away when I needed encouragement. I truly cannot find words adequate enough to express my gratitude and affection for their kindnesses.

Finally, I would like to thank my husband and son, who are my anchors. They have indulged my days of frenzied work schedules when there was little time left over for them; they have tasted myriad dishes for this collection; and they (especially my husband) have given me invaluable advice about the manuscript. Thank you both for your love and support.

Contents

Introduction

As soon as I put down my whisk and turn off the stove, signaling the end of cooking class, students always appear at my side anxious to discuss menus they are planning. Confidently, they list the entrées and desserts for their meals, but when I ask, "What are you serving before dinner?," there are often blank stares. I have seen looks of panic as students tell me they have invited twenty or thirty or forty people over "just for drinks and hors d'oeuvres," but have no idea what to prepare. And the readers of my column on entertaining often write or call me to suggest that I include more appetizer recipes in my weekly articles. Over the years, these requests became so frequent that I began to carry around a mental list of appetizers, for everything from pre-dinner occasions to cocktail parties. Finally, I decided that there was a need for a cookbook devoted entirely to the art of *l'hors d'oeuvrerie*.

Entertaining is one of the great joys in my life, whether at a small, casual, impromptu event or a carefully planned fête for a hundred. So the idea of working on a book of appetizers— quintessential party food—was enticing. I kept three goals in mind while developing these recipes. Paramount was that the dishes be as attractive to the eye as to the palate. Presentation is especially important for "starters," because they indeed give guests the first impression of the style that will define a dinner or party. Consequently, for most of the recipes in this collection, I have provided suggestions for distinctive garnishes. Next, I never forgot that today's hosts lead busy lives. Since it does take time to cook and entertain, I have made every effort in these recipes to help you do so more efficiently. At every step possible, there are make-ahead directions, as well as suggestions for using prepared ingredients such as store-bought puff pastry and phyllo dough, mayonnaise, and smoked or cured meats. Last, I have paid attention to the nutritional concerns of today's cooks. When I first started teaching in the 1970s, eggs, butter, and cream were a given for any serious cook. These ingredients do appear throughout this book, but I have tried to reduce the amounts or I have used alternatives, such as olive oil for butter, without sacrificing taste. I will leave it to some readers to replace butter with margarine or with a butter-margarine spread (which I use frequently myself), or to use egg substitutes rather than eggs or light mayonnaise in place of regular. Since party food is offered in small tastes or as mere nibbles, the amount of rich ingredients will often be less than in an entrée or a dessert. In fact, appetizers may be the only way some people can even try forbidden foods!

The recipes in this book range from traditional ones with new twists to some unique inventions. Many of the dishes reflect my interest in foreign cultures, especially those of France, Italy, and India. Classic French tartlets with unexpected fillings, Italian crostini with tempting toppings, and a host of dishes flavored with curry are redolent of these cuisines. Many of these foods reflect my abiding interest in our own South: Cornbread muffins and biscuits, sliced and filled with savory stuffings, and Creole dipping sauce are links to my Southern heritage.

I have benefited from having a host of willing co-chefs and experimenters for this project, and these recipes have been tested and retested many times. However, keep in mind that using the best and freshest ingredients is essential to the success of any dish. Also remember that to ignore even a small detail can turn a dish that is a sure thing into a near miss.

Working on this book has involved drawing on the technical as well as the artistic skills of many talented professional cooks, food writers, and friends. Appetizers are too often thought of as marginal, less significant foods, and they deserve a new status. They should be works of art, albeit simple ones, perfectly prepared and presented. I hope then that this collection will enable you to create a whole new repertoire of special appetizers that will leave your guests with many memorable first impressions.

Savory Scones, Biscuits, and Muffins

Several years ago, while visiting in Vancouver, British Columbia, a friend and I had afternoon tea at one of the city's well-known hotels. We ordered large, sweet scones and spread them with marmalade and thick cream. Later that night, I ate dinner with a group of food professionals in one of the area's most interesting restaurants. The first thing we sampled was a plate of small savory scones (made without the sugar found in the traditional tea scones) served with herbed butters. They were the hit of the evening and for me the most memorable dish. Since that trip, I have often served such diminutive scones as appetizers, accompanied by a variety of fillings. This chapter includes recipes for such openers: crusty scones with tomato-basil butter and walnut scones with blue cheese and pears.

Warm-from-the-oven, bite-sized biscuits and muffins with special fillings are also perfect but untraditional party food. Try the cornbread muffins filled with Saga blue cheese and prosciutto or the thin crispy buttermilk biscuits spread with cranberry butter and topped with smoked turkey. If your guests are like mine, they will quickly devour these tempting little treats.

Savory Scones with Tomato-Basil Butter

Bite-sized scones filled, while piping hot, with a dollop of creamy tomato-basil butter take only minutes to assemble and bake. The colorful butter can be made ahead and refrigerated or frozen.

Makes 30 to 35 scones

TOMATO-BASIL BUTTER

½ cup peeled, seeded, and chopped ripe tomatoes (1 to 2 medium tomatoes)
8 tablespoons (1 stick) unsalted butter, softened
¾ teaspoon minced garlic
1½ teaspoons fresh thyme or ½ teaspoon dried
3 tablespoons chopped fresh basil, preferred, or 1 tablespoon dried
Salt and freshly ground black pepper to taste

SCONES

2 cups all-purpose flour, sifted
1 teaspoon salt
1 tablespoon baking powder
1 cup plus 2 tablespoons whipping or heavy cream

Several sprigs of basil, for garnish

1. To prepare the tomato butter, place the tomatoes, butter, garlic, thyme, and basil in the bowl of an electric mixer and beat on medium speed until the mixture is smooth and creamy and a light red color, about 3 to 4 minutes. Taste and season generously with salt and pepper.

2. Shape the butter into a log about 1½ inches in diameter and 12 inches long. Wrap tightly in plastic wrap and refrigerate to firm slightly, about 30 minutes. The butter can be prepared and refrigerated for up to 2 days or frozen. If freezing, wrap in aluminum foil and place in an airtight plastic bag for 1 to 2 weeks. Defrost in the refrigerator for 24 hours and bring to room temperature 30 minutes before using.

3. To prepare the scones, sift together the flour, salt, and baking powder into a mixing bowl. Stirring with a wooden spoon, gradually add 1 cup of the cream to form a soft dough. Knead lightly on a floured surface, handling the dough gently to retain the air needed for the scones to rise, about 20 to 30 seconds.

4. On a floured surface, roll out the dough to a ⅜-inch thickness. Using a 1¾-inch cutter, cut out rounds; you should get 30 to 35. Place on ungreased baking sheets. Brush tops of the scones very lightly with the cream left in the measuring cup plus the remaining 2 tablespoons. The scones can be prepared ahead to this point; cover with plastic wrap and refrigerate for up to 6 hours.

5. To bake the scones, preheat the oven to 425°F.

6. Bake in the center of the oven until the scones have risen and are lightly browned, about 15 minutes. The scones are best eaten immediately, but they can be made ahead if necessary. Cool completely and store at cool room temperature in tightly covered plastic bags for up to a day. Reheat the scones in a preheated 350°F. oven, about 10 to 12 minutes.

7. To serve, split the scones and fill with ⅓-inch-thick slices of the tomato butter. Arrange the scones on a serving tray and garnish the tray with a cluster of basil sprigs. Serve hot, as the tomato butter starts to melt.

✳ Santa Fe Scones with Smoked Chicken and Cherry Tomatoes

Chili powder, cayenne pepper, Monterey Jack cheese, and chopped red peppers give these scones a Southwestern flavor. Sliced tomatoes and smoked chicken or turkey make a perfect filling.

Makes 30 to 35 scones

SCONES

2 cups sifted all-purpose flour
1 teaspoon salt
1 tablespoon baking powder
1 teaspoon chili powder
½ teaspoon cayenne pepper
½ teaspoon freshly ground black pepper
4 ounces grated Monterey Jack cheese (about 1 cup)
1 cup minced sweet red pepper
1 cup plus 2 tablespoons whipping or heavy cream

1 pint cherry tomatoes or 5 to 6 plum tomatoes, thinly sliced
10 to 12 ounces smoked chicken or turkey, thinly sliced

1. To prepare the scones, sift together the flour, salt, baking powder, chili powder, cayenne pepper, and black pepper into a mixing bowl. Add the cheese and minced red pepper and toss to coat with the flour mixture. Stirring with a wooden spoon, gradually add 1 cup of the cream to form a soft dough. Knead lightly on a floured surface, handling the dough gently to retain the air needed for the scones to rise, about 20 to 30 seconds.

2. On a floured surface, roll out the dough to a ⅜-inch thickness. Using a 1¾-inch cutter, cut out rounds; you should get 30 to 35. Place on ungreased baking sheets. Brush the tops of the scones lightly with the cream left in the measuring cup plus the remaining 2 tablespoons. The scones can be prepared ahead to this point; cover with plastic wrap and refrigerate for up to 6 hours.

3. When ready to bake the scones, preheat the oven to 425°F.

4. Bake the scones in the center of the oven until they have risen and are lightly browned, about 15 minutes. The scones are best eaten immediately, but they can be made ahead. Cool completely and store at cool room temperature in tightly closed plastic bags for up to a day. Reheat the scones in a preheated 350°F. oven, about 10 to 12 minutes.

5. To serve, split the scones and fill with the sliced tomatoes and smoked chicken or turkey. Arrange on a serving tray and serve warm.

NOTE: A star-shaped cutter (1¾ inches wide) can be used to cut out star-shaped scones instead of round ones.

SERVING: Sometimes I put a sprig of cilantro in with the filling to add extra flavor and more color.

VARIATION: Substitute thin slices of dried beef for the smoked poultry.

Walnut Scones with Blue Cheese

Toasted walnuts give these scones a nutty flavor. These are a good starter for an autumn dinner.

Makes 30 to 35 scones

SCONES

2 cups sifted all-purpose flour
1 teaspoon salt
1 tablespoon baking powder
⅔ cup finely chopped toasted walnuts (page 268)
1¼ cups whipping or heavy cream, plus more if needed

10 to 12 ounces smooth blue cheese, such as Maytag blue or Saga blue, cut into thin slices
2 to 3 ripe Bartlett pears, cored and seeded, cut into ¼-inch wedges
1 bunch watercress, tough stems removed

1. To prepare the scones, sift together the flour, salt, and baking powder into a mixing bowl. Add the walnuts and toss to coat with the flour mixture. Stirring with a wooden spoon, gradually add ½ cup plus 1 tablespoon of the cream to form a soft dough. Knead lightly on a floured surface, handling the dough gently to retain the air needed for the scones to rise, about 20 to 30 seconds.

2. On a floured surface, roll out the dough to a ⅜-inch thickness. Using a 1¾-inch cutter, cut out rounds; you should get 30 to 35. Place on ungreased baking sheets. Brush the tops of the scones very lightly with the cream left in the measuring cup plus the remaining 2 tablespoons. The scones can be prepared ahead to this point; cover and refrigerate for up to 6 hours.

3. To bake the scones, preheat the oven to 425°F.

4. Bake in the center of the oven until the scones have risen and are lightly browned, about 15 minutes. The scones are best eaten immediately, but they can be made ahead. Cool completely and store at room temperature in plastic bags for up to a day. Reheat in a preheated 350°F. oven.

5. To serve, split the scones and fill each one with slices of blue cheese, a pear wedge, and a sprig of watercress. Arrange on a serving tray and serve warm.

Buttermilk Biscuits with Smoked Turkey and Cranberry Butter

During the end-of-the-year holiday season, I spread these thin crisp biscuits with cranberry butter, fill them with slices of smoked turkey and watercress, and serve them in a basket lined with long-needled pine branches.

Makes 24 biscuits

CRANBERRY BUTTER

8 tablespoons (1 stick) unsalted butter, slightly softened
¾ cup canned cranberry sauce with whole cranberries

BISCUITS

2 cups all-purpose flour, sifted
2 teaspoons baking powder
½ teaspoon baking soda
1 tablespoon sugar
½ teaspoon salt
2 tablespoons unsalted butter, chilled and cut into small pieces
4 tablespoons vegetable shortening, chilled and cut into small pieces
¾ cup buttermilk
1 egg yolk

¾ to 1 pound smoked turkey, very thinly sliced
1 bunch watercress, broken into sprigs
Salt and freshly ground black pepper to taste

1. To prepare the cranberry butter, place the butter in the bowl of an electric mixer and beat on medium speed until smooth and creamy. Add the cranberry sauce and mix just to blend. Shape the butter into a log about 1½ inches in diameter and 12 inches long. The cranberry butter can be made in advance. Cover tightly with plastic wrap and refrigerate for up to 2 days or freeze for 1 to 2 weeks. Defrost in the refrigerator and bring to room temperature 30 minutes before using.

2. To prepare the biscuits, preheat the oven to 425°F.

3. Place the flour, baking powder, baking soda, sugar, and salt in a mixing bowl. Using a pastry blender or two knives, cut in the butter and shortening until the mixture resembles the texture of coarse cornmeal.

4. Make a well in the center of the dry ingredients and add ½ cup of the buttermilk and the egg yolk. Stir well with a fork to combine. Continue to stir and add enough of the remaining buttermilk, a little at a time, until the dough is soft and pliable. You may not need to add all the milk. Gather the dough into a ball and knead gently about 10 times.

5. Roll the dough out on a floured work surface to a thickness of ¼ to ⅜ inch. Use a 2-inch cookie cutter to cut out 24 rounds. If necessary, gather the scraps of dough together, shape into a ball, and roll out again so that more rounds can be cut. Transfer the biscuits to a lightly greased baking sheet.

6. Bake the biscuits on the center shelf of the oven until golden, about 10 minutes. Remove from the oven and cool 2 to 3 minutes.

7. Split the biscuits and spread each half with about 1 teaspoon of the cranberry butter. Place several slices of smoked turkey and a watercress sprig on each bottom half. Sprinkle with salt and pepper and top with the other half. Arrange the biscuits on a serving tray or place in a basket lined with branches of long-needled pine or with a napkin.

VARIATION: Substitute the Honey-Mustard Mayonnaise on page 264 for the cranberry butter.

Buttermilk Biscuits with Ham, Orange Marmalade, and Mint

The thin crispy biscuits from the preceding recipe are also delicious filled with sliced ham, a dollop of orange marmalade, and a sprig of mint. These savory biscuit sandwiches make perfect appetizers at brunches.

Makes 24 biscuits

1 recipe Buttermilk Biscuits (page 20)
3 tablespoons unsalted butter, melted
½ pound ham such as honey-baked ham, thinly sliced and cut to fit biscuits
¼ cup orange marmalade
1 bunch mint

1. To assemble the biscuits, halve them and brush the insides with the melted butter. Top each bottom half with several slices of ham, a dollop of orange marmalade, and a sprig of mint. Place the other half on top.

2. To serve, arrange the biscuits on a serving tray or place in a napkin-lined basket. Serve warm.

Corn Muffins with Saga Blue and Prosciutto

These miniature corn muffins are best served warm when the cheese is just starting to melt. The muffins can be baked and filled up to an hour in advance and reheated quickly before serving.

Makes 24 muffins

MUFFINS

2 eggs
¾ cup buttermilk
¼ teaspoon baking soda
¾ teaspoon baking powder
¾ teaspoon salt
4 teaspoons vegetable oil
1 cup yellow cornmeal
Nonstick vegetable cooking cooking spray

6 ounces Saga blue cheese, cut into ¼-inch-thick slices
3 ounces thinly sliced prosciutto

1. To prepare the muffins, preheat the oven to 450°F.

2. In a mixing bowl, lightly mix the eggs and buttermilk. Add the baking soda, baking powder, salt, and oil. Mix well. Add the cornmeal and stir well.

3. Spray two miniature muffin tins (1¾ inches in diameter), preferably non-stick, with vegetable cooking spray. If your tins are not the nonstick variety, spray them twice. Fill each cup about three-quarters full with the cornmeal batter.

4. Place the tins on the center shelf of the oven and bake until the muffins have risen and are just golden in color, about 8 to 10 minutes. Remove from the oven and unmold onto a rack.

5. Let cool about 5 minutes and then slice each muffin in half horizontally. Place slices of cheese cut to fit the muffins on the bottom halves, then place 2 thin slices of prosciutto cut to fit the muffins on top of the cheese. Cover with the muffin tops. The muffins can be prepared up to an hour ahead to this point. Place on a baking sheet lined with aluminum foil, and cover loosely with foil if not serving immediately. Set aside at room temperature.

(continued)

6. To reheat the muffins, preheat the oven to 400°F. Remove the foil covering the muffins and bake on the center oven shelf until the muffins are warm, about 5 minutes. Arrange the muffins on a serving tray. Serve warm.

Corn Muffins du Midi

My Southern heritage and my love of the south of France are combined in this recipe. Piping hot little corn muffins, split and filled with chèvre, tomatoes, fresh basil, and mint, bring to mind the cuisine of both our own South and the Midi of France.

Makes 24 muffins

MUFFINS

2 eggs
¾ cup buttermilk
¼ teaspoon baking soda
¾ teaspoon baking powder
¾ teaspoon salt
4 teaspoons vegetable oil
1 cup yellow cornmeal
Nonstick vegetable cooking spray

6 ounces chèvre, preferably in a log shape, cut into ¼-inch slices
6 cherry tomatoes, cut into ¼-inch slices
24 small basil sprigs, plus more for garnish
24 small mint sprigs, plus more for garnish

1. To prepare the muffins, preheat the oven to 450°F.

2. In a mixing bowl, lightly beat the eggs and buttermilk together. Add the baking soda, baking powder, salt, and oil. Mix well. Add the cornmeal and stir well.

3. Spray two miniature muffin tins (1¾ inches in diameter), preferably nonstick, with vegetable cooking spray. If your tins are not the nonstick variety, spray them twice. Fill each cup about three-quarters full with the cornmeal batter.

4. Place the tins on the center shelf of the oven and bake until the muffins have risen and are just golden in color, about 8 to 10 minutes. Remove from the oven and unmold.

5. Split each muffin in half horizontally. Place a slice of cheese on the bottom half of each muffin, top with a tomato slice, and place a basil sprig and mint sprig on top of each tomato slice. Cover with the muffin tops. Arrange the muffins on a serving tray and garnish the tray with basil and mint sprigs. Serve warm.

Crostini and Open-faced Sandwiches

Crostini, those crisp, toasted slices of bread that the Italians serve with delicious toppings, make perfect hors d'oeuvre fare. In Italy, chicken livers, prosciutto, salami, and cheese are all typical garnishes for these crusty rounds, but more unusual toppings, such as the sautéed wild mushrooms, tomatoes and leeks scented with herbs, or roasted garlic purée included in this chapter are also delicious on crostini.

This section also features little open-faced sandwiches, an American version of crostini. Smoked salmon and Roquefort butter toasts, blue cheese and shrimp toasts, and corned beef and cheese on rye with horseradish cream are particularly attractive combinations.

All of these recipes give advice about how to make these starters well before a party, along with directions for assembling them right before the guests arrive. In this way, you can adapt the preparation time to your own schedule.

Whether used for crostini or open-faced sandwiches, the toasted breads serve the same purpose: They are canvases ready for artistic interpretation. Your success with these recipes should inspire you to create new ones of your own.

Tomato Crostini with Bacon and Basil

Thin slices of French or Italian bread are brushed with butter and olive oil, baked until golden, and then topped with sautéed fresh tomatoes, crisp crumbled bacon, and a julienne of basil. I serve these throughout the summer when tomatoes and fresh herbs are in abundance.

Makes 24 crostini

6 tablespoons olive oil, divided
1/3 cup chopped shallots
2 teaspoons finely chopped garlic
1 1/2 cups peeled, seeded, and coarsely chopped ripe tomatoes or
* drained canned Italian plum tomatoes*
1/4 teaspoon salt, or more to taste
1/4 teaspoon crushed red pepper flakes
1/4 cup chicken stock
Pinch of sugar, optional
3 tablespoons unsalted butter
24 3/8-inch-thick slices French or Italian bread, preferably cut from
* a loaf about 2 1/2 inches in diameter*
6 strips bacon, fried until crisp, drained well, and crumbled
4 tablespoons finely julienned fresh basil leaves
Several sprigs of basil, for garnish

1. To prepare the topping, heat 3 tablespoons of the olive oil in a heavy medium skillet over medium-high heat. When hot, add the shallots and sauté, stirring, 2 minutes. Add the garlic and sauté and stir a minute more. Add the tomatoes, salt, red pepper flakes, and chicken stock and mix well. Cook, stirring often, until all the liquid has evaporated and the mixture is thick and chunky. Taste and, if necessary, add more salt. If the tomato mixture seems too acidic, add a pinch of sugar. The tomato topping can be prepared up to a day ahead. Cool, cover, and refrigerate. Reheat when needed.

2. When ready to prepare the crostini, preheat the oven to 300°F.

3. Place the butter and the remaining 3 tablespoons olive oil in a small saucepan over low heat and stir until the butter is melted. Brush both sides of the bread slices with this mixture and place on a baking sheet. Bake on the center shelf of the oven, turning once, until golden and slightly crisp, about 10 to 12 minutes. The crostini can be made several hours ahead and kept loosely covered with aluminum foil at room temperature.

4. When ready to serve, preheat the oven to 350°F.

5. Spread each crostini generously with the warm tomato mixture. Sprinkle the crumbled bacon on top and place the crostini on a baking sheet. Bake on the center oven shelf until the crostini are hot, about 6 to 8 minutes. Remove and garnish each one with some of the julienned basil.

6. To serve, arrange the crostini on a serving plate and garnish with clusters of basil sprigs.

Roasted Garlic Crostini

When roasted slowly in the oven, whole garlic cloves take on a sweet, less pungent taste and become quite soft in texture. Puréed and blended with butter and olive oil, they make a sublime spread for toasted French or Italian bread.

Makes 24 crostini

2 medium heads garlic
½ cup olive oil, plus more if needed
3 tablespoons unsalted butter
¼ teaspoon freshly ground black pepper, or to taste
24 ⅜-inch-thick slices French or Italian bread, preferably cut from
a loaf 2½ inches in diameter
3 tablespoons chopped fresh chives

1. To prepare the topping, preheat the oven to 400°F.

2. Smash each head of garlic with your hand to break it into cloves. Lightly smash the individual cloves with the back of a large knife so that the papery coating is loosened. Peel off this papery skin.

3. Place the garlic cloves in a small ovenproof ramekin, soufflé, or custard cup. Pour the olive oil over the cloves; the oil should cover them completely. Cover tightly with a double thickness of aluminum foil. Place on the center shelf of the oven and bake until the garlic cloves are very tender, about 20 to 25 minutes. If necessary, bake another 10 to 15 minutes. When the garlic cloves are tender, remove with a slotted spoon and drain. Reserve the oil.

4. Place the garlic cloves, butter, and 1 tablespoon of the reserved oil in a food processor or blender and process until puréed, about 45 to 60 seconds. Transfer to a small bowl and season with the pepper. The garlic purée can be prepared up to 2 days in advance. Cool, cover, and refrigerate.

5. When ready to prepare the crostini, preheat the oven to 300°F.

6. Brush both sides of the bread slices with the remaining reserved olive oil. (Any extra oil can be saved for another use.) Place the bread slices on a large baking sheet. Bake, turning once, until the crostini are light golden brown and crisp, about 10 to 12 minutes. Spread each crostini with a generous teaspoon of the roasted garlic mixture. Place on a baking sheet. The crostini can be prepared 2 to 3 hours ahead to this point. Cover loosely with plastic wrap and leave at room temperature. *(continued)*

7. When ready to serve the crostini, preheat the oven to 350°F.

8. Bake the crostini until warm, about 5 minutes. Sprinkle with the chives and arrange on a serving tray. Serve warm.

VARIATION: The roasted garlic butter/oil mixture is also good spread on broiled tomatoes or baked zucchini or used as a stuffing for boneless chicken breasts.

✳ *Wild Mushroom Crostini*

On a visit to Boston, I had the pleasure of being invited to a potluck Italian dinner given by the Women's Culinary Guild of New England. These *crostini di bosco* were one of several outstanding antipasti served before the meal. A combination of cultivated mushrooms and dried porcini mushrooms sautéed with garlic taste delicious mounded on toasted bread slices.

Makes 24 crostini

1 ounce dried porcini mushrooms (see note)
5 tablespoons unsalted butter
5 tablespoons olive oil
1 pound cultivated white mushrooms, coarsely chopped
2 teaspoons finely chopped garlic
1 teaspoon lemon juice
Pinch finely crumbled rosemary
24 ⅜-inch-thick slices French or Italian bread, preferably cut from
  a loaf 2½ inches in diameter
5 tablespoons chopped fresh parsley
Salt and freshly ground black pepper to taste
Several sprigs of flat-leaf parsley for garnish

1. To prepare the topping, place the dried porcini mushrooms in a small bowl and cover with 1 cup boiling water. Let stand until the mushrooms are completely softened, about 30 minutes. Drain the mushrooms in a sieve, reserving the soaking liquid. Rinse the mushrooms under cold water to remove any dirt or grit, pat dry, and chop coarsely. Strain the soaking liquid again through a sieve and reserve ½ cup.

2. Heat 2 tablespoons each of the butter and oil in a large heavy skillet over medium-high heat until hot. Add the porcini and white mushrooms and sauté, stirring, about 2 to 3 minutes. Add the garlic and lemon juice and sauté and stir 2 to 3 minutes more. Add the reserved soaking liquid and cook, stirring, until all the liquid has evaporated, about 2 to 3 minutes. Stir in half the chopped parsley and the rosemary and season the mixture generously with salt and pepper. The mushroom topping can be prepared up to a day ahead. Cool, cover, and refrigerate. Reheat in a skillet, stirring, when needed.

3. When ready to prepare the crostini, preheat the oven to 300°F.

4. In a small heavy saucepan, heat the remaining 3 tablespoons each of the butter and olive oil until the butter has melted. Brush both sides of the bread slices with this mixture. Place the slices on a baking sheet and bake on the center shelf of the oven, turning once, until golden and crisp, about 10 to 12 minutes. The crostini can be made several hours ahead and kept loosely covered with aluminum foil at room temperature.

5. Mound the warm mushroom mixture on top of the crostini and place the crostini on a baking sheet. The crostini can be prepared 1 hour ahead to this point. Cover loosely with plastic wrap and leave at room temperature.

6. When ready to serve the crostini, preheat the oven to 350°F.

7. Bake the crostini on the center oven shelf for 5 minutes, or until warm. Sprinkle the remaining chopped parsley over the crostini, arrange on a serving tray, and garnish the tray with several parsley sprigs. Serve warm.

SHOPPING: Dried porcini mushrooms have a strong, almost smoky, taste. When sautéed with cultivated white mushrooms, they impart some of this flavor to the white mushrooms. Dried porcini mushrooms are available at specialty food stores and at some supermarkets.

Tomato and Leek Crostini

A colorful sauté of tomatoes and leeks is a good topping. I use fresh tomatoes for these in the summer and canned plum tomatoes during the winter months.

Makes 24 crostini

½ cup plus 2 tablespoons olive oil, divided, plus more if needed
1½ cups chopped leeks (white parts only)
1½ teaspoons finely chopped garlic
1½ pounds ripe tomatoes, peeled, seeded, and chopped, or one
    28-ounce can Italian plum tomatoes, drained well and coarsely
    chopped
½ teaspoon crushed red pepper flakes
¾ teaspoon dried rosemary, crushed
½ teaspoon dried thyme
¼ teaspoon salt, or more to taste
Freshly ground black pepper to taste
24 ⅜-inch-thick slices French or Italian bread, preferably cut from
    a loaf 2½ inches in diameter
Fresh rosemary leaves, for garnish

1. To prepare the topping, heat 4 tablespoons of the olive oil in a large heavy skillet over medium-high heat. When hot, add the leeks and sauté, stirring, until softened, about 3 to 4 minutes. Add the garlic, tomatoes, red pepper flakes, thyme, salt, black pepper, and rosemary. Cook, stirring constantly, about 3 to 4 minutes more. Taste and, if needed, add more salt and black pepper. Remove from the heat and drain the mixture well in a colander or strainer to remove excess liquid. The topping can be prepared a day ahead. Cool, cover, and refrigerate. Reheat before using.

2. To prepare the crostini, preheat the oven to 300°F.

3. Brush both sides of bread slices with the remaining 6 tablespoons of olive oil; use additional oil if necessary. Place on a large baking sheet. Bake, turning once, until the crostini are golden and crisp, about 10 to 12 minutes. The crostini can be made several hours ahead and kept loosely covered with aluminum foil at room temperature.

4. When ready to assemble the crostini, preheat the oven to 350°F.

5. Spread about a tablespoon of the warm tomato mixture on each crostini. Place the crostini on a baking sheet and heat until warm, about 4 to 5 minutes. Arrange the crostini on a serving plate and garnish each one with a pinch of fresh rosemary leaves.

Smoked Salmon and Roquefort Butter Croutons

Smoked salmon and blue cheese are an unexpected but delicious topping for crisp toasted slices of French bread. These savory morsels, which take only a few minutes to assemble, can be completely prepared an hour in advance.

Makes 24 croutons

24 ⅓-inch-thick slices of French bread, cut from a loaf
*   approximately 2½ to 3 inches in diameter*
6 ounces Roquefort cheese, slightly softened
2 tablespoons unsalted butter, slightly softened
10 to 12 ounces smoked salmon, sliced paper-thin
Freshly ground black pepper to taste

1. Preheat the oven to 350°F.

2. Arrange the bread slices on a baking sheet. Bake on the center shelf of the oven until golden brown, about 10 to 15 minutes, turning once. Cool 4 to 5 minutes. The croutons can be prepared 2 to 3 hours ahead and kept loosely covered with aluminum foil at cool room temperature.

3. With an electric mixer set on medium speed or by hand, beat the Roquefort and butter together until smooth and creamy. Spread each crouton with about ½ tablespoon of the mixture.

4. Cut the salmon slices so they fit the top of the croutons. Top each crouton with a single slice of salmon. Season with a grinding of pepper. The croutons can be prepared up to an hour ahead. Cover with plastic wrap and keep at cool room temperature until ready to serve.

Shrimp and Saga Blue Croutons

This, like the preceding recipe, is an easy appetizer in which a blue cheese is paired with seafood. In this combination, toasted bread slices are topped with Saga blue cheese, shrimp, and fresh rosemary.

Makes 24 croutons

5 tablespoons unsalted butter
5 tablespoons olive oil
24 ⅓-inch-thick slices French bread, cut from a loaf 2½ to 3 inches in diameter
10 to 12 ounces Saga blue cheese, with rind, at room temperature
48 medium cooked and peeled shrimp
Chopped fresh rosemary, for garnish

1. In a medium-size skillet, heat 2½ tablespoons each of the butter and oil over medium-high heat until hot. Sauté the bread slices, 4 to 5 at a time, until golden, adding more butter and oil in equal amounts as necessary. The bread slices can be sautéed 4 to 5 hours ahead and kept loosely covered with aluminum foil at cool room temperature.

2. Spread the cooled croutons with the softened Saga blue cheese and top each one with 2 shrimp. Place the croutons on a baking sheet. The croutons can be assembled 1 hour ahead and kept loosely covered with aluminum foil at cool room temperature.

3. When ready to serve the croutons, preheat the broiler and adjust the rack 4 to 5 inches from heat.

4. Broil the croutons, watching carefully, until the cheese melts and the shrimp are heated, about 2 to 3 minutes. Garnish the croutons with a light sprinkling of chopped rosemary.

Curried Shrimp and Lobster Croutons

These little croutons, baked until crisp and spread with a curry-and-chutney-flavored mayonnaise, are garnished with shrimp and lobster meat. They make very easy but very elegant appetizers.

Makes 24 croutons

*24 ¼-inch-thick slices of French bread, cut from a loaf 2½ to 3
    inches in diameter*
6 to 8 tablespoons olive oil
1 cup mayonnaise
¼ cup chopped mango chutney
1 teaspoon curry powder
*12 large shrimp, cooked, peeled, and sliced in half through the
    dorsal (back) side*
6 ounces cooked lobster meat
Cayenne pepper
Sprigs of watercress or lemon leaves, for garnish

1. Preheat the oven to 350°F.

2. Brush each slice of bread lightly on both sides with the olive oil. Place on a baking sheet and bake on the center shelf of the oven until just crisp, about 10 minutes, turning after 5 minutes. Remove from the oven and cool. The croutons can be made 4 to 5 hours ahead and kept loosely covered with aluminum foil at room temperature.

3. To serve, place the mayonnaise in a mixing bowl, add the chutney and curry powder, and mix well. Spread a generous ½ tablespoon of this mixture on top of each crouton. To serve, top each crouton with a shrimp half and some of the lobster meat. Sprinkle the croutons lightly with cayenne pepper. Arrange on a serving tray and garnish with sprigs of watercress or lemon leaves.

NOTE: If you prefer to use all shrimp, use 24 large shrimp, split them, and top each toast with two halves. If you wish to use all lobster meat, 8 ounces should be sufficient. Lobster tails cut into medallions work well.

Deli Pick-ups

These bite-sized sandwiches made with dark rye bread topped with Gruyère cheese, corned beef, and a dollop of horseradish cream are always a crowd pleaser. I serve them at casual get-togethers such as parties after a football or basketball game.

Makes 48 sandwiches

8 slices dark rye bread (or 24 slices party rye)
5 ounces Gruyère cheese, grated (1¼ cups)
½ pound corned beef, thinly sliced
Horseradish cream (recipe follows)
Sprigs of fresh dill or 1½ to 2 teaspoons dried dill

1. Cut each piece of dark rye bread into thirds, then cut each third in half, for a total of 48 pieces. If using party rye, cut each slice in half.

2. Preheat the oven to 350°F.

3. Arrange the rye slices on two baking sheets. Bake for 5 minutes, turn, and bake 5 minutes more. Remove and cool. The bread can be prepared 3 to 4 days ahead and kept in an airtight container.

4. When ready to assemble the sandwiches, preheat the broiler.

5. Place the bread slices on two baking sheets lined with aluminum foil. Sprinkle each piece evenly with ½ teaspoon of the grated Gruyère. Top each with 3 thin slices of corned beef cut to fit the bread, and sprinkle ½ teaspoon more Gruyère on top of the corned beef. Broil 4 to 5 inches from the heat source until the cheese melts, about 1 to 2 minutes.

6. While the sandwiches are still warm, place a dollop of the horseradish cream on top of each one. Sprinkle with the dried dill or top with a small sprig of dill. Serve hot.

VARIATION: You can use miniature pitas (approximately 3-inch diameter) for this recipe. Halve the pitas, fill each half generously with corned beef, and sprinkle with cheese. When ready to serve, heat in a preheated 400°F oven for 8 minutes, or until hot, and then garnish with a dollop of horseradish cream. You will need about a quarter pound more of both the corned beef and the cheese to fill 24 halved pita pockets.

(continued)

HORSERADISH CREAM

Makes about ¾ cup

¾ cup sour cream
1½ tablespoons mayonnaise
2½ teaspoons prepared horseradish
Pinch of salt
⅛ teaspoon cayenne pepper

1. Combine all the ingredients in a mixing bowl. Stir well to blend. If not using immediately, cover and refrigerate. The cream can be made 4 to 5 days ahead and refrigerated; stir before using.

Turnovers, Triangles, and Pinwheels

These appetizers all have one thing in common: They are pastry-wrapped packages with special fillings. They are made with store-bought puff pastry or phyllo dough or with quick homemade pizza dough and can be quickly assembled in advance. The turnovers, made with puff pastry, encase such inviting combinations as barbecued chicken, Black Forest ham and spiced cranberries, and grated Cheddar mixed with chopped scallions. The pinwheels are fashioned from sheets of puff pastry, which are spread or layered with unusual fillings and rolled into log shapes. They can be made ahead and frozen, then simply cut into spirals and baked when needed. The delectable Mushroom and Leek Pinwheels and the crispy Provençal Palmiers are two of my favorites.

The Italians are celebrated for calzones, large half-moon–shaped turnovers prepared with pizza dough; the mini-calzones in this chapter, bite-sized versions of the traditional ones, are perfect as hors d'oeuvres. The homemade pizza dough can be put together in minutes. It rises quickly, and the simple stuffings can be prepared while the dough is resting. Once assembled, the mini-calzones freeze beautifully.

The triangles, shaped from purchased phyllo dough, are especially convenient hors d'oeuvres, for they can be made completely in advance and frozen. Then you can take them straight from the freezer to the oven as needed. Your guests will love the combination of the flaky pastry and robust fillings.

Whether you serve these as pre-dinner nibbles or offer them with an array of foods at a party, they are addictive, so keep that in mind when you are estimating how many you will need!

Chicken Barbecue
Turnovers

At Emeril's, one of New Orleans' best restaurants, I ordered a barbecued pork turnover as an appetizer. When a large flaky puff pastry triangle filled with moist strips of pork coated with a barbecue sauce arrived at the table, I ate it with abandon. After talking with Chef Emeril Lagasse, the creator of this special dish, I came home and devised a slightly different version. My turnovers are bite-sized and filled with smoked chicken instead of pork. By the way, the Barbecue Sauce, made by my friend Jim Budros, must be made with Coca-Cola, not another brand.

Makes 32 turnovers

1 17¼-ounce package frozen puff pastry (containing 2 sheets
   pastry), defrosted
8 ounces smoked chicken, cut into ¼-inch cubes
½ cup plus 1½ tablespoons Barbecue Sauce (recipe follows)
1 large egg, slightly beaten

1. On a floured work surface, roll out each sheet of puff pastry to a 12- × 12-inch square and trim to make sides even. Cut sixteen 3-inch squares from each sheet, for a total of 32 squares.

2. Place the chicken and Barbecue Sauce in a mixing bowl and mix well. Place about ½ tablespoon of the filling on one diagonal half of each square. Brush the edges of each square with a little of the beaten egg. Fold each square neatly in half to form a triangle, and press the edges with the tines of a fork to seal. Place the turnovers on two aluminum foil-lined baking sheets. The turnovers can be prepared ahead to this point, covered with plastic wrap, and refrigerated for at least 1 hour or up to a day. They can also be frozen. Cover with plastic wrap and then wrap tightly with aluminum foil. Defrost the frozen turnovers for 24 hours in the refrigerator before baking.

3. When ready to bake the turnovers, preheat the oven to 350°F.

4. Brush the tops of the turnovers with beaten egg. Bake in the preheated oven until golden, about 20 minutes. Remove and cool 5 minutes.

5. Arrange the turnovers on a napkin-lined serving plate or place in a napkin-lined basket. Serve warm.

(continued)

Makes about 1½ cups

1 cup Coca-Cola
1 cup ketchup
1 cup A-1 sauce
¼ cup Worcestershire sauce
1 teaspoon liquid smoke
½ teaspoon garlic powder
1 tablespoon cider vinegar

1. Combine all the ingredients in a large heavy saucepan and mix well. Cook, stirring occasionally, over low to medium heat, until the sauce has reduced by half and is quite thick, about 1 hour.

2. Remove from the heat and cool. Cover tightly and refrigerate. The sauce can be stored in the refrigerator for up to 4 weeks. It's best made at least 1 day in advance.

NOTE: Leftover barbecue sauce can be stored for 3 to 4 weeks in the refrigerator. It's delicious brushed over grilled chicken, pork chops, or spareribs.

Black Forest Ham and Spiced Cranberry Turnovers

Light, airy puff pastry rectangles filled with thinly sliced ham and spiced cranberries are perfect appetizers to serve during the holiday season.

Makes about 60 turnovers

1 17¼-ounce package frozen puff pastry (containing 2 sheets pastry), defrosted
Spiced Cranberries (recipe follows)
1 pound Black Forest or other baked ham, sliced paper-thin
Bunch of watercress, for garnish

1. Preheat the oven to 350°F.

2. Cut each of the puff pastry sheets lengthwise into 6 equal strips about 1⅜ inches wide, for a total of 12 strips. Then cut each of the strips crosswise at 2-inch intervals to yield approximately 60 rectangles, each about 2 × 1⅜ inches. Discard any excess dough or save for another use.

3. Arrange the rectangles on two ungreased baking sheets and place in the center of the oven. Bake until the rectangles are crisp and golden, about 15 minutes. Remove from the oven and cool to room temperature. The turnovers can be made several hours ahead to this point and kept loosely covered with aluminum foil at cool room temperature.

4. Slice open each rectangle so that it will open like a book. Spread about ½ teaspoon of the spiced cranberries inside each puff, and top the cranberries with 3 slices of ham cut to fit the puffs. Close each puff like a book.

5. To serve, place several sprigs of watercress in the center of a serving tray. Arrange the turnovers around the watercress.

VARIATIONS: Let your imagination be your guide for other fillings for these turnovers. Sliced turkey can replace the ham; mango chutney, the spiced cranberries; or you can try slices of roast beef with a favorite horseradish relish or tomato salsa. The possibilities are unlimited.

(continued)

SPICED CRANBERRIES

Makes 1¾ to 2 cups

½ cup sugar
2 cups fresh cranberries, divided
¼ teaspoon cinnamon
⅛ teaspoon ground cloves
⅛ teaspoon freshly grated nutmeg

1. Place ¾ cup water, the sugar, 1 cup of the cranberries, the cinnamon, cloves, and nutmeg in a medium-size, heavy saucepan over medium-high heat. Stir to dissolve the sugar, and bring to a boil. Cook, stirring only occasionally, until the berries pop and the mixture is the consistency of a loose sauce, about 10 minutes.

2. Add the remaining cup of cranberries and cook another 4 to 5 minutes. Remove and cool to room temperature. The cranberries can be made ahead; cover and refrigerate for up to 3 days.

Cheddar and Scallion Turnovers

Nothing could be easier to assemble than these savory pastry squares. A sheet of store-bought puff pastry is spread with honey mustard, sprinkled with grated Vermont Cheddar and chopped scallions, and topped with a second pastry sheet. The two sheets are pressed and rolled firmly together to incorporate the filling into the pastry, and then cut into bite-sized squares. The pastries can be prepared well in advance of serving and are baked to a rich golden brown.

Makes 64 turnovers

1 17¼-ounce package frozen puff pastry (containing 2 sheets pastry), defrosted
8 teaspoons honey mustard
1 cup finely grated Vermont Cheddar cheese
¼ cup chopped scallions

1. Roll 1 puff pastry sheet out on a lightly floured work surface to a 12-inch square. Cut the pastry sheet in half so that you have two 6- × 12-inch sheets.

2. Spread one half sheet with 4 teaspoons of the honey mustard. Sprinkle with half the cheese, then with half the scallions. Place the second half sheet neatly over the filling and lightly roll a rolling pin over the pastry, just to press together the dough, without stretching it. Trim the edges to make them even and discard the trimmings.

3. Cut the filled pastry rectangle into 32 squares by cutting the short side of the dough into 4 equal strips 1½ inches wide and the long side into 8 equal strips 1½ inches wide. Transfer the squares to a lightly greased aluminum foil-lined baking sheet.

4. Repeat the process with the second sheet of puff pastry and the remaining filling ingredients. The pastry squares can be prepared up to a day in advance, covered with plastic wrap, and refrigerated. The squares can also be frozen. Cover with plastic wrap and then wrap foil tightly over the plastic wrap. Defrost the frozen squares in the refrigerator for 24 hours before baking.

5. When ready to bake the turnovers, preheat the oven to 400°F.

6. Bake until the turnovers are puffed and golden, about 10 minutes. Arrange on a serving tray and serve hot.

Spinach-Blue Cheese Mini-Calzones

Calzones, half-moon—shaped turnovers, made with pizza dough and stuffed with different fillings, have become such a popular menu item in many restaurants that I decided to try making miniature versions to serve at cocktail parties. In this one, sautéed spinach and shallots are combined with crumbled Roquefort and cream cheese. They can be assembled completely ahead of time and either refrigerated or frozen until time to be baked.

Makes 24 mini-calzones

1 recipe Pizza Dough (page 96; prepare through Step 2, then proceed as directed below)

1 tablespoon vegetable oil
¼ cup chopped shallots
1 10-ounce package frozen chopped spinach, defrosted and squeezed dry in a clean kitchen towel
4 ounces Saga blue, rind removed, cut into chunks
2 ounces cream cheese, cut into chunks
¼ teaspoon salt, or to taste
1 large egg, lightly beaten
4 to 5 large flat-leaf spinach leaves, for garnish

1. Punch down the dough and divide it in half. Roll one half on a floured surface into a very thin 12-inch circle and, using a 3-inch cutter, cut out 12 rounds. If necessary, reroll the scraps and cut out more rounds. Repeat with the remaining dough. You should have 24 small rounds. Cover and refrigerate while you prepare the filling.

2. Heat the oil in a medium skillet over medium-high heat. When hot, add the shallots and sauté, stirring, until softened, about 2 minutes. Add the spinach and cook and stir 3 minutes more. Add the cheeses and cook, stirring, until the cheese has melted. Taste and season with salt as needed. Because the blue cheese and cream cheese are salty, you may not need to add salt. Remove the mixture from the pan.

3. Brush the edges of each pizza round with some of the beaten egg. Place a generous teaspoon of the filling on one half of each round. Fold in half, press the edges to seal, and place 1½ inches apart on lightly greased baking sheets.

The mini-calzones can be prepared ahead, covered with plastic wrap, and refrigerated for 3 to 4 hours. They can also be frozen: Wrap in plastic wrap, then in aluminum foil. Defrost in the refrigerator before baking.

4. When ready to bake, preheat oven to 400°F.

5. Brush the tops of the calzones with beaten egg. Bake until golden, about 8 to 10 minutes. Remove and cool 2 to 3 minutes. Place a cluster of spinach leaves on a serving plate, and arrange the calzones on the plate. Serve warm.

Ricotta and Brie Mini-Calzones

Brie and ricotta cheeses combined with scallions, basil, and chopped fresh tomatoes make an irresistible filling for crisp calzones. These appetizers can be made ahead and refrigerated or frozen.

Makes 24 mini-calzones

1 recipe Pizza Dough (page 96; prepare through Step 2, then proceed as directed below)

4 ounces Brie, with rind, cut into ½-inch chunks
¾ cup part-skim ricotta cheese
2 tablespoons minced scallions
2 tablespoons chopped fresh basil or 2 teaspoons dried
1 teaspoon chopped fresh rosemary or ¼ teaspoon dried
¼ teaspoon cayenne pepper
Salt to taste
1 large egg, lightly beaten
3 tablespoons chopped seeded ripe tomato
Several sprigs of basil, for garnish

1. Punch down the dough and divide it in half. Roll one half on a floured surface into a very thin 12-inch circle and, using a 3-inch cutter, cut out 12

49

rounds. If necessary, reroll the scraps and cut out more rounds. Repeat with the remaining dough. You should have 24 small rounds. Cover and refrigerate while you make the filling.

2. Place the Brie and ricotta in a food processor fitted with the metal blade or in a blender, and process until smooth, 30 to 45 seconds. Remove the mixture to a mixing bowl and stir in the scallions, basil, rosemary, and cayenne pepper. Taste and season with salt as needed.

3. Brush the edges of each pizza round with some of the beaten egg. Place a teaspoon of the filling on one half of each round. Top the cheese mixture with ½ teaspoon of the chopped tomato. Fold the rounds in half, press the edges to seal, and place on lightly greased baking sheets. The calzones can be prepared ahead, covered with plastic wrap, and refrigerated for 3 to 4 hours. They can also be frozen: Wrap in plastic wrap, then in aluminum foil. Defrost in the refrigerator before baking.

4. When ready to bake, preheat the oven to 400°F.

5. Brush the tops of the calzones with beaten egg. Bake until golden, about 8 to 10 minutes. Remove and cool 2 to 3 minutes. Arrange the calzones on a serving plate, and garnish with a cluster of basil sprigs.

Camembert and Walnut Phyllo Bundles

These golden phyllo packages can be prepared a day in advance. Simply bake until crisp just before serving.

Makes 60 bundles

8 ounces Camembert cheese, with rind, cut into cubes, at room temperature
1 teaspoon dried rosemary, crumbled
¼ teaspoon cayenne pepper
1 egg, lightly beaten
3 tablespoons coarsely chopped walnuts
15 sheets phyllo (14 × 18 inches), thawed if frozen
1 cup (2 sticks) unsalted butter, melted
Several sprigs of rosemary, for garnish

1. Using an electric mixer, beat the cheese in a small bowl until smooth. Beat in the rosemary, cayenne pepper, and egg. Stir in the nuts.

2. Butter two large baking sheets. Place 1 phyllo sheet on a work surface. Keep the remainder of the phyllo covered with a slightly damp towel. Brush the phyllo sheet lightly with the melted butter. Top with a second phyllo sheet, brush lightly with butter, and top with a third phyllo sheet. Brush lightly with butter. Cut the stacked phyllo lengthwise into 3½ inch-wide strips. Then cut crosswise into 3½ inch-wide squares.

3. Place 1 teaspoon of the filling in the center of each square. Gather the corners together over the center and crimp firmly to form "purses." Transfer to the prepared baking sheets, spacing 1 inch apart. Brush the tops lightly with butter.

4. Repeat with the remaining pastry, butter, and filling. Refrigerate the phyllo purses for at least 1 hour before baking. The purses can be prepared a day ahead. Cover with plastic wrap and refrigerate.

5. When ready to bake the phyllo, preheat the oven to 350°F.

6. Bake the pastries until crisp and golden brown, about 20 to 22 minutes. Cool 5 minutes. Arrange on a serving platter, and garnish the platter with rosemary sprigs.

Curried Beef Triangles

These spicy phyllo packages reflect my love of Indian food. They are filled with a mixture of browned ground beef, onion, garlic, mango chutney, almonds, and currants all generously seasoned with curry powder.

Makes 32 triangles

½ tablespoon olive oil

¾ pound lean beef ground round

1 large clove garlic, peeled and finely chopped

½ cup finely chopped onion

¾ cup mango chutney, coarsely chopped

¼ cup currants, softened in boiling water for 10 minutes and drained

¼ cup slivered almonds

1 tablespoon dry unflavored bread crumbs

1 tablespoon curry powder

¼ teaspoon salt

¼ teaspoon freshly ground black pepper

⅛ teaspoon cayenne pepper

8 sheets phyllo (14 × 18 inches), thawed if frozen

About 12 tablespoons (1½ sticks) unsalted butter, melted

1. Heat the olive oil in a heavy medium skillet over medium-high heat until hot. Add the ground round, garlic, and onion. Cook, stirring and breaking up the meat until the beef is browned, about 4 to 5 minutes. Pour off the excess fat and discard.

2. Lower the heat and add the chutney, currants, almonds, bread crumbs, curry powder, salt, black pepper, and cayenne pepper. Cook a minute more, stirring. Remove from the heat and set aside.

3. Place a sheet of phyllo dough on a work surface with a short side in front of you. Keep the remaining phyllo sheets covered with a damp towel as you work. With scissors or a sharp knife, cut the dough lengthwise into 4 equal strips. Brush 1 strip generously with the melted butter. Place a generous tablespoon of the filling at the bottom of the strip. Fold a corner up over the filling, then continue folding as if folding a flag to the end of the strip. Place the phyllo triangle seam side down on a buttered jelly roll pan or other baking sheet with sides and brush the top with more butter. Repeat with the remaining filling and phyllo. The triangles can be made up to a day in advance to this point.

Cover the baking sheets with lightly dampened kitchen towels, cover tightly with plastic wrap, and refrigerate. The triangles can also be frozen. If freezing, do not brush the tops with butter. Place on greased baking sheets and cover with plastic wrap and then aluminum foil.

4. When ready to bake the triangles, preheat the oven to 375°F.

5. Bake the triangles until golden, about 15 minutes. If you have frozen the phyllo triangles, do not defrost. Uncover, brush with melted butter, and bake until golden and hot, about 30 minutes. Serve warm in a napkin-lined basket.

Asparagus and Prosciutto Triangles

Thin asparagus spears and prosciutto mixed with ricotta, Parmesan cheese, and fresh herbs fill these crisp phyllo triangles. They can be prepared completely in advance and refrigerated or frozen.

Makes about 36 triangles

½ cup plus 2½ tablespoons whole-milk ricotta cheese
6 tablespoons grated imported Parmesan cheese
¼ cup chopped fresh basil or 4 teaspoons dried, but fresh is preferable
1½ tablespoons chopped fresh chives
1½ tablespoons chopped fresh flat-leaf parsley
1½ ounces prosciutto, sliced ¹⁄₁₆ inch thick and finely chopped
½ pound thin asparagus spears
½ tablespoon unsalted butter
3 tablespoons chopped scallions
1½ teaspoons finely chopped garlic
Freshly ground black pepper to taste
1 egg yolk, lightly beaten
8 tablespoons (1 stick) unsalted butter, melted
6 sheets phyllo (14 × 18 inches), thawed if frozen
¼ cup dry unflavored bread crumbs
Several sprigs of flat-leaf parsley, for garnish
Several sprigs of basil, for garnish

1. To prepare the filling, place the ricotta, Parmesan cheese, basil, chives, parsley, and prosciutto in a mixing bowl. Set aside.

2. Trim the tough ends from the asparagus spears. Cut the asparagus on the diagonal into ½-inch pieces. Cook in lightly salted boiling water to cover until just tender, 2 to 3 minutes only. Remove, place in a colander, and rinse under cold running water to cool. Pat dry and add to the ricotta mixture.

3. Heat ½ tablespoon of butter in a small heavy skillet over medium-high heat. When melted and hot, add the scallions and garlic and sauté, stirring constantly, until just tender, about 2 minutes. Remove and add to the ricotta mixture.

4. Season the ricotta mixture with several grinds of black pepper. Then add the egg yolk and mix well to blend all the ingredients. Set aside while you prepare the phyllo sheets.

5. Melt the remaining butter in a small saucepan over moderate heat. Place a phyllo sheet on a work surface with a long end facing you and brush generously with the melted butter. Cover the remaining phyllo sheets with a lightly dampened kitchen towel so they do not dry out. Cut the sheet into 6 equal strips, each about 2¾ × 14 inches. Place a generous teaspoon of the filling in a bottom corner of a strip. Fold a corner over the strip, then continue folding as if folding a flag to the end of the strip. Place the phyllo triangle seam side down on a greased baking sheet and brush the top with more butter. Repeat with the remaining filling and phyllo. The triangles can be made a day ahead. Cover with lightly dampened kitchen towels and plastic wrap and refrigerate or, if you want to freeze them, omit the final brushing of butter. Place the triangles on greased baking sheets and cover with plastic wrap and then with aluminum foil.

6. When ready to bake, preheat the oven to 375°F. Bake on the center rack until golden, about 15 minutes. If you have frozen the triangles, do not defrost. Uncover, brush with butter, and bake until golden and hot, about 30 minutes.

Mushroom and Leek Pinwheels

The inspiration for this recipe came from talented cooking teacher Marlene Sorosky. While giving a class at my school, she spread sheets of store-bought puff pastry with pesto, then rolled the dough tightly into logs, which could be refrigerated or frozen until needed. Just before baking, pinwheels were cut from the logs and arranged on baking sheets. Then they were quickly popped into the oven. So delectable were these easy appetizers, I decided to try some new fillings and created the two variations that follow.

Makes about 80 pinwheels

4½ tablespoons unsalted butter
1½ pounds mushrooms, finely chopped
1 tablespoon finely chopped garlic
½ cup chopped leeks
¾ cup chicken stock
12 ounces cream cheese, broken into chunks
½ teaspoon salt
¼ teaspoon freshly ground black pepper
4 tablespoons chopped fresh chives or parsley
1 17¼-ounce package frozen puff pastry (containing 2 sheets pastry), defrosted

1. To prepare the filling, melt the butter in a large heavy skillet over medium-high heat. When hot, add the mushrooms and sauté, stirring, for 3 to 4 minutes. Add the garlic and leeks and sauté, stirring, 2 to 3 minutes more. Add the stock and cook over high heat until all the liquid has evaporated, about 5 to 6 minutes longer.

2. Lower the heat and add the cream cheese. Cook, stirring constantly, until the cheese has melted. Add the salt and pepper. Stir in the chives. Refrigerate until well chilled.

3. Roll each sheet of puff pastry out on a lightly floured work surface to a 12- × 14-inch rectangle. Spread half of the filling on each sheet, going all the way to the edges except for a ½-inch border on one of the long sides. Roll up the pastry, starting with the long side without the border, tightly into a coil. Moisten the ½-inch border lightly with water and press to seal the end. Wrap the rolls in plastic and freeze to firm, about 45 minutes. The logs can be

56

prepared to this point in advance and refrigerated for up to 2 days. They can also be frozen for 2 to 3 weeks. Cover the plastic-wrapped logs tightly with aluminum foil. Defrost in the refrigerator for 24 hours before baking.

4. To make the pinwheels, slice ¼-inch-thick slices from each roll. You should get about 40 pinwheels from each roll. Arrange on two large baking sheets lined with lightly greased aluminum foil. The pinwheels can be prepared to this point in advance. Cover the baking sheets with plastic wrap and refrigerate for up to 6 hours.

5. When ready to bake, preheat the oven to 450°F.

6. Bake the pinwheels about 12 to 14 minutes. Using a spatula, turn the pinwheels over and bake for an additional 5 to 8 minutes, until golden brown and crispy. Watch them carefully as they bake. Remove with a spatula and arrange on a napkin-lined serving tray. Serve hot.

NOTE: If using a food processor to chop the mushrooms, process in small batches so that the mushrooms are chopped to an even consistency.

Herb-Garlic Cheese and Prosciutto Pinwheels

Creamy garlic-scented herbed cheese and paper-thin slices of prosciutto are another tempting combination of flavors for crispy puff pastry spirals. If you are in a hurry, use store-bought herb-garlic cheese; the pinwheels will take even less time to assemble.

Makes about 80 pinwheels

1 17¼-ounce package frozen puff pastry (containing 2 sheets pastry), defrosted
10 to 12 ounces herb-garlic cheese, either store-bought or homemade (page 264)
6 ounces lean prosciutto, sliced paper-thin

1. Roll each sheet of puff pastry out on a lightly floured work surface to a 12- × 14-inch rectangle. Spread half of the cheese on each sheet, going all the way to the edges except for a ½-inch border on one of the long sides. Arrange the prosciutto slices evenly on top of the cheese. Roll up the pastry, starting at the long side without the border, tightly into a coil. Moisten the ½-inch border lightly with water and press to seal the end. Wrap the rolls in plastic and freeze to firm, about 45 minutes. The logs can be prepared to this point in advance and refrigerated for up to 2 days. They can also be frozen for 2 to 3 weeks. Cover the plastic-wrapped logs tightly with aluminum foil. Defrost in the refrigerator for 24 hours before baking.

2. To make the pinwheels, slice ¼-inch-thick slices from each roll. You should get about 40 pinwheels from each roll. Arrange on two large baking sheets lined with lightly greased aluminum foil. The pinwheels can be prepared to this point in advance. Cover the baking sheets with plastic wrap and refrigerate for up to 6 hours.

3. When ready to bake, preheat the oven to 450°F.

4. Bake the pinwheels about 12 to 14 minutes. Using a spatula, turn the pinwheels over and bake for an additional 5 to 8 minutes, until golden and crisp. Watch carefully as they bake. Remove with a spatula and arrange on a napkin-lined serving tray. Serve hot.

Provençal Palmiers

The unmistakable flavors of Provence—olives, tomatoes (sun-dried in this case), garlic, basil, thyme, and fennel seeds—are combined and mixed with Parmesan cheese to make the filling for these crisp, flaky palmiers. The palmiers, made with puff pastry spirals like the traditional sweet version, are also known as elephant's ears.

Makes 52 to 56 palmiers

1 cup imported olives such as Alphonso or Kalamata, pitted and finely chopped
¼ cup sun-dried tomatoes packed in oil, drained and finely chopped
2 teaspoons finely chopped garlic
2 teaspoons dried basil
1 teaspoon dried thyme
1 teaspoon fennel seeds, lightly crushed
1¼ cups grated imported Parmesan cheese, divided (about 6 ounces)
1 17¼-ounce package frozen puff pastry (containing 2 sheets pastry), defrosted
Several sprigs of basil, for garnish
Several sprigs of thyme, for garnish

1. Combine the olives, sun-dried tomatoes, garlic, basil, thyme, fennel seeds, and ½ cup of the Parmesan cheese in a mixing bowl and stir well to mix.

2. Lightly flour a work surface and place 1 puff pastry sheet on it. Sprinkle the sheet evenly with 1 tablespoon of the Parmesan cheese and press the cheese in with a rolling pin. Turn the pastry over and repeat with another tablespoon of cheese.

3. Spread half the olive filling evenly over the pastry sheet. Cover the filling with a sheet of waxed paper and press the filling evenly into the pastry with a rolling pin.

4. Starting with one of the longer sides, roll up the pastry tightly like a jelly roll, stopping at the center of the pastry sheet. Repeat with the other side, so that there are 2 rolls that meet in the center.

5. Repeat with the second pastry sheet. The rolls can be prepared ahead, wrapped individually in plastic wrap, and refrigerated for 1 to 2 days. They can also be frozen. Wrap the plastic-wrapped rolls in aluminum foil. Defrost in the refrigerator for 24 hours before baking.

6. Using a sharp knife, cut ⅜-inch slices from the rolls. You should get 26 to 28 slices from each. Place the palmiers on ungreased baking sheets, cover with plastic wrap, and refrigerate until firm, about 30 minutes. The palmiers can be refrigerated for up to 1 day.

7. When ready to bake, preheat the oven to 450°F.

8. Sprinkle each palmier with about ¼ teaspoon of the remaining Parmesan cheese. Bake, 1 sheet at a time, about 6 to 8 minutes. Then remove from the oven, turn the palmiers over, and sprinkle each with another ¼ teaspoon Parmesan cheese. Bake until golden brown, about 4 to 6 minutes more. Remove to a rack to cool and crisp.

9. Serve warm or at room temperature on a serving tray. Garnish the tray with basil and thyme sprigs.

Tartlets and Tarts

The sizable number of entries in this chapter amazes me, for my early attempts at pastry-making were near disasters. The savory French tarts I first turned out had soggy crusts and dry, overcooked fillings. But practice (and Julia Child's books and a food processor!) helped change all that. The dough used for all the tartlets and tarts in this section is one of the best (read: foolproof) recipes in my repertoire. When used for large 9-inch tarts, the dough is weighted down with foil and weights, but small tartlet shells can be baked successfully with no weights. Instructions are given for making bite-sized individual tartlets in mini-muffin tins, or large 9-inch tarts that can be cut into wedges. The fillings, most of which can be partially or completely prepared ahead, have been inspired by frequent eating forays to France and Italy. Combinations such as chèvre, hazelnut, and mint, Gorgonzola and red peppers, or fillings of pesto, Italian sausage and tomatoes are redolent of these two European cuisines.

Among the less traditional offerings in this chapter are savory flans, or crustless tarts. The Angel Hair Flans, in fact, are one of the most popular appetizers I have ever served and, like the other flans included here, can be completely made in advance. Cheese-filled polenta tarts, made by molding cooked polenta into tart pans, and toasted tarts shaped with slices of bread are other special offerings. The unique Southwest tart has a lime-scented cream cheese base that is topped with fresh pineapple salsa.

These tartlets could be offered with drinks before a dinner or served as part of a more extensive menu for a cocktail party.

Savory Tart Dough

This dough can be made in a processor or by hand, and is tender, crisp, and golden when baked. Talented pastry chef Nick Malgieri shared his secret of using baking powder in pastry dough.

Makes enough for 24 3-inch tart sheets or 1 9-inch tart shell

1½ cups all-purpose flour
½ teaspoon salt
½ teaspoon baking powder
8 tablespoons (1 stick) unsalted butter, well chilled and cut into
    small pieces
1 large egg yolk
2 to 3 tablespoons cold water

1. *Food Processor Method:* Place the flour, salt, and baking powder in the container of a food processor fitted with the metal blade. Place the butter on top of the flour. Process, pulsing the machine on and off, for several seconds, until the mixture resembles oatmeal flakes. Add the egg yolk and 2 tablespoons cold water and process about 30 seconds. The dough should hold together when pinched between your fingers. If necessary, add up to an additional 1 tablespoon cold water.

Hand Method: Place the flour, salt, and baking soda in a bowl and cut in the butter with a pastry blender or two knives until the mixture resembles oatmeal flakes. Gradually work in the egg yolk and 2 tablespoons cold water, mixing just until the dough holds together when pinched between your fingers. If necessary, add up to an additional 1 tablespoon cold water.

2. Place the crumbly mixture on a board or counter top and smear the dough with the heel of your hand to blend. Shape into a ball, then flatten the dough into a disc. Cover with plastic wrap and refrigerate for 1 hour or overnight. The dough can also be frozen. Cover tightly with plastic wrap, then with aluminum foil, and freeze. Defrost in the refrigerator before using.

3. *For tartlets:* Place the dough on a lightly floured work surface and roll out to a ⅛-inch thickness. With a 3-inch-round cookie cutter, cut 24 circles from the dough. Press the circles of dough into two nonstick mini-muffin tins with 12 molds, each 1¾ inch in diameter. With a fork, prick holes in the bottom of the tartlet shells.

For a 9-inch tart: On a lightly floured work surface, roll the dough out to a circle about 12 inches in diameter and between ⅛ and ¼ inch thick. Fit the dough into a 9-inch tart pan with a removable bottom, and trim it so ½ inch of dough extends over the edge. Fold the overhanging dough in and press it against the sides of pastry shell. Prick the bottom of the shell with a fork.

4. Freeze the tart shell(s) to firm, about 15 minutes. Or you can freeze for up to 1 to 2 weeks; cover the tart shell(s) with plastic wrap, then with aluminum foil. Defrost in the refrigerator.

Pesto Tartlets

Most frequently used as a sauce for pasta, pesto can also be used in many other dishes. These tarts are filled with fresh mozzarella and Parmesan, and then topped with some pesto as a garnish. For a 9-inch tart, increase the filling by half.

Makes 24 tartlets or 1 9-inch tart

1 recipe Savory Tart Dough (page 63)

6 ounces fresh mozzarella cheese, crumbled
¼ cup grated imported Parmesan cheese
½ cup Toasted Pine Nut Pesto (page 262)
¼ cup pine nuts, toasted (page 268), for garnish
Small fresh basil leaves or sprigs of basil, for garnish

1. Preheat the oven to 375°F.

2. *For tartlets:* Bake the tartlet shells 15 minutes.

For a 9-inch tart: Line the tart shell with aluminum foil and fill it with pie weights or dried beans. Bake the shell until the crust is set, about 10 minutes. Remove the weights or beans and continue to bake until golden, about 15 minutes more.

The tart shell(s) can be baked up to 4 hours ahead. Cool, cover loosely with foil, and leave at cool room temperature.

3. When ready to fill and bake the tarts, preheat the oven to 375°F.

4. *For tartlets:* Fill each tartlet shell half full with the mozzarella cheese and sprinkle with the Parmesan cheese. (For a 9-inch tart, increase the filling ingredients by half.) Bake until the pastry is browned and the cheese has melted, about 15 to 20 minutes. Remove the tartlets from the pans and, while they are still hot, spoon about 1 teaspoon of the pesto on top of each and garnish with a few pine nuts.

For a 9-inch tart: Increase the filling by one half. Spread the mozzarella cheese evenly in the tart shell and sprinkle with the Parmesan. Bake until the filling is piping hot, about 25 to 30 minutes. Remove, spread the pesto on top, and sprinkle with the pine nuts. Cut into 10 wedges.

5. To serve, place the tart(s) on a serving tray. Garnish each tartlet with a small basil leaf; garnish the 9-inch tart with several basil sprigs arranged in the center of the tart.

SHOPPING: Fresh mozzarella is sold in Italian groceries or specialty food stores. White rather than pale yellow, and soft rather than firm, it is quite different from processed mozzarella.

SERVING: These tarts, whether made large or small, are best assembled and baked just prior to serving. If necessary, completely baked tarts can be cooled, unmolded, wrapped tightly in plastic wrap and then in aluminum foil, and frozen. To reheat, place the frozen tarts on a baking sheet, covered loosely with foil, in a preheated 350°F. oven until defrosted and heated through, about 20 to 25 minutes for tartlets and 30 to 40 minutes for a large tart. The crust will not be quite as crisp, but the tarts will still taste good.

Curried Onion Tartlets

Mild onions, sautéed until a rich deep brown in color, then seasoned with curry powder, make an untraditional but delicious filling. A dollop of chutney used as a garnish to complement the curried filling is a nice extra touch.

Makes 24 tartlets or 1 9-inch tart

1 recipe Savory Tart Dough (page 63)

3 tablespoons unsalted butter, divided
1½ pounds (2 large) Vidalia onions or mild yellow or white onions, chopped (4 cups)
1 tablespoon white wine vinegar
¼ cup brown sugar
½ teaspoon curry powder
Salt to taste, optional

1. Preheat the oven to 375°F.

2. *For tartlets:* Bake the tartlet shells 15 minutes.

For a 9-inch tart: Line the tart shell with aluminum foil and fill it with pie weights or dried beans. Bake the shell until the crust is set, about 10 minutes. Remove the weights or beans and continue to bake until golden, about 15 minutes more.

The tart shell(s) can be baked up to 4 hours ahead. Cool, cover loosely with foil, and leave at cool room temperature.

3. To prepare the filling, melt 1½ tablespoons of the butter in a large heavy skillet over medium-high heat. Add the onions, vinegar, and brown sugar. Cook, stirring, until all the liquid has evaporated, about 12 to 15 minutes. Then, as the onions begin to brown, lower the heat and add the remaining 1½ tablespoons butter. Cook the onions slowly until they caramelize, or take on a dark brown glazed appearance, about 10 to 15 minutes longer. Stir in the curry powder and cook 1 or 2 minutes more. Taste and, if desired, season lightly with salt. Remove from the heat. The filling can be made a day ahead, covered, and refrigerated, then reheated before using.

4. When ready to bake, preheat the oven to 375°F.

5. *For tartlets:* Fill each shell with about 1 tablespoon of the onion mixture. Bake until the crust is lightly browned, about 15 to 20 minutes. Remove the tartlet from the pans.

For a 9-inch tart: Spread the onion mixture evenly over the bottom of the pastry shell. Bake until the filling is hot, about 20 to 25 minutes. Remove from the pan.

6. To serve the tart(s), place on a serving tray. Serve the tartlets individually, or cut the 9-inch tart into 10 wedges.

SERVING: Fruit Chutney (page 266) or a good-quality commercial chutney makes a delicious garnish spooned over the tartlets or spread over a large 9-inch tart.

These tarts, whether made small or large, are best assembled and baked just prior to serving. If necessary, completely baked tarts can be cooled, unmolded, wrapped tightly in plastic wrap and then in aluminum foil, and frozen. To reheat, place the frozen tarts on a baking sheet, covered loosely with foil, in a preheated 350°F. oven until defrosted and heated through, about 20 to 25 minutes for tartlets and 30 to 40 minutes for a large tart. The crust will not be quite as crisp, but the tarts will still taste good.

Italian Sausage and Tomato Tartlets

Sautéed Italian sausage, chopped tomatoes, and fresh basil, ingredients I use often as a topping for pizza or pasta, are equally good baked in savory pastry shells.

Makes 24 tartlets or 1 9-inch tart

1 recipe Savory Tart Dough (page 63)

6 ounces sweet Italian bulk sausage
⅛ teaspoon cayenne pepper
2 to 3 plum tomatoes, unpeeled, seeded, and cut into ¼-inch dice (enough to make ½ cup), or ½ cup well-drained and chopped canned Italian tomatoes
3 tablespoons chopped fresh basil or 3 teaspoons dried
¾ cup whipping or heavy cream
3 large egg yolks
¼ teaspoon salt
Freshly ground white pepper to taste
Small fresh basil leaves or sprigs of basil, for garnish

1. Preheat the oven to 375°F.

2. *For tartlets:* Bake the tartlet shells 15 minutes.

For a 9-inch tart: Line the tart shell with aluminum foil and fill it with pie weights or dried beans. Bake the shell until the crust is set, about 10 minutes. Remove the weights or beans and continue to bake until golden, about 15 minutes more.

The tart shell(s) can be baked up to 4 hours ahead. Cool, cover loosely with foil, and leave at cool room temperature.

3. To prepare the filling, place a heavy skillet over medium-high heat and add the sausage. Brown the sausage, breaking it up into small pieces with a wooden spoon. Add the cayenne pepper, tomatoes, and basil and stir and cook 2 to 3 minutes more. The filling can be made up to a day ahead. Cool, cover, and refrigerate.

4. When ready to bake, preheat the oven to 375°F.

5. *For tartlets:* Fill each tartlet shell with some of the sausage mixture. Whisk together the cream, egg yolks, salt, and white pepper, preferably in a large measuring cup with a spout. Carefully pour the cream mixture into tartlet shells, filling each about two-thirds to three-quarters full. Bake until the filling is set and the crust is lightly browned, about 15 to 20 minutes.

For a 9-inch tart: Spread the sausage mixture evenly over the bottom of the pastry shell. Whisk together the cream, egg yolks, salt, and white pepper. Carefully pour the cream mixture into the tart shell. Bake until the filling is set and the crust is lightly browned, about 20 to 25 minutes.

Remove the tart(s) from the oven and, when cool enough to handle, lift from the pan(s).

To serve, place on a serving tray. Garnish each tartlet with a basil leaf, or garnish the 9-inch tart with a cluster of basil sprigs. Serve the tartlets individually, or cut a 9-inch tart into 10 wedges.

SERVING: These tarts are good with a glass of Chianti or Barolo.

These tarts, whether made small or large, are best assembled and baked just prior to serving. If necessary, completely baked tarts can be cooled, unmolded, wrapped tightly in plastic wrap and then in aluminum foil, and frozen. To reheat, place the frozen tarts on a baking sheet, covered loosely with foil, in a preheated 350°F. oven until defrosted and heated through, about 20 to 25 minutes for tartlets and 30 to 40 minutes for a large tart. The crust will not be quite as crisp, but the tarts will still taste good.

Smoked Gouda and Leek Tartlets

Sautéed leeks and smoked Gouda seasoned with a hint of fresh rosemary make a tempting filling for appetizer tarts. Served hot from the oven, they melt in your mouth.

Makes 24 tartlets or 1 9-inch tart

1 recipe Savory Tart Dough (page 63)

1 tablespoon olive oil
2 leeks, white parts only, chopped (1 cup)
1 teaspoon chopped fresh rosemary, or ⅓ teaspoon dried
1 cup grated smoked Gouda (about 4 ounces)
¾ cup whipping or heavy cream
3 large egg yolks
¼ teaspoon salt
Freshly ground white pepper to taste

1. Preheat the oven to 375°F.

2. *For tartlets:* Bake the tartlet shells 15 minutes.

For a 9-inch tart: Line the tart shell with aluminum foil and fill it with pie weights or dried beans. Bake the shell until the crust is set, about 10 minutes. Remove the weights or beans and continue to bake until golden, about 15 minutes more.

The tart shell(s) can be baked up to 4 hours ahead. Cool, cover loosely with foil, and leave at cool room temperature.

3. To prepare the filling, heat the olive oil in a heavy skillet over medium-high heat. When the oil is hot, add the chopped leeks, reduce the heat to medium, and sauté the leeks until softened, about 4 minutes. Add the rosemary and stir to mix. The leeks can be sautéed 2 to 3 hours ahead. Cool and leave at room temperature.

4. When ready to bake, preheat the oven to 375°F.

5. *For tartlets:* Divide the leek mixture evenly among the tartlet shells. Top the leek filling in each tartlet with about 2 teaspoons of the cheese. Whisk together the cream, egg yolks, salt, and pepper, preferably in a large measuring cup with a spout. Carefully pour the custard mixture into the tartlet shells, filling

70

them about two-thirds to three-quarters full. Bake until the filling is set and the crust is lightly browned, about 15 to 20 minutes.

For a 9-inch tart: Spread the leek mixture in the tart shell. Sprinkle with the cheese. In a small bowl, whisk together the cream, egg yolk, salt, and pepper to blend. Pour this mixture into the tart. Bake until the filling is set and the crust is lightly browned, about 20 to 25 minutes.

Remove the tart(s) from the oven and, when cool enough to handle, lift from the pan(s).

6. To serve, place on a serving tray. Serve the tartlets individually, or cut the 9-inch tart into 10 wedges.

SERVING: The large 9-inch tart makes a delicious main course for a light meal. I often serve a salad of Belgian endive, spinach, and walnuts in a mustard vinaigrette dressing along with it.

These tarts, whether made small or large, are best assembled and baked just prior to serving. If necessary, completely baked tarts can be cooled, unmolded, wrapped tightly in plastic wrap and then in aluminum foil, and frozen. To reheat, place the frozen tarts on a baking sheet, covered loosely with foil, in a preheated 350°F. oven until defrosted and heated through, about 20 to 25 minutes for tartlets and 30 to 40 minutes for a large tart. The crust will not be quite as crisp, but the tarts will still taste good.

Chèvre, Hazelnut, and Mint Tartlets

Makes 24 tartlets or 1 9-inch tart

1 recipe Savory Tart Dough (page 63)

8 ounces chèvre
4 tablespoons grated imported Parmesan cheese
4 tablespoons coarsely chopped hazelnuts
¼ cup fresh mint leaves, cut into fine julienne strips, for garnish

1. Preheat the oven to 375°F.

2. *For tartlets:* Bake the tartlet shells 15 minutes.

For a 9-inch tart: Line the tart shell with aluminum foil and fill it with pie weights or dried beans. Bake the shell until the crust is set, about 10 minutes. Remove the weights or beans and continue to bake until golden, about 15 minutes more.

The tart shell(s) can be baked up to 4 hours ahead. Cool, cover loosely with foil, and leave at cool room temperature.

3. When ready to bake, preheat the oven to 375°F.

4. *For tartlets:* Fill each tartlet shell with about 1½ teaspoons of the chèvre, sprinkle with ½ teaspoon of the Parmesan cheese, and top with ½ teaspoon of the hazelnuts. Place on the middle shelf of the oven and bake until the pastry is golden and the cheese has melted, about 15 to 20 minutes.

For a 9-inch tart: Spread the chèvre evenly in the tart shell. Sprinkle with the Parmesan cheese and top with the hazelnuts. Bake until the filling is set and the crust is lightly browned, about 20 to 25 minutes.

Remove the tart(s) from the oven and, when cool enough to handle, lift from the pan(s).

5. To serve, place on a serving tray and garnish with the julienned mint. Serve the tartlets individually, or cut the 9-inch tart into 10 wedges.

SERVING: These tarts, whether made small or large, are best assembled and baked just prior to serving. If necessary, completely baked tarts can be cooled, unmolded, wrapped tightly in plastic wrap and then in aluminum foil, and frozen. To reheat, place the frozen tarts on a baking sheet, covered loosely with foil, in a preheated 350°F. oven until defrosted and heated through, about 20 to 25 minutes for tartlets and 30 to 40 minutes for a large tart. The crust will not be quite as crisp, but the tarts will still taste good.

Monterey Jack Cheese and Salsa Tartlets

These spicy tarts are filled with a custard mixture made piquant by the addition of grated hot Monterey Jack cheese and garnished with a colorful salsa and fresh basil.

Makes 24 tartlets or 1 9-inch tart

1 recipe Savory Tart Dough (page 63)

4 ounces Monterey Jack cheese with jalapeño peppers, grated
   (1 cup)
3 tablespoons chopped fresh basil
¾ cup whipping or heavy cream
3 large egg yolks
¼ teaspoon salt
Freshly ground white pepper to taste
½ cup mild salsa, drained well, for garnish
24 small fresh basil leaves, for garnish

1. Preheat the oven to 375°F.

2. *For tartlets:* Bake the tartlet shells 15 minutes.

For a 9-inch tart: Line the tart shell with aluminum foil and fill it with pie weights or dried beans. Bake the shell until the crust is set, about 10 minutes. Remove the weights or beans and continue to bake until golden, about 15 minutes more.

The tart shell(s) can be baked up to 4 hours ahead. Cool, cover loosely with foil, and leave at cool room temperature.

3. When ready to bake, preheat the oven to 375° F.

4. *For tartlets:* Combine the grated cheese with the chopped basil and divide this mixture among the tart shells. Whisk together the cream, egg yolks, salt, and pepper, preferably in a large measuring cup with a spout. Carefully pour the custard mixture into the tartlet shells, filling them about two-thirds to three-quarters full. Bake until the filling is set and the crust is lightly browned, about 15 to 20 minutes.

For a 9-inch tart: Combine the grated cheese with the chopped basil and spread it in the bottom of the tart shell. In a small bowl, whisk together the cream, egg yolk, salt, and pepper to blend. Pour this mixture into the tart shell.

(continued)

Bake until the filling is set and the crust is lightly browned, about 20 to 25 minutes.

Remove the tart(s) from the oven and, when cool enough to handle, lift from the pan(s).

5. To serve, place on a serving tray. Garnish each tartlet with a teaspoon of the salsa and a basil leaf. Or make a border with the salsa on top of the 9-inch tart and arrange the basil leaves in a decorative pattern on the salsa. Serve the tartlets individually, or cut the 9-inch tart into 10 wedges.

SHOPPING: If fresh basil is not available, chopped cilantro, which adds a totally different taste, also works well.

SERVING: These tarts, whether made small or large, are best assembled and baked just prior to serving. If necessary, completely baked tarts can be cooled, unmolded, wrapped tightly in plastic wrap and then in aluminum foil, and frozen. To reheat, place the frozen tarts on a baking sheet, covered loosely with foil, in a preheated 350°F. oven until defrosted and heated through, about 20 to 25 minutes for tartlets and 30 to 40 minutes for a large tart. The crust will not be quite as crisp, but the tarts will still taste good.

Asparagus and Prosciutto Tartlets

These golden tarts filled with asparagus, mushrooms, and prosciutto are perfect for special occasions in the spring. They are delicious with champagne or a crisp dry white wine. For a 9-inch tart, increase the filling by half (using 2 eggs).

Makes 24 tartlets or 1 9-inch tart

1 recipe Savory Tart Dough (page 63)

15 medium asparagus spears (about 1 pound)
2 tablespoons unsalted butter
½ cup chopped scallions, including about 2 inches of the green stems
¾ cup chopped mushrooms
2 ounces prosciutto, thinly sliced and coarsely chopped
½ teaspoon lemon juice
¼ teaspoon salt, or to taste
Freshly ground black pepper to taste
1 large egg
½ cup whipping or heavy cream
¼ cup grated imported Parmesan cheese

1. Preheat the oven to 375°F.

2. *For tartlets:* Bake the tartlet shells 15 minutes.

For a 9-inch tart: Line the tart shell with aluminum foil and fill it with pie weights or dried beans. Bake the shell until the crust is set, about 10 minutes. Remove the weights or beans and continue to bake until golden, about 15 minutes more.

The tart shell(s) can be baked up to 4 hours ahead. Cool, cover loosely with foil, and leave at cool room temperature.

3. To prepare the filling, cut the tough ends from the asparagus and discard. (For a 9-inch tart, increase the filling ingredients by one-half [using 2 eggs].) Blanch the asparagus in lightly salted boiling water to cover until just tender, about 3 minutes. Remove, place in a colander, and refresh under cold running water. Pat dry. Cut the spears into ¼-inch slices.

4. Heat the butter in a medium heavy skillet over medium-high heat. Add the asparagus and sauté, stirring constantly, for 1 minute. Add the scallions and cook and stir a minute more. Add the mushrooms and cook, stirring, until all the liquid evaporates, about 2 to 3 minutes. Stir in the prosciutto, lemon juice, salt, and pepper and cook a minute more. Taste and adjust the seasonings if necessary. The filling can be made to this point up to a day ahead; cover with plastic wrap and refrigerate.

5. When ready to bake, preheat the oven to 375°F.

6. *For tartlets:* Divide the asparagus mixture evenly among the tartlet shells. Whisk together the cream, egg, salt, and pepper, preferably in a large measuring cup with a spout. Carefully pour the custard mixture into the tartlet shells, filling them about two-thirds to three-quarters full. Sprinkle with the Parmesan cheese. Bake until the filling is set and the crust is lightly browned, about 15 minutes.

For a 9-inch tart: Spread the asparagus mixture evenly over the bottom of the tart shell. In a small bowl, whisk together the cream, eggs, salt, and pepper to blend. Pour this mixture into the tart. Sprinkle with the Parmesan cheese. Bake until the filling is set and the crust is lightly browned, about 20 to 25 minutes.

Remove the tart(s) from the oven and, when cool enough to handle, lift from the pan(s).

7. To serve, place the tart(s) on a serving tray. Serve the tartlets individually, or cut the 9-inch tart into 10 wedges.

SERVING: These tarts, whether made small or large, are best assembled and baked just prior to serving. If necessary, completely baked tarts can be cooled, unmolded, wrapped tightly in plastic wrap and then in aluminum foil, and frozen. To reheat, place the frozen tarts on a baking sheet, covered loosely with foil, in a preheated 350°F. oven until defrosted and heated through, about 20 to 25 minutes for tartlets and 30 to 40 minutes for a large tart. The crust will not be quite as crisp, but the tarts will still taste good.

VARIATION: Broccoli florets, blanched for 3 to 4 minutes and then coarsely chopped, can be used in place of asparagus.

Watercress Tartlets

I make these tarts in early spring (around the time of St. Patrick's Day) when good watercress appears in the market.

Makes 24 tartlets or 1 9-inch tart

1 recipe Savory Tart Dough (page 63)

2 bunches watercress (about 8 ounces total)
2 tablespoons unsalted butter
¼ teaspoon freshly grated nutmeg
⅔ cup whipping or heavy cream
2 large eggs
¼ teaspoon salt, or to taste
Freshly ground black pepper
¼ cup grated Jarlsberg cheese
1½ teaspoons grated lemon zest
Several sprigs of watercress, for garnish

1. Preheat the oven to 375°F.

2. *For tartlets:* Bake the tartlet shells 15 minutes.

For a 9-inch tart: Line the tart shell with aluminum foil and fill it with pie weights or dried beans. Bake the shell until the crust is set, about 10 minutes. Remove the weights or beans and continue to bake until golden, about 15 minutes more.

The tart shell(s) can be baked up to 4 hours ahead. Cool, cover loosely with foil, and leave at cool room temperature.

3. To prepare the filling, rinse and dry the watercress. Remove and discard the tough stems. Melt the butter in a large heavy skillet over medium-high heat. When hot, add the watercress and cook, stirring, until wilted, about 2 to 3 minutes.

4. Place the watercress in a food processor fitted with the steel blade or in a blender. Process several seconds until puréed. Then add the nutmeg, cream, and eggs and process until the mixture is blended. Remove and place in a mixing bowl. Add the salt and pepper, and stir in the lemon zest. The watercress filling can be made 2 to 3 hours ahead; cover and refrigerate.

5. When ready to bake, preheat the oven to 375°F.

6. *For tartlets:* Divide the watercress mixture among the tartlet shells. Sprinkle the cheese evenly on top. Bake until the filling is set and the crusts are lightly browned, about 15 to 20 minutes.

For a 9-inch tart: Pour the watercress mixture into the tart. Sprinkle the cheese on top. Bake until the filling is set and the crust is lightly browned, about 20 to 25 minutes.

Remove the tart(s) from the oven and, and when cool enough to handle, lift from pan(s).

7. To serve, place the tarts on a serving tray. Garnish the tray with a cluster of watercress sprigs. Serve the tartlets individually or cut a 9-inch tart into 10 wedges.

SERVING: These tarts, whether made small or large, are best assembled and baked just prior to serving. If necessary, completely baked tarts can be cooled, unmolded, wrapped tightly in plastic wrap and then in aluminum foil, and frozen. To reheat, place frozen tarts on a baking sheet, covered loosely with foil, in a preheated 350°F. oven until defrosted and heated through, about 20 to 25 minutes for tartlets and 30 to 40 minutes for a large tart. The crust will not be quite as crisp, but the tarts will still taste good.

Chile Verde Tartlets

Mild green chilies, Monterey Jack cheese, and a generous seasoning of cayenne pepper are the dominant flavors of these special, not too spicy, tarts created by my friend and student Elly Persing, who lived for many years in New Mexico. Serve these tartlets before a Southwestern-style meal.

Makes 24 tartlets or 1 9-inch tart

1 recipe Savory Tart Dough (page 63)

4 tablespoons unsalted butter
½ cup finely chopped shallots
2 4-ounce cans mild chilies, well drained and very finely chopped
¼ teaspoon cayenne pepper
¼ teaspoon salt, or to taste
1 cup whipping or heavy cream
¾ cup grated Monterey Jack cheese
Sprigs of cilantro, for garnish

1. Preheat the oven to 375°F.

2. *For tartlets:* Bake the tartlet shells 15 minutes.

For a 9-inch tart: Line the tart shell with aluminum foil and fill it with pie weights or dried beans. Bake the shell until the crust is set, about 10 minutes. Remove the weights or beans and continue to bake until golden, about 15 minutes more.

The tart shell(s) can be baked up to 4 hours ahead. Cool, cover loosely with foil, and leave at cool room temperature.

3. To prepare the filling, heat the butter in a medium-size heavy skillet over medium-high heat. When hot, add the shallots and cook, stirring, for 2 minutes. Add the chilies and cook and stir a minute more. Add the cayenne pepper, salt, and cream and cook, stirring, until the cream has thickened slightly, about 3 minutes. Add the cheese and stir until melted. The filling can be made a day ahead. Cover and refrigerate.

4. When ready to bake, preheat the oven to 375°F.

5. *For tartlets:* Divide the chile mixture among the tartlet shells, filling them two-thirds to three-quarters full. Bake until the filling is set and the crust is lightly browned, about 15 to 20 minutes.

For a 9-inch tart: Fill the tart shell with the chile mixture. Bake until the filling is set and the crust is lightly browned, about 20 to 25 minutes.

Remove the tart(s) from the oven and, when cool enough to handle, lift from the pan(s).

6. To serve, place the tart(s) on a serving tray and garnish with cilantro sprigs. Serve the tartlets individually or cut the 9-inch tart into 10 wedges.

SERVING: These tarts, whether made small or large, are best assembled and baked just prior to serving. If necessary, completely baked tarts can be cooled, unmolded, wrapped tightly in plastic wrap and then in aluminum foil, and frozen. To reheat, place the frozen tarts on a baking sheet, covered loosely with foil, in a preheated 350°F. oven until defrosted and heated through, about 20 to 25 minutes for tartlets and 30 to 40 minutes for a large tart. The crust will not be quite as crisp, but the tarts will still taste good.

Belgian Endive and Ham Tartlets

Belgian endive and ham, a classic French combination, make a sophisticated tart filling. The slightly bitter endive takes on a sweet taste when sautéed and the ham adds a complementary salty touch.

Makes 24 tartlets or 1 9-inch tart

1 recipe Savory Tart Dough (page 63)

4 tablespoons unsalted butter
4 cups chopped Belgian endive (about 4 medium endives)
½ teaspoon sugar
3 ounces ham, very thinly sliced and diced
¼ teaspoon salt
⅔ cup whipping or heavy cream
2 large egg yolks
½ teaspoon freshly grated nutmeg
Freshly ground black pepper to taste
2 to 3 tablespoons grated imported Gruyère cheese
3 to 4 endive leaves, for garnish
4 to 5 whole chives, for garnish
2 tablespoons chopped fresh chives, for garnish

1. Preheat the oven to 375°F.

2. *For tartlets:* Bake the tartlet shells 15 minutes.

For a 9-inch tart: Line the tart shell with aluminum foil and fill it with pie weights or dried beans. Bake the shell until the crust is set, about 10 minutes. Remove the weights or beans and continue to bake until golden, about 15 minutes more.

The tart shell(s) can be baked up to 4 hours ahead. Cool, cover loosely with foil, and leave at cool room temperature.

3. To prepare the filling, place the butter in a large heavy skillet (a cast-iron skillet works well) over medium-high heat. When hot, add the chopped endive and cook, stirring, until the endive starts to wilt, about 4 to 5 minutes. Sprinkle with the sugar and stir and cook another 2 minutes. Add the ham and toss and cook another minute. Taste and add salt if needed. The sautéed endive and ham mixture can be prepared a day ahead. Cool, cover, and refrigerate.

(continued)

81

4. When ready to bake, preheat the oven to 375°F.

5. *For tartlets:* Fill each tart shell with about 1 to 1½ teaspoons of the endive mixture. Whisk together the cream, egg yolks, salt, nutmeg, and pepper, preferably in a large measuring cup with a spout. Carefully pour the custard mixture into the tartlet shells, filling them about two-thirds to three-quarters full. Sprinkle the top of the tart(s) with the grated Gruyère. Bake until the filling is set and the crust is lightly browned, about 15 to 20 minutes.

For a 9-inch tart: Spread the endive mixture evenly in the bottom of the tart shell. In a small bowl, whisk together the cream, egg yolks, salt, nutmeg, and pepper to blend. Pour this mixture into the shell. Sprinkle Gruyère over the filling. Bake until the filling is set and the crust is lightly browned, about 20 to 25 minutes.

Remove the tart(s) from the oven, and when cool enough to handle, remove from the pan(s). To serve, arrange the endive leaves in a fan-shaped cluster on a serving plate. Arrange the whole chives between the endive leaves. Place the tart(s) on the serving plate and sprinkle with the chopped chives. Serve the tartlets individually or cut a 9-inch tart into 10 wedges.

SERVING: These tarts, whether made small or large, are best assembled and baked just prior to serving. If necessary, completely baked tarts can be cooled, unmolded, wrapped tightly in plastic wrap and then in aluminum foil, and frozen. To reheat, place the frozen tarts on a baking sheet, covered loosely with foil, in a preheated 350°F. oven until defrosted and heated through, about 20 to 25 minutes for tartlets and 30 to 40 minutes for a large tart. The crust will not be quite as crisp, but the tarts will still taste good.

Gorgonzola and Roasted Red Pepper Tartlets

These tartlets, made without a custard base, are filled simply with Gorgonzola, cream cheese, chopped roasted red peppers, and sliced prosciutto. If the shells are prepared in advance and the peppers are roasted ahead, they take only a few minutes to assemble. This recipe works best prepared just as tartlets.

Makes 24 tartlets

1 recipe Savory Tart Dough (page 63)

2 ounces Gorgonzola, crumbled
1 large roasted sweet red pepper (page 269, chopped, see note)
3 ounces cream cheese, softened
2 ounces prosciutto, thinly sliced and coarsely chopped
1 tablespoon chopped fresh flat-leaf parsley
1 tablespoon chopped fresh chives
Several sprigs of flat-leaf parsley, for garnish
Whole chives, for garnish

1. Preheat the oven to 375°F.

2. Bake the tartlet shells 15 minutes. The shells can be baked up to 4 hours ahead. Cool, cover loosely with foil, and leave at cool room temperature.

3. In a small bowl, mix together the Gorgonzola and cream cheese until blended. Place a ½ to ¾ teaspoon of the Gorgonzola-cream cheese mixture in each tart shell. Then top with a ½ teaspoon of the chopped red pepper. Place another ½ teaspoon of the Gorgonzola-cream cheese mixture over the red pepper. Finally, top each tart with a little of the chopped prosciutto. The tarts can stand, loosely covered, at room temperature for an hour before baking.

4. When ready to bake, preheat the oven to 375°F. Bake the tartlets until the cheese has melted and the filling is hot, about 15 to 20 minutes.

5. Remove the tarts from the oven and cool 3 to 5 minutes. When cool enough to handle, remove from the pans and arrange on a serving tray. Sprinkle with the chopped herbs, and garnish the tray with a bouquet of parsley and chives. Serve warm.

SHOPPING: If you do not have the time to roast red peppers, you can substitute commercially prepared roasted red peppers, which are packaged in glass jars.

SERVING: The bouquet of fresh parsley and chives for the garnish on the tray looks particularly attractive tied with a raffia bow.

These tartlets are best assembled and baked just prior to serving. If necessary, completely baked tarts can be cooled, unmolded, wrapped tightly in plastic wrap and then in aluminum foil, and frozen. To reheat, place the frozen tartlets on a baking sheet, covered loosely with foil, in a preheated 350°F. oven until defrosted and heated through, about 20 to 25 minutes. The crust will not be quite as crisp, but the tartlets will still taste good.

Angel Hair Flans

At a dinner I attended at the Folger Library in Washington, D.C., these wonderful little pasta flans were served as a side dish. Made by baking cooked angel hair pasta with a mixture of eggs, cream, and cheese, they became the hit of the party. I re-created the delicious pasta custards in my own kitchen, scaling down the size so they could be offered as appetizers.

Makes 24 flans

Nonstick vegetable cooking spray
1 tablespoon salt, divided
3 ounces angel hair pasta (capellini)
3 large eggs
1 cup whipping or heavy cream
1/2 teaspoon freshly grated nutmeg
Freshly ground black pepper to taste
1 cup grated imported Parmesan cheese, divided
Sprigs of watercress, for garnish

1. Preheat the oven to 350°F. Spray two nonstick mini-muffin tins (with 12 1¾-inch molds each) with the nonstick vegetable cooking spray.

2. Bring 2 quarts of water to a boil and add 2 teaspoons of the salt and the

84

pasta. Cook the pasta until tender, about 4 to 5 minutes. Drain well in a colander, then pat dry with a clean kitchen towel. Divide the pasta evenly among the mini-muffin tins.

3. In a mixing bowl, place the eggs, cream, nutmeg, the remaining 1 teaspoon salt, a generous grating of pepper, and ⅔ cup of the Parmesan cheese. Using a whisk, mix well to blend. Pour or ladle the mixture into the molds. Sprinkle the tops of the flans with the remaining ⅓ cup Parmesan cheese.

4. Bake on the center shelf of the oven until the flans are set, puffed, and lightly browned, about 15 to 20 minutes. Remove from the oven and cool 10 minutes. The flans will deflate, losing their puffiness. The flans can be made up to 3 days in advance. Cool, cover with plastic wrap, and refrigerate. Reheat in a preheated 350°F. oven until heated through, about 10 to 15 minutes.

5. To serve, remove the flans by lifting gently from the molds. Arrange on a serving plate and garnish with sprigs of watercress. Serve warm.

NOTE: The flans can be unmolded and reheated in a microwave if desired.

SERVING: Sometimes I use a whole bunch of watercress and arrange a border of the sprigs around the edge of a rimmed tray to create a nest effect. Then I place the flans in the center of the tray.

VARIATION: You can make these flans in 1-cup custard cups or ramekins. Garnished with sautéed shrimp or scallops and vegetables, they make a striking first course for a dinner or an unusual entrée for a luncheon. One recipe will yield 6 large custards.

Confetti Angel Hair Flans

This variation on the preceding recipe is the invention of my good friend and student Elly Persing. She added grated Monterey Jack cheese and chopped red and green peppers to the basic recipe. The results are delicious.

Makes 36 flans

Nonstick vegetable cooking spray
2½ teaspoons salt, divided
3 ounces angel hair pasta (capellini)
½ cup finely diced mixed sweet red and green peppers
4 large eggs
1⅓ cups whipping or heavy cream
Freshly ground black pepper to taste
1¼ cups grated Monterey Jack cheese with jalapeño peppers
3 tablespoons chopped fresh parsley, for garnish

1. Preheat the oven to 350°F. Spray three mini-muffin tins (each with 12 1¾-inch molds) with the nonstick vegetable cooking spray.

2. Bring 2 quarts of water to a boil and add 2 teaspoons of the salt and the pasta. Cook until tender, about 4 to 5 minutes. Drain the pasta well in a colander, then pat dry with a clean kitchen towel. Divide the pasta evenly among the mini-muffin tins. Sprinkle the diced peppers evenly over the pasta.

3. In a mixing bowl, place the eggs, cream, the remaining ½ teaspoon of salt, a grating of pepper, and the cheese. Using a whisk, mix well to blend. Pour or ladle the mixture into the molds.

4. Bake on the center shelf of the oven until the flans are set, puffed, and lightly browned, about 15 to 20 minutes. Remove from the oven and cool 10 minutes. The flans will deflate, losing their puffiness. The flans can be made up to 3 days in advance. Cool, cover with plastic wrap, and refrigerate. Reheat in a preheated 350°F. oven until heated through, about 10 to 15 minutes.

5. To serve, remove the flans by lifting gently from the molds. Arrange on a serving plate. Sprinkle with the chopped parsley.

NOTE: The flans can be unmolded and reheated in a microwave if desired.

SERVING: These flans, with red and green bursts of color, make a festive hors d'oeuvre at Christmastime. I arrange the flans on trays garnished with branches of long-needled pine.

Smoked Cheddar and Leek Flans

These individual baked flans are made by simply combining eggs and crème fraîche with sautéed leeks and smoked Cheddar cheese. Since these "tarts" are made without a pastry crust, they can be assembled in only a few minutes.

Makes 30 flans

Nonstick vegetable cooking spray
2 tablespoons unsalted butter
*2¼ cups chopped leeks (about 4 medium leeks) (save the green
    stems for garnish, optional)*
1 cup crème fraîche (see note)
2 large eggs
2 large egg yolks
1¼ cups grated smoked Cheddar cheese (about 5 ounces), divided
Pinch of freshly grated nutmeg
Salt to taste
2 tablespoons chopped fresh chives, for garnish

1. Preheat the oven to 400°F. Spray three nonstick mini-muffin tins (each with 12 1¾-inch molds) with the nonstick vegetable cooking spray.

2. Heat the butter in a large heavy skillet over medium-high heat. When hot, add the leeks and sauté, stirring, until softened, about 6 to 7 minutes. Remove from the heat.

3. Combine the crème fraîche, eggs, and yolks in a mixing bowl. Add the sautéed leeks, 1 cup of the cheese, the nutmeg, and the salt. Ladle or spoon 2 tablespoons each of this mixture into the prepared molds; you should be able to fill 30 molds. Sprinkle the remaining ¼ cup cheese over the flans.

4. Bake the flans until they are set and slightly puffed, about 15 to 20 minutes. Remove from the oven and cool 5 minutes. The flans will deflate, losing their puffiness. The flans can be made up to 3 days in advance. Cool, cover with plastic wrap, and refrigerate. Reheat in a preheated 350°F. oven until heated through, about 10 to 15 minutes.

5. To serve, unmold the flans and sprinkle with the chopped chives. Arrange on a serving plate.

(continued)

NOTE: To prepare crème fraîche, combine 1 cup heavy or whipping cream and ⅓ cup sour cream in a medium-sized bowl and mix well. Let stand, uncovered, in a warm spot for 6 to 7 hours or overnight until thickened. Makes 1⅓ cups. Crème fraîche can be covered and stored in the refrigerator for up to 1 week.

NOTE: The flans can be unmolded and reheated in a microwave if desired.

SERVING: For a special presentation, I blanch the green parts of the leeks in boiling water for 10 to 15 seconds to intensify the color. Then, I drain and pat the greens dry and cut slender leaf shapes from them. The leek "leaves" look very attractive overlapping each other as a border on the serving tray, with the flans in the center of the tray.

Fresh Tomato and Polenta Tarts

Years ago, I attended a cooking class given by talented Italian chefs from the celebrated CIGA hotel chain. Bowls of hot polenta, made simply by simmering cornmeal in a hot liquid, were part of the menu and my favorite dish of the meal. Since then, I have used polenta in countless recipes. In this one, cooked polenta is molded in mini-muffin tins and then garnished with chopped tomatoes and oregano.

Makes 36 tartlets

Nonstick vegetable cooking spray
3 cups chicken stock
1 cup yellow cornmeal
1¼ cups grated imported Parmesan cheese, divided
Salt to taste
1 cup diced unpeeled but seeded ripe tomatoes
1½ teaspoons chopped fresh oregano or ½ teaspoon dried
1 teaspoon very finely minced garlic
Freshly ground black pepper to taste
Several sprigs of oregano, for garnish

1. Lightly grease three mini-muffin tins (with 12 1¾-inch molds each) with the nonstick vegetable cooking spray.

2. Pour the chicken stock into a large heavy saucepan and bring to a boil over medium-high heat. When boiling, gradually add the cornmeal in a fine stream, whisking constantly. When all the cornmeal has been added, continue to cook, whisking constantly, until the mixture is quite thick, about 5 minutes. Remove from the heat and stir in 1 cup of the Parmesan cheese. Season to taste with salt. If using canned stock, you may not need to add salt.

3. Fill the muffin tins with the polenta, pressing down with your fingertips to make sure the polenta is firmly packed, two-thirds to three-quarters full, into the molds. With your thumb, make a slight indentation in the center of each tart. The polenta tarts can be made a day ahead to this point. Cool, cover, and refrigerate for 15 to 30 minutes to become firm. They can also be frozen. Defrost in the refrigerator before baking.

4. When ready to serve the tarts, preheat the oven to 350°F. Unmold the tarts and arrange, round, indented side up, on a baking sheet.

5. To prepare the topping, combine the tomatoes, oregano, garlic, and pepper. Spoon a little topping on top of each tart. Heat the tarts in the oven until hot, about 10 to 12 minutes. (Or heat using a microwave-proof container in a microwave until hot.)

6. To serve, arrange the tarts on a serving tray and sprinkle with the remaining ¼ cup Parmesan cheese. Garnish the tray with sprigs of oregano.

SHOPPING: If fresh oregano is not available, fresh basil is a good substitute.

Toast Tartlets with Chèvre, Tomatoes, and Walnuts

These toasted bread cups are filled with chèvre, chopped plum tomatoes, walnuts, and fresh herbs. I make them in the summer months when perfect tomatoes and fresh basil and mint are easy to find in the market.

Makes 24 tartlets

Toast Tartlets

24 slices extra-thin firm white bread
4 tablespoons unsalted butter, melted
2 tablespoons olive oil
1 teaspoon minced garlic

Filling

1 cup chopped unpeeled but seeded tomatoes (about 3 to 4 plum
    tomatoes)
Salt
¼ cup toasted walnuts (page 268)
¼ cup finely chopped fresh basil
4 teaspoons chopped fresh mint
2 teaspoons minced garlic
4 teaspoons olive oil
Freshly ground black pepper to taste
4 ounces chèvre

1. To prepare the toast tartlet shells, preheat the oven to 375°F.

2. Remove the crusts from the bread and cut a 3-inch round from each slice. (Save the trimmings for another use.) Roll each round with a rolling pin so that it is thin and firm. Combine the melted butter, olive oil, and garlic in a small bowl and stir to mix. Brush the bread rounds lightly on both sides with the butter mixture. Then mold the rounds into two nonstick mini-muffin tins (each with 12 1¾-inch molds).

3. Bake the tartlet shells until golden, about 10 minutes. The toast tartlet shells can be prepared up to a day in advance. Leave in the molds, cover tightly with plastic wrap, and refrigerate.

4. When ready to assemble the tartlets, place the chopped tomatoes in a sieve or colander and salt lightly. Let drain for 30 minutes.

5. Place the drained tomatoes in a bowl with the walnuts, basil, mint, garlic, and olive oil. Toss to mix and season with salt and pepper to taste.

6. Whip the chèvre to a smooth consistency with a mixer. Place a scant teaspoon of chèvre in each toast cup. Top the chèvre with 1 tablespoon of the tomato mixture. The tarts may be assembled 2 to 3 hours in advance to this point. Cover loosely with plastic wrap and leave at cool room temperature.

7. When ready to serve, preheat the oven to 350°F.

8. Transfer the bread cups to a baking sheet. Bake until warm, about 5 to 7 minutes. Arrange on a serving tray and serve warm.

Cheese-Filled Polenta Tartlets

These little polenta tarts with their surprise cheese filling are among my favorite appetizers. The taste of the rich combination of cooked cornmeal and melted cheese is, for me, heaven. The tarts can be made completely in advance and refrigerated or frozen until needed.

Makes 18 tartlets

Nonstick vegetable cooking spray
1½ cups chicken stock
½ cup yellow cornmeal
⅓ cup grated imported Parmesan cheese
½ tablespoon unsalted butter
Salt to taste
1 egg white, lightly beaten
4 ounces Herb-Garlic Cheese (page 264)
Flat-leaf parsley leaves and sprigs, for garnish

1. Spray two nonstick mini-muffin tins (with 12 1¾-inch molds each) with the nonstick vegetable cooking spray.

(continued)

2. Place the stock in a medium heavy saucepan over medium-high heat and bring to a boil. When boiling, add the cornmeal very slowly in a thin stream, whisking constantly. Continue to whisk until the mixture is very thick, about 5 minutes. Whisk in the Parmesan cheese and butter. Remove the pan from the heat. Taste, and if desired, add salt. If you used canned stock, which is often salty, you may need very little or no additional salt.

3. Place 1 tablespoon of the warm polenta mixture in 18 of the muffin molds and pat with your fingers to smooth. Let cool slightly. Then make a slight indentation in the center of each tart with your fingertips.

4. Brush the edges of each polenta tart with some of the egg white. Pat ½ teaspoon of the cheese in each mold, then pat a teaspoon of the polenta mixture over the cheese, and use your fingers or a spatula to smooth the top. The tarts can be made 1 to 2 days in advance, if covered with plastic wrap, and refrigerated. Or they can be covered with plastic wrap and refrigerated. Or they can be covered with plastic wrap and then with aluminum foil and frozen. If the tarts have been frozen, defrost overnight in the refrigerator before baking.

5. When ready to bake, preheat the oven to 350°F. Bake the tarts, uncovered, until hot, about 20 to 25 minutes. Remove the tarts from the oven and cool a minute or two. Carefully lift the tarts out of the molds and arrange on a serving platter. Place a parsley leaf on top of each tart. Arrange the tarts on a serving tray and garnish the tray with sprigs of flat-leaf parsley.

VARIATIONS: Roquefort or another blue cheese without a rind is also delicious as a filling. In place of the parsley leaf garnish, place a small piece of chopped walnut on top of each tart.

Monterey Jack cheese with jalapeño peppers is also a fine variation. Use a small piece of finely chopped sweet red pepper as a garnish on top of each tart. Homemade chili also makes a good filling.

Southwestern Tart

This Southwestern-style "tart" is a dish I created with the help of my good friend and cooking pal Jim Budros. We spread a mixture of cream cheese and sour cream flavored with lime in a pie plate and topped it with Jim's delicious pineapple salsa. The pie is baked until hot and served warm with tortilla chips.

Makes 1 9-inch tart

8 ounces cream cheese, softened
2 tablespoons milk
½ cup sour cream
¼ teaspoon grated lime zest
¼ teaspoon coarsely ground black pepper

1½ cups diced (cut into ½-inch cubes) fresh pineapple (see note)
1 small mango, peeled and cut into ½-inch dice; or 1 large peach
    (frozen peaches will work) or nectarine, peeled and cut into
    ½-inch dice; or 2 ripe plums, unpeeled but pitted and diced
1 sweet red pepper, cut into ¼-inch dice
1 small jalapeño pepper, or more for a hotter taste, seeded and
    chopped (see note)
3 scallions, including about 2 inches of the green stems, finely
    chopped
1½ teaspoons finely chopped garlic
2 tablespoons chopped fresh cilantro
3½ tablespoons lime juice

Tortilla chips (regular corn tortilla chips or blue corn tortilla chips
    or a combination)

1. To prepare the tart, place the cream cheese, milk, and sour cream in the bowl of a food processor fitted with the metal blade. Process until the mixture is smooth. Add the lime zest and pepper and process only a few seconds to blend. Spread the mixture in a 9-inch Pyrex pie plate or other oven-to-table dish. The tart can be prepared up to 2 days in advance to this point; cover and refrigerate.

2. To prepare the salsa, combine the pineapple, mango, both peppers, the scallions, garlic, and cilantro in a medium-size nonaluminum mixing bowl. Stir to mix. Add the lime juice and stir to blend. The salsa can be prepared a day ahead. Cover and refrigerate. Bring to room temperature 30 minutes before using.

3. When ready to assemble the tart, preheat the oven to 350°F.

4. Drain the pineapple salsa in a large sieve or colander. Spread the drained salsa evenly on top of the cream cheese mixture in the pie plate. Place on the center shelf of the preheated oven and bake for 15 minutes to heat.

5. Remove from the oven and place the tart on a large serving tray. Surround with mounds of tortilla chips. Use a small knife to spread the cheese and salsa on the chips or dip the chips into tart and eat.

SHOPPING: To save time, buy fresh, peeled pineapple, available in the produce section of many grocery stores.

NOTE: When seeding and chopping jalapeño peppers, it is wise to wear rubber gloves. The tissues around your eyes, nose, mouth, and ears are very sensitive to the oils and fumes of hot peppers. If, by mistake, you rub any of these areas with your fingers after handling hot peppers, you will feel a burning sensation.

VARIATION: When I am trying to reduce calories, I make this tart with light cream cheese and light sour cream. It is not as rich and thick as the original, but still tastes very good.

Pizzettes and Galettes

I don't think there is a more popular food in America than pizza. Its appeal is universal. Although most people think of pizza as a main course, small bite-sized pizzas, which I call *pizzettes*, or large pizzas cut into small servings, make superb appetizers. And they are quite manageable, even for the busiest cook.

The dough for these pizzettes and pizzas is easy to assemble and rises in about an hour's time because it is prepared with quick-rising yeast. The pizza rounds can be cut out, prebaked, and either stored in an airtight container for a few days or frozen. The toppings, for the most part, can be made ahead, and the pizzas put together and baked briefly when needed.

The pizzas in this chapter are not ordinary run-of-the-mill types. Apples and Brie, potatoes and chives, and smoked salmon and herbed cream cheese are some of the unexpected but delicious toppings. For several of these pizzas, the dough is replaced with flour tortillas, which become quite crisp when baked and work well as a base for Southwestern-inspired garnishes.

Galettes are flaky pastry rounds of French origin that can be made with either sweet or savory toppings. Savory galettes prepared with store-bought puff pastry crusts are unusual but easy appetizers. The ones included here are topped with walnuts and chèvre or eggplant, tomato, and ricotta.

Pizza Dough

This pizza dough, made with quick-rising yeast, is easy to assemble, and when rolled thin, makes a crispy crust for pizza toppings.

1½ cups all-purpose flour, plus up to 1 tablespoon more if needed
1 package quick-rising active dry yeast
½ teaspoon salt
½ teaspoon sugar
1 tablespoon olive oil
½ cup warm water (115° to 125°F.), plus up to 1 tablespoon more if needed

1. *Food Processor Method:* Place the 1½ cups flour, the yeast, salt, and sugar in the bowl of a food processor fitted with the metal blade and process until the mixture is combined. Combine the olive oil and the ½ cup warm water in a measuring cup with a spout. With the motor running, add the liquids through the feed tube in a steady stream. Continue processing until the dough forms a ball and cleans the side of the bowl. If the dough seems too wet, add up to a tablespoon additional flour; if it seems too dry, add up to a tablespoon more water. Process for 30 seconds to knead the dough. Remove the dough and place on a lightly floured surface. Knead a few times to form a smooth ball.

Mixer Method: Place ¾ cup of the flour, the yeast, salt, sugar, olive oil, and the ½ cup warm water in the bowl of an electric mixer. Beat on medium speed until the dough forms a shaggy mass. Add the remaining ¾ cup flour and beat until a smooth ball of dough is formed. If the dough seems too wet, add up to a tablespoon additional flour; if it seems too dry, add up to a tablespoon more water. Remove the dough and place on a lightly floured surface. Knead a few times to form a smooth ball.

Hand Method: Place ¾ cup of the flour, the yeast, salt, sugar, olive oil, and the ½ cup warm water in a mixing bowl and stir with a spoon to blend. Stir in the remaining ¾ cup flour, ¼ cup at a time, and mix until a smooth ball of dough is formed. If the dough seems too wet, add up to a tablespoon additional flour; if it seems too dry, add up to a tablespoon more water. Remove the dough from the bowl and knead on a lightly floured surface until smooth and soft, about 3 to 4 minutes.

2. Place the ball of dough in a greased mixing bowl and let rise in a warm place until almost doubled in bulk, about 45 to 60 minutes.

3. Punch down the dough. Divide it in half. On a lightly floured surface roll out each half to a very thin 12-inch round. The specialness of these pizzas comes from the very thin dough, which gets crispy when baked.

For 30 pizzettes: Using a 2½-inch cutter, cut out 15 rounds from each 12-inch dough round. If necessary, reroll the scraps to get 15 rounds. Prick the surface of each small round all over with the tines of a fork.

For 2 11-inch pizzas: Fold over the outer ½-inch edge of each 12-inch round and pinch to make a rim. Prick the rounds all over with the tines of a fork.

4. Place the small or large rounds on two lightly greased baking sheets. Cover with plastic wrap and then with aluminum foil, and refrigerate for up to a day. Bring to room temperature for 30 minutes before baking. Or freeze and defrost in the refrigerator before baking.

Saga Blue and Apricot Pizzettes

Smooth, creamy slices of blue cheese and tart dried apricots are an untraditional savory pizza topping. These pizzas are best served only as pizzettes, not as large pizzas. They take only minutes to assemble, after the dough has been prepared.

Makes 30 pizzettes

30 pizzettes made from 1 recipe Pizza Dough (page 96)

8 ounces Saga blue cheese, with rind, well chilled
30 dried apricot halves (buy dried apricots with a soft texture)
30 small sprigs of mint, for garnish

1. Preheat the oven to 450°F.

2. Bake the pizza rounds for 5 minutes, until just lightly colored. Remove from the oven. The pizza rounds can be baked 1 to 2 days ahead. Cool completely and store in an airtight container at room temperature. They can also be frozen; wrap tightly in plastic wrap and then in aluminum foil. Defrost in the refrigerator before using, and reheat to "dry out" for 2 to 4 minutes in a 450°F. oven.

3. When ready to assemble the pizzas, preheat the oven to 450°F.

4. Cut ⅛-inch-thick slices from the cheese and trim to fit the tops of the pizzas. Top each pizza with 2 slices. Flatten the apricots by pressing with your fingers; then place one apricot, hollow side up, over the cheese on each pizza. Place another thin slice of Saga blue over each apricot.

5. Bake until the cheese has melted, about 5 to 6 minutes. Remove and garnish each pizzette with a mint sprig. Arrange the pizzettes on a serving tray.

SHOPPING: Saga blue is my favorite choice for these pizzas because of its very smooth texture and because the rind adds a sharp taste. However, if unavailable, Maytag Blue or another smooth creamy blue cheese can be substituted.

NOTE: If you have trouble finding soft dried apricots, soak the dried apricots for 10 to 15 minutes in hot water to soften. Pat dry and then use as directed.

Smoked Salmon, Cream Cheese, and Dill Pizzettes

Pizzettes topped with dill and lemon-scented cream cheese and paper-thin slices of smoked salmon make truly sophisticated appetizers. I serve these cocktail pizzas for very special occasions.

Makes 30 pizzettes or 2 11-inch pizzas

8 ounces cream cheese, at room temperature
½ tablespoon fresh dill or ½ teaspoon dried
1½ teaspoons grated lemon zest
2½ teaspoons lemon juice
6 to 8 ounces smoked salmon, thinly sliced
3 tablespoons chopped fresh chives
30 pizzettes or 2 pizzas made from 1 recipe Pizza Dough (page 96)

1. To prepare the topping, place the cream cheese, dill, lemon zest, and lemon juice in a mixing bowl and stir to mix well. The cream cheese topping can be made a day ahead; cover and refrigerate. Bring to room temperature 30 minutes before using.

2. When ready to assemble the pizzas, preheat the oven to 450°F.

3. Bake the pizza rounds until light golden and crisp, about 8 to 10 minutes. Remove and cool 2 to 3 minutes.

4. *For pizzettes:* Spread each round with a scant tablespoon of the cream cheese mixture and top with 2 to 3 slices of salmon, trimmed to fit the pizzette. Garnish with the chopped chives.

For large pizzas: Spread each pizza with half the cream cheese mixture. Arrange half the salmon slices over the cheese mixture on each pizza. Garnish with the chopped chives.

5. Arrange the pizzas on a serving tray. Serve pizzettes individually, or cut large pizzas into 15 wedges each.

NOTE: Do not rebake these pizzas after they are assembled, because the smoked salmon will lose its bright color.

Spicy Tomato and Brie Pizzettes

These thin, crisp pizza rounds are topped with a robust tomato sauce, Brie, crumbled bacon, and a garnish of chopped fresh basil. I serve these at open houses during football season as well as at fancy cocktail receptions. No matter what the occasion, people always ask for seconds.

Makes 30 pizzettes or 2 11-inch pizzas

30 pizzettes or 2 pizzas made from 1 recipe Pizza Dough (page 96)

1 recipe Quick Tomato Sauce (page 261)

1 teaspoon crushed red pepper flakes
2 tablespoons olive oil
8 ounces Brie with the rind, cut into 1/4-inch cubes
6 ounces sliced bacon, fried until crisp and crumbled, optional
4 tablespoons julienned fresh basil

1. Preheat the oven to 450°F.

2. Bake the pizza rounds for 5 minutes, until just lightly colored. Remove from the oven. The pizza rounds can be baked 1 to 2 days ahead. Cool completely and store in an airtight container at cool room temperature. They can also be frozen; wrap tightly in plastic wrap and then in aluminum foil. Defrost in the refrigerator before using, and reheat to "dry out" for 2 to 4 minutes in a 450°F. oven.

3. When ready to assemble the pizzas, preheat the oven to 450°F. If the tomato sauce was made ahead, reheat until hot. Stir in the red pepper flakes. Set aside.

4. Brush the tops of the pizzas lightly with olive oil.

For pizzettes: Spread each pizzette with about a tablespoon of the tomato sauce. Scatter a few cubes of the Brie over the sauce. If using bacon, sprinkle it over the top of each pizza.

For large pizzas: Spread each round with half the sauce. Then top each one with half of the Brie and bacon.

5. Bake the pizzas until the cheese melts and the pizzas are hot, about 5 minutes. Remove from the oven and sprinkle with the julienned basil. Serve pizzettes individually, or cut large pizzas into 15 wedges each.

VARIATION: Garnish with sliced olives (Kalamata, Niçoise, or ripe green olives) in place of the bacon.

Fennel and Prosciutto Pizzettes

You can prepare the tomato sauce and sauté the fennel and prosciutto ahead, so that all that is necessary before baking is a quick assembly of these delicious pizzas.

Makes 30 pizzettes or 2 11-inch pizzas

30 pizzettes or 2 pizzas made from 1 recipe Pizza Dough (page 96)
1 recipe Quick Tomato Sauce (page 261)

2 medium fennel bulbs
4 tablespoons olive oil, divided
4 ounces prosciutto, sliced ¼ inch thick and cut into ¼-inch dice
¾ cup grated Italian fontina cheese (3 ounces)
¼ cup grated imported Parmesan cheese (1 ounce)
2 teaspoons fennel seeds, crushed

1. Preheat the oven to 450°F.

2. Bake the pizza rounds for 5 minutes, until just lightly colored. Remove from the oven. The pizza rounds can be baked 1 to 2 days ahead. Cool completely and store in an airtight container at cool room temperature. They can also be frozen; wrap tightly in plastic wrap and then in aluminum foil. Defrost in the refrigerator before using, and reheat to "dry out" for 2 to 4 minutes in a 450°F. oven.

(continued)

3. Remove the feathery stems from the fennel bulbs, place them in a large glass or a vase filled with water, and set aside at room temperature. Cut the fennel bulbs in half lengthwise and cut out and discard the tough triangular cores. Coarsely chop the bulbs.

4. Heat 2 tablespoons of the olive oil in a medium-size heavy skillet over medium-high heat. When hot, add the chopped fennel and sauté, stirring, until softened, about 8 minutes. Remove from the heat and stir in the prosciutto. The fennel and prosciutto can be prepared a day ahead. Cool, cover, and refrigerate. Bring to room temperature 15 to 20 minutes before using.

5. When ready to assemble the pizzas, preheat the oven to 450°F. If the tomato sauce was made ahead, reheat until hot. Set aside.

6. *For pizzettes:* Spread each pizza with about a tablespoon of the tomato sauce. Top the pizzas with the fennel/prosciutto mixture. Combine the cheeses and sprinkle over the pizzas, then sprinkle the crushed fennel seeds over the cheese.

For large pizzas: Spread each round with half the sauce, and top each with half the fennel/prosciutto mixture. Combine the cheeses and spread half over each pizza. Then sprinkle each pizza with the fennel seeds.

7. Bake until the cheese melts and the pizzas are hot, about 5 minutes. Arrange the pizzas on a serving tray and garnish the tray with the reserved fennel stems. Serve pizzettes individually, or cut large pizzas into 15 wedges each.

Apple and Brie Pizzettes

Makes 30 pizzettes or 2 11-inch pizzas

30 pizzettes or 2 pizzas made from 1 recipe Pizza Dough (page 96)

3 medium tart red apples
3 tablespoons lemon juice
2½ tablespoons honey mustard
10 to 12 ounces Brie, with rind, well chilled or slightly frozen
2 tablespoons chopped fresh flat-leaf parsley
2 tablespoons coarsely chopped walnuts or almonds
Several sprigs of flat-leaf parsley, for garnish

1. Preheat the oven to 450°F.

2. Bake the pizza rounds for 5 minutes, until just lightly colored. Remove from the oven. The pizza rounds can be baked 1 to 2 days ahead. Cool completely and store in an airtight container at room temperature. They can also be frozen; wrap tightly in plastic wrap and then in aluminum foil. Defrost in the refrigerator before using, and reheat to "dry out" for 2 to 4 minutes in a 450°F. oven.

3. Stem and core the apples, but do not peel. Cut into ⅛-inch-thick slices. Toss the slices in the lemon juice and set aside.

4. *For pizzettes:* Spread each pizza with ¼ teaspoon of the honey mustard. Cut ⅛-inch-thick slices from the Brie and trim to fit the tops of the pizzas. Top each pizza with 2 slices Brie, arrange 2 to 3 apple slices trimmed to fit the pizza over the Brie, and top with another slice of Brie.

For large pizzas: Spread each pizza with half the mustard. Cut the Brie into ⅛-inch slices. Cover each pizza with one third of the Brie slices. Arrange the apple slices on top of the Brie, and top the apples with the remaining Brie.

5. Bake the pizzas until the cheese has melted and the pizzas are hot, about 5 minutes. Remove and sprinkle with the chopped parsley and nuts.

6. Arrange the pizzas on a serving plate garnished with a cluster of parsley sprigs. Serve pizzettes individually, or cut large pizzas into 15 wedges each.

SHOPPING: Although I use tart red apples such as Winesap or McIntosh for these pizzas, Granny Smiths and a whole variety of sweet apples such as Red and Golden Delicious can be substituted with successful results.

Primavera Pizzettes

If vegetables are so good with pasta, why not on pizza? One of my favorites is pizzettes topped with a nutmeg-scented cheese sauce and slices of tender, young asparagus spears.

Makes 30 pizzettes or 2 11-inch pizzas

30 pizzettes or 2 pizzas made from 1 recipe Pizza Dough (page 96)

1 cup whipping or heavy cream
¼ cup grated imported Parmesan cheese
⅛ teaspoon freshly grated nutmeg
15 medium asparagus spears (about 1 pound)

1. Preheat the oven to 450°F.

2. Bake the pizza rounds for 5 minutes, until just lightly colored. Remove from the oven. The pizza rounds can be baked 1 to 2 days ahead. Cool completely and store in an airtight container at room temperature. They can also be frozen; wrap tightly in plastic wrap and then in aluminum foil. Defrost in the refrigerator before using, and reheat to "dry out" for 2 to 4 minutes in a 450°F. oven.

3. To prepare the topping, place the cream in a medium-size heavy saucepan over medium-high heat. When the cream is hot, gradually add the cheese, whisking constantly, until the cheese has melted and the sauce is smooth. Stir in the nutmeg. The sauce can be made up to a day ahead. Cover and refrigerate. Reheat, stirring, before using.

4. To prepare the asparagus, cut off the tough ends and discard. Blanch the asparagus in lightly salted boiling water to cover until just tender, about 3 minutes. Remove, place in a colander, and refresh under cold running water. Pat dry. The asparagus can be prepared up to a day ahead. Wrap in plastic wrap and refrigerate.

5. When ready to assemble the pizzas, preheat the oven to 450°F.

6. *For pizzettes:* Spread each pizza with a heaping teaspoon of the sauce. Slice the asparagus spears in half lengthwise, then cut each half into 3 equal pieces. Place 3 pieces, including an asparagus tip, parallel to each other on top of each pizza.
    For large pizzas: Spread each pizza with half the sauce. Slice the asparagus in half lengthwise and arrange in a spoke pattern on top of each pizza.

104

7. Bake the pizzas for 5 minutes, until hot. Arrange the pizzas on a serving plate. Serve pizzettes individually, or cut large pizzas into 15 wedges each.

VARIATIONS: You can use the same sauce but vary the topping. Try thin julienned slices of prosciutto and cooked peas; sautéed thinly sliced sea scallops topped with chives and lemon zest; or shrimp, sautéed and cut in half through the dorsal (back) side, topped with chopped scallions and parsley.

Tomato and Olive Pizzettes

I created this tomato and olive sauce to serve with sautéed chicken, but Shirley Pogodinski, the chef at the president's house at Amherst College, told me that she tried a version of the sauce as a topping for pizza and that her husband was crazy about the resulting dish. When I tested this new recipe, my spouse was equally enthusiastic. In fact, he regularly suggests that I include these piquant pizzas for party menus.

Makes 30 pizzettes or 2 11-inch pizzas

30 pizzettes or 2 pizzas made from 1 recipe Pizza Dough (page 96)

5 tablespoons olive oil
1 cup chopped onions
1 tablespoon chopped garlic
2½ cups peeled, seeded, and chopped ripe tomatoes or drained canned Italian plum tomatoes
¾ cup chicken stock
24 Kalamata olives, pitted and sliced
12 green olives, pitted and sliced
6 tablespoons unsalted butter, cut into pieces
Salt and freshly ground black pepper to taste
½ cup grated Monterey Jack cheese (about 2 ounces)
Flat-leaf spinach leaves, for garnish

1. Preheat the oven to 450°F.

2. Bake the pizza rounds for 5 minutes, until just lightly colored. Remove from

105

the oven. The pizza rounds can be baked 1 to 2 days ahead. Cool completely and store in an airtight container at cool room temperature. They can also be frozen; wrap tightly in plastic wrap and then in aluminum foil. Defrost in the refrigerator before using, and reheat to "dry out" for 2 to 4 minutes in a 450°F. oven.

3. To prepare the topping, heat the olive oil until hot in a large heavy skillet over medium-high heat. Add the onions and sauté, stirring, until softened, about 5 minutes. Add the garlic, then the tomatoes, and sauté 2 minutes. Add the stock and olives and cook, stirring frequently, until the liquid has evaporated, about 5 to 8 minutes. Stir in the butter, about a tablespoon at a time. Taste and season as desired with salt and pepper. Because the olives are salty, you may not need to add any salt. The sauce can be made 1 to 2 days ahead. Cool, cover, and refrigerate. The sauce can also be frozen; cool, cover, and freeze. Defrost in the refrigerator or in a microwave before using.

4. When ready to assemble the pizzas, preheat the oven to 450°F. Reheat the sauce to warm.

5. *For pizzettes:* Spread each pizza with a generous tablespoon of the sauce. Sprinkle with the cheese.

For large pizzas: Spread half the sauce over each pizza round. Sprinkle with the cheese.

6. Bake until the cheese has melted and the pizzas are hot, about 5 to 6 minutes. Remove from the oven. Arrange a bed of spinach leaves on a serving tray, and place the pizzas on top. Serve pizzettes individually, or cut large pizzas into 15 wedges each.

SHOPPING: Be sure to use high-quality Kalamata and green olives for this dish. I often go to specialty food stores or delis where they are sold in bulk rather than prepackaged.

Potato and Chive Pizzettes

One spring day on a visit to Boston, I ordered a potato pizza as a first course at Biba's, a superb restaurant in the heart of the city. When a small, crisp pizza topped with paper-thin slices of potatoes and a garnish of sour cream, chives, and caviar arrived, I could hardly wait to taste it. It was so good that after finishing it, I immediately made my way to an open area of the restaurant where the pizzas were cooked in a wood-burning oven, and asked the baker how the dish was prepared. In creating my version, I added Monterey Jack cheese and decided to omit the caviar.

Makes 30 pizzettes or 2 11-inch pizzas

30 pizzettes or 2 pizzas made from 1 recipe Pizza Dough (page 96)

2 large baking potatoes, about 10 ounces each, unpeeled
½ cup whipping or heavy cream
Salt and coarsely ground black pepper to taste
½ teaspoon dried thyme
2 teaspoons very finely minced garlic
1 cup sour cream, divided
2 cups grated Monterey Jack cheese
4 tablespoons chopped fresh chives
Small bunch of chives, for garnish
Several sprigs of thyme, for garnish

1. Preheat the oven to 450°F.

2. Bake the pizza rounds for 5 minutes, until just lightly colored. Remove from the oven. The pizza rounds can be baked 1 to 2 days ahead. Cool completely and store in an airtight container at cool room temperature. They can also be frozen; wrap tightly in plastic wrap and then in aluminum foil. Defrost in the refrigerator before using, and reheat to "dry out" for 2 to 4 minutes in a 450°F. oven.

3. To prepare the topping, preheat the oven to 350°F.

4. Cut the potatoes into ⅛-inch-thick slices using a sharp knife, or slice in a food processor fitted with a 2-millimeter blade. Arrange overlapping potato slices in rows on an aluminum foil-lined greased baking sheet with sides. Drizzle the potatoes with the cream, season with the salt and pepper, and sprinkle with the thyme and garlic. Bake until tender, about 15 to 20 minutes.

(continued)

Remove from the oven. The potatoes can be prepared up to a day in advance. Cool, cover with plastic wrap, and refrigerate.

5. When ready to assemble the pizzas, preheat the oven to 450°F.

6. *For pizzettes:* Spread each pizza with a scant teaspoon of the sour cream. Arrange 2 to 3 overlapping potato slices on top of the sour cream. Sprinkle the cheese over the potatoes, then sprinkle with the chopped chives.

For large pizzas: Spread each pizza with ⅓ cup of the sour cream. Arrange half the prepared potatoes, overlapping the slices, on top of each pizza. Spread the cheese over the potatoes, then sprinkle with the chopped chives.

7. Bake the pizzas until hot, about 5 to 8 minutes. Watch carefully to make certain the crusts do not burn. Remove from the oven and place dollops of the remaining sour cream over the tops of the pizzas. Arrange on a serving tray. Garnish the tray with small mixed bouquets of chives and thyme. Serve pizzettes individually, or cut large pizzas into 15 wedges each.

SERVING: One of my cooking assistants serves these pizzas on a tray with three small bowls—one of extra sour cream, one of extra chives, and another of crumbled fried bacon—as garnishes.

BLT Pizzettes

Bacon, lettuce, and tomato sandwiches are my favorite, bar none, so I decided to try a pizza version of this classic combination. The only change I made was in the "L word." Sautéed leeks, I discovered, taste much better than shredded lettuce in the topping. Because there is no cheese in this topping, these pizzas are somewhat difficult to serve if made in the 11-inch size and so are best prepared as pizzettes.

Makes 30 pizzettes

30 pizzettes made from 1 recipe Pizza Dough (page 96)

¾ pound thinly sliced smoked bacon
1½ tablespoons olive oil, preferably extra virgin, plus extra for
*   drizzling over pizzas*
¾ cup very finely chopped leeks (1 to 2 large leeks)
3 large ripe tomatoes, cored, seeded, and chopped (about 2 cups)
Salt and freshly ground black pepper to taste
1½ tablespoons balsamic vinegar
3 tablespoons chopped flat-leaf parsley
Several sprigs of flat-leaf parsley, for garnish

1. Preheat the oven to 450°F.

2. Bake the pizza rounds for 5 minutes, until just lightly colored. Remove from the oven. The pizza rounds can be baked 1 to 2 days ahead. Cool completely and store in an airtight container at room temperature. They can also be frozen; wrap tightly in plastic wrap and then in aluminum foil. Defrost in the refrigerator before using, and reheat to "dry out" for 2 to 4 minutes in a 450°F. oven.

3. To prepare the topping, fry the bacon, in several batches, in a large heavy skillet over medium heat. Remove and drain on paper towels. Crumble into small pieces. Or cook in batches in the microwave. Drain, cool, and crumble.

4. Pour off all the bacon fat from the skillet and add 1½ tablespoons of the olive oil. Place over medium heat and when the oil is hot, sauté the leeks until softened, 2 to 3 minutes. Remove and drain on paper towels.

5. Place the tomatoes in a mixing bowl. Season with salt and pepper, then add the leeks and toss to mix. The bacon and the tomato/leek mixture can be prepared 1 to 2 hours ahead and kept at cool room temperature. If the bacon loses its crispness, reheat in a 350°F. oven for 10 minutes, or reheat in the microwave.

(continued)

6. When ready to assemble the pizzas, preheat the oven to 450°F.

7. Toss the tomato/leek mixture with the balsamic vinegar. Spread each pizzette with about a tablespoon of the tomato/leek mixture, and sprinkle some of the crumbled bacon on top.

8. Bake the pizzas until hot, about 5 to 6 minutes. Sprinkle the pizzettes with the chopped parsley, drizzle with olive oil, and arrange on a serving tray. Garnish the tray with clusters of parsley sprigs. These pizzettes should be eaten soon after being taken from the oven; if allowed to sit for a long time, they will become soggy.

Roasted Red Pepper and Shrimp Pizzettes

Sautéed shrimp, puréed roasted red peppers and chopped fresh basil make an irresistible combination of both colors and tastes for a pizza topping.

Makes 30 pizzettes or 2 11-inch pizzas

30 pizzettes or 2 pizzas made from 1 recipe Pizza Dough (page 96)

2 medium sweet red peppers, roasted (page 269)
3½ tablespoons olive oil, divided
2½ tablespoons unsalted butter
¼ teaspoon salt
Freshly ground black pepper to taste
30 medium shrimp, peeled and deveined
4 tablespoons chopped fresh basil
Several sprigs of basil, for garnish

1. Preheat the oven to 450°F.

2. Bake the pizza rounds for 5 minutes, until just lightly colored. Remove from the oven. The pizza rounds can be baked 1 to 2 days ahead. Cool completely and store in an airtight container at cool room temperature. They can also be frozen; wrap tightly in plastic wrap and then in aluminum foil. Defrost in the refrigerator before using. Reheat to "dry out" for 2 to 4 minutes in a 450°F. oven.

3. Place the roasted peppers in a food processor or blender and purée until smooth, about 1 minute. Add 1 tablespoon of the olive oil and process to blend, 10 seconds more. Season with the salt and pepper. Set the purée aside. The purée can be prepared up to a day ahead. Cover and refrigerate.

4. When ready to assemble the pizzas, preheat the oven to 450°F.

5. Heat the remaining 2½ tablespoons olive oil and the butter in a large heavy skillet over medium-high heat. When hot, add the shrimp and sauté, stirring constantly. until curled and pink, about 2 to 3 minutes. Remove and drain on paper towels. Split each shrimp in half through the dorsal (back) side.

6. *For pizzettes:* Spread each pizza round with a scant teaspoon of the purée. Top with 2 shrimp halves.

(continued)

For large pizzas: Spread each pizza with half of the purée. Arrange half of the shrimp on top of each pizza.

7. Bake the pizzas until hot, about 5 minutes. Remove from the oven. Sprinkle with the chopped basil. Arrange the pizzas on a serving plate and garnish the plate with sprigs of basil. Serve pizzettes individually, or cut large pizzas into 15 wedges each.

SERVING: Because of their rich deep red color, these pizzettes work well as Valentine appetizers. Use a heart-shaped cutter about 2½ inches at the widest point to cut out the dough.

Asparagus and Fontina Pizzettes

Fresh asparagus, lemon zest, dill, and fontina cheese are the simple ingredients used to top these appealing vegetable pizzas. I serve them at spring luncheons and dinners.

Makes 30 pizzettes or 2 11-inch pizzas

30 pizzettes or 2 pizzas made from 1 recipe Pizza Dough (page 96)

24 medium asparagus spears (about 1½ pounds)
2½ to 3 tablespoons olive oil
6 ounces grated Italian fontina cheese
Freshly ground black pepper to taste
4 teaspoons grated lemon zest (from 2 lemons)
3 tablespoons chopped fresh dill or 1 tablespoon dried
Sprigs of dill, for garnish

1. Preheat the oven to 450°F.

2. Bake the pizza rounds for 5 minutes, until just lightly colored. Remove from

112

the oven. The pizza rounds can be baked 1 to 2 days ahead. Cool completely and store in an airtight container at cool room temperature. They can also be frozen; wrap tightly in plastic wrap and then in aluminum foil. Defrost in the refrigerator before using. Reheat to "dry out" for 2 to 4 minutes in a 450°F. oven.

3. To prepare the asparagus, cut off the tough ends and discard. Blanch the asparagus in lightly salted boiling water until just tender, about 3 minutes. Remove, place in a colander, and refresh under cold running water. Pat dry. Cut the asparagus on the diagonal into ½-inch pieces. The asparagus can be prepared a day ahead. Wrap in plastic wrap and refrigerate.

4. When ready to assemble the pizzas, preheat the oven to 450°F.

5. *For pizzettes:* Brush the pizza rounds lightly with olive oil and sprinkle each one with about a teaspoon of the grated cheese. Top the pizzas with the asparagus pieces, and sprinkle the black pepper, lemon zest, and chopped dill over the asparagus.

For large pizzas: Brush each round lightly with olive oil. Sprinkle each with half the cheese. Top each pizza with half the asparagus pieces. Sprinkle the black pepper, lemon zest, and dill over the asparagus.

6. Bake the pizzas until hot, about 5 minutes. Remove from the oven. Arrange on a serving plate and garnish with sprigs of dill. Serve pizzettes individually, or cut large pizzas into 15 wedges each.

SHOPPING: If available, use fresh dill in this recipe. Although dried dill will work, fresh has a more intense flavor.

✳ *Brie and Red Onion Pizzettes*

Lang Bell, the husband of my assistant, Emily Bell, has a passion for Brie served with sweet red onions. At his request, Emily and I created these easy pizzas simply topped with slices of Brie and onion.

Makes 30 pizzettes or 2 11-inch pizzas

30 pizzettes or 2 pizzas made from 1 recipe Pizza Dough (page 96)

10 ounces Brie, with rind, well chilled or slightly frozen
1 large sweet red onion, peeled, halved lengthwise, and cut into
*   paper-thin slices*
2½ tablespoons finely chopped green pepper
Coarsely ground black pepper to taste

1. Preheat the oven to 450°F.

2. Bake the pizza rounds for 5 minutes, until just lightly colored. Remove from the oven. The pizza rounds can be baked 1 to 2 days ahead. Cool completely and store in an airtight container at room temperature. They can also be frozen; wrap tightly in plastic wrap and then in aluminum foil. Defrost in the refrigerator before using. Reheat to "dry out" for 2 to 4 minutes in a 450°F. oven.

3. When ready to assemble the pizzas, preheat the oven to 450°F.

4. *For pizzettes:* Cut ⅛-inch-thick slices from the Brie and trim so they fit the top of the pizzas. Top each pizza with 2 slices Brie, leaving a ¼-inch border around the edge since the cheese will spread when baked. Arrange 1 or 2 onion slices, enough to cover the cheese, on top. Sprinkle pizzas with the chopped green pepper and season with the black pepper.
    For large pizzas: Cut ⅛-inch-thick slices from the Brie, and place half the slices on top of each pizza round. Arrange half the onion slices on top of each pizza. Sprinkle the pizzas with the chopped green pepper and freshly ground black pepper.

5. Bake until the cheese has melted and the pizzas are hot, about 5 to 6 minutes. Remove from the oven. Arrange the pizzas on a serving tray. Serve pizzettes individually, or cut large pizzas into 15 wedges each.

SHOPPING: Use Vidalia onions when they are in season.

Smoked Cheddar and Onion Pizzettes

Sautéed onions seasoned with a hint of rosemary atop a creamy mixture of melted smoked Cheddar cheese and butter make an unusual but enticing pizza combination. Since these pizzas are quite robust in flavor, I most often serve them when the weather is cold and my guests seem to have heartier appetites.

Makes 30 pizzettes or 2 11-inch pizzas

30 pizzettes or 2 pizzas made from 1 recipe Pizza Dough (page 96)

3 tablespoons olive oil, plus extra for brushing the pizzas
4 cups thinly sliced onions (about 2 to 3 medium onions)
1¾ teaspoons dried rosemary, crushed
8 ounces smoked Cheddar cheese, grated
4 tablespoons unsalted butter, softened
6 rosemary sprigs, for garnish

1. Preheat the oven to 450°F.

2. Bake the pizza rounds for 5 minutes, until just lightly colored. Remove from the oven. The pizza rounds can be baked 1 to 2 days ahead. Cool completely and store in an airtight container at cool room temperature. They can also be frozen; wrap tightly in plastic wrap and then in aluminum foil. Defrost in the refrigerator before using. Reheat to "dry out" for 2 to 4 minutes in a 450°F. oven.

3. To prepare the topping, heat 3 tablespoons of the olive oil in a large heavy skillet over medium heat. When hot, add the onions and sauté, stirring, until softened and lightly browned, about 4 to 5 minutes. Stir in the dried rosemary and stir and cook a minute more. Remove from the heat.

4. Place the grated Cheddar and butter in a food processor fitted with the metal blade and process until the mixture is smooth, 10 to 15 seconds. Both the Cheddar spread and the onions can be prepared several hours ahead. Cover and keep at cool room temperature.

5. When ready to assemble the pizzas, preheat the oven to 450°F.

6. *For pizzettes:* Brush the pizza rounds very lightly with olive oil. Spread each round with about ½ tablespoon of the Cheddar mixture. Top with a scant tablespoon of the sautéed onions.

(continued)

For large pizzas: Brush the pizza rounds lightly with olive oil. Spread each pizza with half the Cheddar mixture. Arrange half the onions on top of each pizza.

7. Bake until the cheese melts and the pizzas are hot, about 5 to 6 minutes. Garnish each pizzette with 2 to 3 fresh rosemary leaves, or garnish large pizzas with clusters of rosemary sprigs placed in the center of each. Arrange the pizzas on a serving tray. Serve pizzettes individually, or cut large pizzas into 15 wedges each.

Sonoran Pizzas

I first tasted these mouth-watering pizzas at Sienna, a fabulous restaurant in South Deerfield, Massachusetts. The talented chef, Jonathan Marohn, grew up in Arizona savoring Southwestern cuisine, and these "tortilla" pizzas topped with peppered dried beef, julienned peppers, Monterey Jack cheese, tomatoes, and sour cream reflect his background.

Makes 36 portions

½ teaspoon cumin

½ teaspoon garlic powder

½ teaspoon cayenne pepper

¼ teaspoon chili powder

2½ ounces dried beef, thinly sliced (see note)

7 tablespoons olive oil, divided

1 green pepper, stem, seeds, and membranes removed, cut into
⅛-inch-wide julienne strips

1 sweet red pepper, stem, seeds, and membranes removed, cut into
⅛-inch-wide julienne strips

6 8-inch flour tortillas

8 ounces Monterey Jack cheese, grated

4 plum tomatoes or 4 small regular tomatoes, unpeeled but seeded
and chopped

¼ cup sour cream

1. Combine the cumin, garlic powder, cayenne pepper, and chili powder in a mixing bowl and stir to blend.

2. Stack the slices of dried beef and cut into ¼-inch-wide julienne strips. Add the julienned dried beef to the spice mixture and toss to coat well. Set aside.

3. Heat 4 tablespoons of the olive oil in a medium heavy skillet over medium-high heat. Add the julienned peppers and sauté, stirring, until the peppers are softened, about 4 to 5 minutes. Add the dried beef with all of the spice mixture and stir and cook another 2 minutes. Remove from the heat and set aside.

4. When ready to assemble the pizzas, preheat the oven to 350°F.

5. Place the flour tortillas on two aluminum foil-lined baking sheets. Brush the tops of the tortillas with the remaining olive oil. Place the tortillas in the oven for 5 to 6 minutes, just to crisp. Remove from the oven. Sprinkle each tortilla with some of the grated cheese (about 4 or 5 tablespoons each) and then spread with the dried beef and pepper mixture. Top with the chopped tomatoes. The pizzas can be assembled an hour ahead and left at cool room temperature.

6. When ready to bake, preheat the oven to 350°F.

7. Bake the pizzas until the cheese has melted, the tortillas are crisp, and the edges have started to brown lightly, about 10 to 12 minutes. Watch *carefully* so the tortillas do not burn. Remove from the oven and cut each tortilla into 6 wedges. Arrange the wedges on a serving plate. Place a small dab of the sour cream in the middle of each wedge, and serve warm.

SHOPPING: Some of my cooking students were reluctant to make this dish because they were unexcited by the idea of using dried beef. Much to their surprise, they loved the taste of the paper-thin strips of beef coated with the piquant mixture of cumin, garlic powder, cayenne pepper, and chili powder. I use Armour's 95 percent fat-free dried beef.

VARIATION: One of my students substitutes a large boneless chicken breast cut into very thin slices for the beef in this recipe. She marinates the chicken in the dry spice mixture, increasing the cumin to ¾ teaspoon and the chili powder to ½ teaspoon, for two hours in the refrigerator. The chicken is then sautéed with the peppers. It is a delicious variation.

Santa Monica Pizzas

Inspired by a good friend and true bon vivant, Bert Sonnenfeld, who told me of a special pizza topped with avocado and cilantro he had sampled in Santa Monica, I developed these little tortilla pizzas.

Makes 36 portions

6 8-inch flour tortillas
6 tablespoons chèvre (3 to 4 ounces), at room temperature
1½ cups grated Monterey Jack cheese with jalapeño peppers (about 6 ounces)
1 large ripe avocado, peeled, pitted, and sliced into very thin wedges
4 medium plum tomatoes (about ¾ pound total), seeded, diced, and well drained
6 tablespoons chopped scallions
Salt and freshly ground black pepper to taste
1½ teaspoons chili powder
1½ teaspoons ground cumin
⅓ cup chopped fresh cilantro
Several sprigs of cilantro, for garnish

1. Preheat the oven to 350°F.

2. Place the tortillas on a baking sheet and bake until crisp, 6 to 8 minutes.

3. Lay the tortillas on a work surface. Spread each with 1 tablespoon of the chèvre. Sprinkle about ¼ cup of the Monterey Jack cheese over each tortilla. Arrange 5 to 6 avocado slices over the cheese. Divide the diced tomatoes evenly and arrange on top of each pizza. Divide the scallions evenly and sprinkle over the tomatoes. Sprinkle each pizza with salt and pepper. Combine the chili powder and cumin and sprinkle over each pizza. The pizzas can be assembled 30 minutes ahead and left uncovered at cool room temperature.

4. When ready to bake, preheat the oven to 350°F.

5. Place the tortillas on two aluminum foil-lined baking sheets. Bake until the tortillas are hot and crisp and the edges start to brown lightly, about 10 to 12 minutes. Watch *carefully* so the tortillas do not burn. Remove from the oven and sprinkle with the chopped cilantro. Cut each pizza into 6 wedges. Arrange the wedges on a serving plate and garnish the plate with sprigs of cilantro.

Walnut Galette

For this unusual appetizer, a round of store-bought puff pastry is baked and spread with a mixture of chèvre and Parmesan cheese. Walnut halves, tossed with thyme, oregano, lemon zest, and black pepper, are placed over the cheese layer and the galette is reheated.

Makes 1 9-inch galette

1 sheet frozen puff pastry (from a 17¼-ounce package of 2 sheets pastry), defrosted
5 to 6 ounces chèvre, at room temperature
⅓ cup grated imported Parmesan cheese
1½ tablespoons grated lemon zest, divided
1 cup walnut halves, toasted (page 268) and coarsely chopped
½ teaspoon dried thyme
½ teaspoon dried oregano
⅛ teaspoon freshly ground black pepper
1 tablespoon extra-virgin olive oil
Sprigs of thyme and oregano, for garnish

1. Preheat the oven to 350°F.

2. Roll out the puff pastry sheet to a 10½-inch square, and trim to make a 10½-inch circle. Then, using a 9-inch plate or tart pan bottom, trace a circle in the center of the dough. Roll the edges of the pastry tightly up to the traced circle and pinch to form a rim. Transfer the pastry circle to a baking sheet and bake until golden, about 20 minutes. Check the pastry after the first 5 minutes and, if the bottom is puffed, pierce with a fork to deflate the pastry. Remove from the oven and cool 10 minutes.

3. Combine the chèvre, Parmesan cheese, and ½ tablespoon of the lemon zest in a bowl and stir to mix. Spread the mixture over the bottom of the galette. Combine the walnuts, the remaining 1 tablespoon lemon zest, the dried herbs, pepper, and olive oil in a bowl and toss to mix well. Spread over the cheese layer. The galette can be assembled 1 to 2 hours ahead and left at cool room temperature.

4. When ready to serve, preheat the oven to 350°F.

5. Bake the galette until it is hot and the cheese has melted, about 8 to 10 minutes. Remove from the oven and garnish the center of the galette with clusters of fresh thyme and oregano. Cut into wedges to serve.

SERVING: This is best eaten when warm, but can be served at room temperature.

120

Eggplant and Tomato Galette

Made with store-bought puff pastry, these picture-perfect galettes are topped with herbed cheeses and thin slices of eggplant and tomatoes. The recipe is the invention of a talented cooking teacher and inveterate gardener, my good friend June McCarthy. She created the dish one year when she had a bumper crop of tomatoes and eggplant.

Makes about 32 portions

1 17¼-ounce package frozen puff pastry (containing 2 sheets pastry), thawed
2 medium eggplants, unpeeled, cut into ⅛-inch-thick rounds
Salt
5 plum tomatoes, unpeeled, cut into ⅛-inch-thick slices
15 ounces part-skim ricotta cheese
2 teaspoons finely chopped garlic
6 tablespoons chopped fresh basil, or 2 tablespoons dried
2 teaspoons minced fresh rosemary, or ⅔ teaspoon dried
1 tablespoon minced fresh oregano, or 1 teaspoon dried
¼ teaspoon crushed red pepper flakes
Freshly ground black pepper to taste
12 ounces mozzarella cheese, grated
2 to 4 tablespoons olive oil
½ cup grated imported Parmesan cheese
Basil leaves, sprigs of rosemary, or sprigs of oregano, for garnish

1. Place a sheet of puff pastry on a floured work surface and roll into a 14-inch square. Transfer the pastry to a large unrimmed baking sheet. Using a pastry brush dipped in water, brush a 1-inch border along all sides of the pastry square. Roll the edges of the pastry in 1 inch and pinch to form a standing rim about ½ inch high. At each of the corners there will be a little excess dough; press into a ball shape. Use the back of a knife to make a pattern in the pastry rim. Repeat with the second sheet of puff pastry. Chill the galette shells until firm, about 30 minutes. The pastry shells can be prepared up to a day ahead. Cover tightly with plastic wrap and refrigerate.

2. Place the eggplant slices on a baking sheet and sprinkle generously with salt. Let stand for 30 minutes. Place the eggplant in a colander and rinse under cold running water. Drain and pat dry. Place the tomato slices on paper towels to drain.

(continued)

3. In a small bowl, mix together the ricotta cheese, garlic, herbs, red pepper flakes, ¼ teaspoon salt, and black pepper to taste. Spread half the cheese mixture on each puff pastry shell. Sprinkle with the mozzarella cheese. The galettes can be prepared 4 to 5 hours ahead to this point. Cover and refrigerate. Cover the sliced tomatoes and eggplant separately and refrigerate.

4. When ready to bake the galettes, preheat the oven to 425°F.

5. Arrange slightly overlapping slices of eggplant on each puff pastry square and then top with slightly overlapping tomato slices. Drizzle about 1 to 2 tablespoons olive oil over each galette and sprinkle with the Parmesan cheese.

6. Bake in the lower part of the oven until the crust is a rich dark golden brown and the vegetables are tender, about 40 minutes. Remove to a cooling rack for 2 to 3 minutes. Garnish each galette with a bouquet of basil, rosemary, or oregano sprigs. Cut each galette into 16 squares. Serve warm.

Dips, Relishes, and Salsas

Dips are, without a doubt, the quintessential cocktail food. I cannot remember the last time I was at a party and a dip was not passed. More often than not, however, the same dips are offered over and over again. With this in mind, I created a variety of new dips and sauces and added innovative touches to some old and familiar ones. Warm acorn squash dip, made with a purée of squash seasoned with curry, and served with apple wedges and sausage, is as unusual as it is delectable. Spicy Creole dip garnished with green and wax beans and Far East dipping sauce with tempura-fried scallions are other uncommon dips and garnishes.

Relishes and salsas, like dips, are ideal make-ahead party dishes. I especially love Corn and Red Pepper Relish with Spicy Tortilla Chips, Summer Garden Tomato and Eggplant Relish with Toasted Pita Triangles, and Roasted Red Pepper Salsa with Cornbread Wedges.

Summer Garden Tomato and Eggplant Relish with Pita Toasts

Make this relish during the summer when tomatoes and eggplant are in their prime and fresh rosemary and basil, essential flavorings for the dish, are available. The raisins and pine nuts add an unexpected but welcome taste.

Makes 48 portions

TOMATO RELISH

(Makes about 2 cups)

½ cup pine nuts
1 small eggplant (about 14 ounces), unpeeled and cut into ¼-inch
   dice
½ teaspoon salt, or more to taste
¼ cup olive oil
¾ cup chopped onions
1½ tablespoons finely chopped garlic
½ cup raisins
1 pound Italian plum tomatoes, halved, seeded, and diced
1 tablespoon fresh thyme, preferred, or 1 teaspoon dried
1 teaspoon fresh rosemary, preferred, or ⅓ teaspoon dried
2 tablespoons finely chopped fresh basil, preferred, or 2 teaspoons
   dried
Freshly ground black pepper to taste

Toasted Pita Triangles (page 267), made from 3 pitas (a total of
   48 triangles)

Sprig of basil, for garnish

1. To prepare the relish, place the pine nuts in a medium skillet over medium-high heat. Cook, stirring constantly and shaking the pan, until the nuts are golden, about 3 to 4 minutes. Remove and set aside.

2. Place the eggplant dice in a colander, and sprinkle the eggplant with the ½ teaspoon salt. Place the colander over a bowl to catch any liquid that drains from the salted eggplant. Toss the mixture several times and let sit 30 minutes. Then pat the eggplant dry and set aside.

3. Heat the olive oil in a large heavy skillet over medium-high heat. Add the eggplant and stir and cook for 4 to 5 minutes. Add the onions and stir and cook for 2 minutes more. Add the garlic, raisins, toasted pine nuts, and ½ cup of the diced tomatoes. Cook a minute more. Add the thyme, rosemary, and basil and stir. Remove from the heat and stir in the remaining diced tomatoes. Taste and add salt and pepper as desired. Let the relish sit for at least an hour before serving so that the flavors blend. The relish can be prepared a day ahead, covered, and refrigerated. Bring to room temperature before serving.

4. To serve, mound the relish in a small bowl. Place the bowl on a serving plate and surround with the pita triangles. Garnish with a sprig of fresh basil.

Corn and Red Pepper Relish with Spicy Tortilla Chips

Made with fresh corn and diced red peppers, this colorful relish is served mounded on crisp baked tortilla chips seasoned with cayenne pepper. You can make the chips as spicy and hot as you like by adjusting the amount of pepper sprinkled over them. This works well as part of a summer barbecue menu.

Makes 40 portions

CORN RELISH

(Makes about 2 cups)
4 tablespoons olive oil
2 large sweet red peppers, seeds and membranes removed, diced
2 cups chopped onions
4 teaspoons chopped garlic
2 cups corn kernels, fresh or frozen (if frozen, defrost and pat dry)
6 tablespoons cider vinegar
4 tablespoons sugar
1/2 teaspoon dry mustard
Generous pinch of cayenne pepper
1 1/2 teaspoons salt
3 tablespoons chopped fresh cilantro

5 8-inch flour tortillas
5 tablespoons olive oil
1 1/2 to 2 1/2 teaspoons cayenne pepper, to taste

1. To prepare the relish, heat the olive oil in a large heavy skillet over medium-high heat. When hot, add the red peppers and sauté, stirring, for 3 to 4 minutes. Add the onions and garlic and cook and stir until the onions are softened, about 3 minutes more. Add the corn and cook 2 minutes more. Meanwhile, combine the vinegar and sugar in a small bowl and stir to dissolve the sugar. Stir into the corn mixture. Add the mustard, cayenne pepper, and salt and stir. Cook, stirring frequently, until the liquid has evaporated, about 5 minutes. Remove from the heat and cool. The relish can be made a day ahead to this point, covered, and refrigerated. Bring to room temperature before serving. When ready to serve, stir in the cilantro.

2. To prepare the tortilla chips, preheat the oven to 350°F. and arrange the racks in the center of the oven. *(continued)*

3. Brush both sides of each tortilla with the olive oil. Stack the tortilla rounds and cut in half, then cut each stack of halves into 4 equal triangles. Each tortilla will yield 8 triangles, for a total of 40. Place the triangles on baking sheets. Using a fine-mesh strainer, sprinkle half the cayenne pepper over the triangles. Bake for 5 minutes. With a spatula, turn the triangles. Sprinkle with the remaining cayenne pepper. Bake for 4 to 5 minutes more, or until crisp. Remove the chips from the oven and cool. The tortilla triangles can be made 3 to 4 days ahead. Store in an airtight container.

4. To serve, place the corn and red pepper relish in a bowl and surround with the tortilla chips. Mound the relish on the chips to eat.

VARIATIONS: Leftover relish can be quite versatile. Try blanching zucchini boats and fill them with the relish. The relish is also good mixed with cooked white rice. Or, if you happen to have some zucchini soup on hand, put a tablespoon of the relish in the bottom of each bowl before pouring in the soup.

Roasted Red Pepper Salsa with Cornbread Wedges

When I was growing up in the South, cornbread was a staple on my mother's table. Now, I serve slices of this hot robust bread topped with herbed red pepper salsa.

Makes 40 portions

RED PEPPER SALSA

(Makes about 1¾ cups)

4 large sweet red peppers, roasted (page 269)
1 tablespoon chopped fresh oregano or 1 teaspoon dried
2 tablespoons chopped fresh basil or 2 teaspoons dried
1 teaspoon salt
½ teaspoon freshly ground black pepper
Several drops hot pepper sauce
1 teaspoon lime juice

CORNBREAD

2 large eggs
1¼ cups buttermilk
½ teaspoon baking soda
1 teaspoon baking powder
1 teaspoon salt
1 tablespoon sugar
1½ cups yellow cornmeal
½ cup all-purpose flour
4 tablespoons unsalted butter or vegetable oil

Small bunch of oregano, for garnish
Small bunch of basil, for garnish

1. To prepare the salsa, place the roasted peppers in a food processor fitted with the metal blade. Pulse just until coarsely chopped. Place the peppers in a small bowl and season with the oregano, basil, salt, pepper, hot pepper sauce, and lime juice. The salsa can be prepared up to 2 days in advance. Cover with plastic wrap and refrigerate.

2. To prepare the cornbread, preheat the oven to 425°F. Adjust a rack to the center position.

(continued)

3. In a mixing bowl, lightly mix the eggs and buttermilk together. In another bowl, combine the baking soda, baking powder, salt, sugar, cornmeal, and flour and mix well. Stir the dry ingredients into the liquids and mix well.

4. Heat the butter or vegetable oil in a 12-inch cast-iron or other heavy 12-inch ovenproof skillet. When the butter or oil is very hot, pour it into the batter and stir to mix, then pour the batter into the hot skillet and immediately put it in the oven. Bake until the bread is firm to the touch, about 15 to 20 minutes. Invert the pan over a plate to unmold the bread. Cut into 20 wedges and slice each wedge in half horizontally for a total of 40 wedges.

5. To serve, place the red pepper salsa in a serving bowl and place on a serving plate. Arrange the cornbread wedges in a sunburst pattern around the sauce. Garnish the platter with a bunch of fresh basil and oregano.

SERVING: The cornbread, which takes only a few minutes to assemble and about 15 minutes to bake, is best served hot from the oven.

Tomato Dill Salsa with Toasted Pita Triangles

This is a welcome hors d'oeuvre for friends who are watching calories and cholesterol. Made with low-fat yogurt and fresh herbs, it is a crowd pleaser and does not give the slightest hint that it could be considered "diet food"!

Makes 32 portions

TOMATO DILL SALSA

(Makes about 2 cups)
1 cup low-fat plain yogurt
1 cup peeled, seeded, and chopped ripe tomatoes, well drained (see note)
¼ cup minced fresh dill, preferred, or 1 tablespoon dried
¼ teaspoon salt, or more to taste
¼ teaspoon coarsely ground black pepper, or more to taste

Toasted Pita Triangles (page 267), made from 2 pitas (a total of 32 triangles)

Sprigs of dill, for garnish

1. To prepare the salsa, place the yogurt, tomatoes, and dill in a mixing bowl and stir to mix well. Add the salt and pepper and mix. Taste and add additional salt and pepper if desired. The salsa can be made up to a day ahead. Cover and refrigerate. Drain, if necessary, before using.

2. To serve, place the salsa in a small serving bowl and place the bowl in the center of a serving plate. Arrange the pita triangles around the bowl in overlapping circles. Garnish the sauce with sprigs of dill.

NOTE: To peel tomatoes, plunge into boiling water for 15 to 20 seconds. Remove and cool. With a sharp paring knife, remove the skins. Halve the tomatoes horizontally and squeeze to remove the seeds. Then chop the tomatoes.

Roasted Red Pepper Sauce with Summer Green Beans

Created by my friend Kathy Lane, a talented caterer, this bright sauce is made by combining homemade mayonnaise with puréed roasted red peppers, Parmesan cheese, and fresh basil. It is perfectly complemented by tender, blanched summer green beans.

Makes 10 servings

2 pounds green beans, trimmed
2 tablespoons salt

RED PEPPER SAUCE

(Makes about 2½ cups)
2 large sweet red peppers, roasted (page 269)
Cooked Egg Mayonnaise (page 263)
⅓ cup grated imported Parmesan cheese
1 clove garlic, peeled and minced
3 tablespoons chopped fresh basil
½ teaspoon salt
½ teaspoon freshly ground black pepper

Sprigs of basil, for garnish

1. To prepare the beans, bring 5 quarts of water to a boil and add the 2 tablespoons salt. Add the beans and cook, uncovered, until tender, 8 to 10 minutes. The time will vary slightly, depending on the size and texture of the beans; taste a bean to check for doneness. Drain the beans in a colander and rinse them under cold running water. Pat dry. The beans may be prepared a day in advance. Wrap them in a kitchen towel and then in plastic wrap and refrigerate until needed.

2. To prepare the sauce, purée the red peppers in a food processor fitted with the metal blade or in a blender. Drain. Stir into the mayonnaise. Add the cheese, garlic, basil, and the ½ teaspoon salt, and mix well. The sauce can be made up to a day ahead. Cover and refrigerate. Bring to room temperature before using.

3. Serve the sauce in a small glass bowl, garnished with basil sprigs. Place on a platter and arrange the green beans around the bowl.

Toasted Sesame Mayonnaise with Asparagus Spears

Dark roasted Oriental sesame oil, one of the most aromatic of all oils, and toasted sesame seeds lift store-bought mayonnaise to new heights in this recipe. Long, sleek asparagus spears for dipping are my favorite garnish.

Makes 10 servings

SESAME MAYONNAISE

(Makes about 1½ cups)
1½ cups mayonnaise (Hellmann's or Best Foods is preferred)
1 tablespoon lemon juice
2 tablespoons Oriental sesame oil
2½ tablespoons sesame seeds, toasted (page 269), divided

2½ pounds medium asparagus spears

1. To prepare the sesame mayonnaise, place the mayonnaise in a mixing bowl and add the lemon juice, sesame oil, and 2 tablespoons of the sesame seeds. Whisk well to blend. The sesame mayonnaise can be prepared 1 to 2 days ahead. Cover and refrigerate.

2. To prepare the asparagus, break off and discard the tough ends. Trim the ends with a knife so the spears are an even length. Parboil the asparagus in boiling salted water to cover until just tender, about 3 minutes. Remove, drain in a colander, and place under cold running water to stop the cooking process and maintain the bright green color of the asparagus. Pat the asparagus dry. The asparagus can be cooked a day in advance. Wrap in clean kitchen towels, place in plastic bags, and refrigerate. Bring to room temperature before using.

3. To serve, place the mayonnaise in a shallow serving bowl and sprinkle with the remaining ½ tablespoon sesame seeds. Place the bowl in the center of a large serving plate. Arrange the asparagus spears in a spoke pattern around the bowl of mayonnaise.

SERVING: The mayonnaise looks attractive served mounded in "cups" made with radicchio leaves.

Tempura-Fried Scallions with Far East Dipping Sauce

Scallions, coated with a light batter and fried quickly until golden, are perfect for dipping in a tangy sauce made with rice wine vinegar, soy sauce, sesame oil, and fresh ginger. The sauce can be assembled well in advance of serving, and the fried scallions will stay crisp in a low oven for more than half an hour.

Makes 8 to 10 servings

DIPPING SAUCE

(Makes about 1 cup)
6 tablespoons soy sauce
6 tablespoons rice wine vinegar
3 tablespoons Oriental sesame oil
1 tablespoon very finely julienned peeled gingerroot

1 large egg, separated
3 tablespoons vegetable oil
¾ cup all-purpose flour
Generous pinch of salt
Pinch of sugar
6 bunches scallions, root ends and all but 2 inches of the green stems removed
Vegetable oil for deep-frying

1. To prepare the sauce, combine the soy sauce, vinegar, and sesame oil in a bowl and whisk to blend. Add the ginger. The sauce can be made a day ahead. Cover and refrigerate. Bring to room temperature before serving.

2. Place the egg yolk in a mixing bowl. Add ¾ cup water and the 3 table-spoons vegetable oil and whisk thoroughly to blend. Combine the flour, salt, and sugar, and, using a fine-mesh sieve, sift over the egg mixture. Whisk to incorporate the flour into the liquid. The batter can be made an hour ahead. Cover with plastic wrap and refrigerate.

3. When ready to fry the scallions, preheat the oven to 275°F.

4. Beat the egg white until soft peaks form. Fold the beaten white into the batter.

5. In a wok, heat 1 cup vegetable oil over medium-high heat. When the oil is hot, hold a scallion by the green stem and dip it in the batter, covering all but an inch of the green stem. Twirl to remove excess batter and place in the hot oil. Repeat with 2 more scallions. Cook the scallions, 3 at a time only to ensure even cooking, for 1 to 2 minutes, turning once, until lightly golden. Remove with a slotted spoon and drain on paper towels. Then transfer the fried scallions to a baking sheet and place, uncovered, in the oven. Continue frying, adding additional oil if needed, until all the scallions are cooked. The fried scallions will retain their crispness in the oven for 30 to 45 minutes.

6. To serve, place the sauce in a small bowl and place on a tray. Arrange the fried scallions on the tray.

SERVING: For an especially attractive presentation, line a wicker tray with lemon or tea leaves (available at florist shops). Put the bowl of sauce in one corner of the tray and arrange the scallions around it. When fresh ginger flowers are available, I use them as a garnish.

Creole Dipping Sauce with Green and Wax Beans

My college friend Martha Garland Davis, whose family lives in New Orleans, shared this recipe with me long ago. Her relatives serve the sauce with boiled shrimp, but I discovered that it is equally good with vegetables, especially fresh beans. Because the dipping sauce can be made several days in advance, it is a staple on party menus at our house.

Makes 10 servings

CREOLE SAUCE

(Makes about 1½ cups)

½ cup vegetable or olive oil
1 small clove garlic, peeled
¼ cup coarsely chopped scallions
¼ cup coarsely chopped celery
½ teaspoon salt
¼ teaspoon cayenne pepper
3 drops hot pepper sauce
1½ teaspoons paprika
1 tablespoon ketchup
¼ cup tarragon vinegar
2 tablespoons horseradish mustard or Dijon mustard

1 pound wax beans
1 pound green beans
2 tablespoons salt
Several sprigs of flat-leaf parsley, for garnish

1. To prepare the sauce, place all the ingredients in a blender or food processor and process until the mixture is smooth, about a minute. The sauce can be made 2 to 3 days ahead. Cover and refrigerate.

2. To prepare the beans, bring 4 quarts of water to a boil and add the salt. Add the beans and cook until just tender, about 8 minutes. Remove, place in a colander, and rinse under cold water. Drain and pat dry. The beans can be prepared a day ahead. Cover and refrigerate. Bring beans to room temperature before using.

3. To serve, place the sauce in a bowl. Garnish with parsley sprigs. Arrange the beans in a spoke pattern around the bowl of sauce.

SERVING: I often put the sauce in a small glass dessert bowl and arrange the beans in a footed goblet-style vase.

VARIATION: This sauce is also delicious with other vegetables such as celery sticks or red and green pepper sticks.

Neal's Dill Dip with New Potatoes

Neal Cavanaugh, one of Columbus, Ohio's most talented caterers and special-events planners, introduced me to this recipe.

Makes 8 to 10 servings

DILL DIP

(Makes about 2 cups)
1 cup mayonnaise (Hellmann's or Best Foods is preferred)
1 cup sour cream
2 teaspoons lemon juice
2 tablespoons dried dill
1 teaspoon celery salt
¼ teaspoon salt
1½ tablespoons minced onions

2 pounds small new potatoes (preferably 1 to 1½ inches in diameter), unpeeled
Sprigs of dill, for garnish
6-inch wooden skewers

1. To prepare the dip, place all the ingredients in the work bowl of a food processor fitted with the metal blade or in a blender. Process until the mixture is smooth, about 45 to 60 seconds. Remove, cover, and refrigerate to chill. The dip can be made 1 to 2 days ahead. Bring to room temperature 15 minutes before serving.

2. To prepare the potatoes, bring a large pot of water to a boil. Salt the water lightly, add the potatoes, and cook until tender when pierced with a knife, about 10 to 15 minutes, depending on the size of the potatoes. The potatoes can be cooked a day ahead. To reheat, place the potatoes in boiling water for 1 to 2 minutes, drain, and pat dry. Or heat in a microwave on high power for 30 seconds, or until hot.

3. To serve, place a bowl of the dill dip on a serving tray. Halve the warm potatoes and arrange them around the sauce. Garnish the plate with sprigs of fresh dill. Offer skewers to spear the potatoes and dip them in the dill sauce.

VARIATION: In the spring, I blanch asparagus spears as well and serve them warm along with the new potatoes.

138

Warm Acorn Squash Dip with Apples and Sausage

A purée of cooked acorn squash seasoned with curry powder is delicious served warm with skewers of apple wedges and sautéed slices of kielbasa sausage. I created this for a special Thanksgiving dinner shared with family and friends.

Makes 10 to 12 servings

ACORN SQUASH DIP

(Makes about 1½ cups)
1 large acorn squash (about 2 pounds)
½ teaspoon salt
½ teaspoon curry powder
½ teaspoon chicken bouillon granules
¼ cup sour cream

2 tablespoons vegetable oil
1 pound kielbasa sausage, cut diagonally into ½-inch slices
4 Golden Delicious apples or 4 red Bartlett pears or a combination,
  cored but not peeled, cut into eighths
6-inch wooden skewers

1. To prepare the dip, cut the unpeeled squash in half and scoop out and discard the seeds. Place the squash halves cut side down in a microwave-proof dish. Fill the dish with ½ inch of water. Microwave the squash until very tender, about 13 to 14 minutes or longer on high power. Or, to use a conventional oven, place the squash halves cut side down in a baking dish filled with ½ inch water. Bake in a preheated 350°F. oven until tender, about 1 hour and 20 to 30 minutes.

2. When the squash is just cool enough to handle, scoop out the flesh and place in a food processor fitted with the metal blade or in a blender. Process until smooth, about 20 seconds. Add the salt, curry powder, and chicken bouillon granules and process just to blend. Add the sour cream and process for an additional 10 seconds to incorporate. The dip can be made a day ahead. Cool, cover, and refrigerate.

3. When ready to serve, heat the vegetable oil in a large heavy skillet over medium-high heat. When hot, add the kielbasa and cook, stirring and turning

139

the slices, until lightly browned. Remove and drain on paper towels.

4. Place the dip in a medium heavy saucepan over low heat, and stir constantly until hot or heat in a microwave-proof dish in a microwave. Transfer to a serving bowl. Place the bowl on a serving tray and surround with the apple or pear wedges and kielbasa slices. Offer skewers so your guests can spear pieces of fruit and sausage to dip in the warm sauce.

VARIATION: Dark brown Boston bread, available canned, is good with this dip, sliced and cut into small pieces. Although the kielbasa is delicious, it can be omitted.

Sesame Sauce with Sea Scallops

The inspiration for this dish came from my good friends, both talented cooks, Rich Terapak and Steve Stover, who created this aromatic sauce to serve over seafood-filled wontons. I simply sauté sea scallops until golden, sprinkle them with chives, and arrange them on skewers accompanied by a bowl of the warm sauce and another of toasted sesame seeds for dipping.

Makes about 50 to 60 portions

SESAME DIPPING SAUCE

(Makes about 1¾ cups)
3 cups chicken stock, preferably only lightly salted
1½ tablespoons cornstarch dissolved in 2 tablespoons cold water
2 tablespoons very finely minced peeled gingerroot
1½ tablespoons soy sauce
1½ tablespoons Oriental sesame oil
1½ tablespoons unsalted butter or margarine

4 tablespoons unsalted butter or margarine, plus more if needed
4 tablespoons vegetable oil, plus more if needed
2 pounds medium sea scallops (about 50 to 60 scallops), rinsed and patted dry
3 tablespoons very finely chopped fresh chives or parsley
¾ cup sesame seeds, toasted (page 269)
6-inch wooden skewers
2 to 3 small branches lemon leaves, for garnish

1. To prepare the sauce, place the chicken stock in a medium heavy saucepan over high heat. Bring to a boil and boil until the stock has reduced by half. Add the cornstarch and water mixture and stir until the sauce has thickened and lightly coats the back of a spoon, about 2 to 3 minutes. Add the ginger, soy sauce, sesame oil, and butter or margarine and stir well to blend. Simmer, stirring often, for 10 minutes. Remove from the heat. Cool slightly before serving. The sauce can be made a day ahead. Cover and refrigerate. Reheat to warm when needed.

2. To cook the scallops, heat 2 tablespoons each of the butter and oil in a large heavy skillet over medium-high heat. Add just enough scallops to fit comfortably in a single layer and sauté, turning once, until the scallops are opaque and light golden, about 1 to 2 minutes per side. Remove to a side dish and cover loosely with foil to keep warm. Pour off any liquid from the scallops that has accumulated in the pan. Add the remaining 2 tablespoons each butter or margarine and oil and cook the remaining scallops in the same way. If necessary, use more butter and oil in equal amounts to cook all the scallops. Sprinkle the cooked scallops with the chopped chives or parsley. When cool enough to handle, place each scallop on a 6-inch wooden skewer.

3. To serve, place a bowl of the warm sauce and a bowl of the sesame seeds on a serving tray. Arrange the skewered scallops around the bowls. Garnish the tray with branches of lemon leaves. To eat, dip a skewered scallop in the sauce and then into sesame seeds.

Nancy Kennick's Mustard Sauce with Sea Scallops

Nancy Kennick, a truly gifted cook and hostess, is a new friend and neighbor. A bowl mounded with this creamy, piquant mustard sauce and surrounded with breaded scallops was the mouth-watering hors d'oeuvre she served my husband and me one summer evening. The sauce can be assembled ahead and the sautéed scallops kept warm in a low oven for up to an hour.

Makes about 60 portions

MUSTARD SAUCE

(Make about 1½ cups)
4 tablespoons powdered mustard
2 tablespoons sugar
1 teaspoon salt
1 tablespoon unsalted butter, softened
2 large eggs, well beaten
4 tablespoons cider vinegar
½ cup whipping or heavy cream

1½ pounds medium sea scallops
⅔ cup all-purpose flour
1 teaspoon salt
Freshly ground black pepper to taste
2 large eggs, plus 1 additional egg if needed
2 cups dry unflavored bread crumbs
4 tablespoons vegetable oil, plus more if needed
4 tablespoons unsalted butter, plus more if needed
Sprigs of watercress, for garnish
6-inch wooden skewers

1. To prepare the sauce, combine the mustard, 2 tablespoons water, the sugar, and the salt in the top of a double boiler set over simmering water. Stir constantly until the mixture is smooth. Then add the butter and stir until melted and incorporated. Add the eggs and vinegar and whisk constantly until the mixture thickens, about 2 minutes. Remove from the heat, transfer to a mixing bowl, and cool to room temperature.

(continued)

2. Whip the cream until firm but not stiff and fold into the mustard mixture. The sauce can be made 2 to 3 days in advance. Cover and refrigerate.

3. To prepare the scallops, preheat the oven to 200°F. Rinse and pat the scallops dry. Combine the flour, the salt, and the pepper to taste and spread on a dinner plate. Place the 2 eggs and 2 tablespoons water in a bowl and whisk well to mix. Spread the bread crumbs on another dinner plate. Dredge the scallops in the flour mixture, dip in the egg mixture, and then dredge in the bread crumbs. Whisk together an additional egg with 1 tablespoon water if needed to coat all the scallops.

4. Heat 2 tablespoons each of the oil and butter in a large heavy skillet over medium-high heat. When hot, add the scallops a few at a time and sauté, turning once or twice, until golden. Remove and drain on paper towels. Continue, adding oil and butter in equal amounts as needed, until all the scallops are sautéed. The scallops can be placed on a baking sheet and kept warm in a preheated 200°F. oven for up to 1 hour.

5. To serve, place a bowl of the mustard sauce on a serving tray. Surround with the warm scallops and garnish the tray with watercress. Offer wooden skewers for spearing the scallops and dipping them in the sauce.

SHOPPING: Do not substitute bay scallops for the sea scallops in this recipe. The smaller bay scallops tend to get dry during sautéing and are not as succulent as the larger sea scallops.

Orange-Sherry Mayonnaise with Shrimp

My assistant, Emily Bell, and I discovered that orange zest and dry sherry do wonders for store-bought mayonnaise. We serve this sauce with shellfish such as shrimp, scallops, or crab.

Makes about 50 portions

ORANGE-SHERRY MAYONNAISE

(Makes about 1 cup)
1 cup mayonnaise (Hellmann's or Best Foods is preferred)
1 tablespoon dry sherry
2¼ teaspoons grated orange zest

1 large navel orange
3 tablespoons unsalted butter, plus more if needed
3 tablespoons olive oil, plus more if needed
2 pounds large shrimp (21/30 count), peeled and deveined
Lemon leaves or tea leaves, for garnish

1. To prepare the sherry mayonnaise, whisk the mayonnaise, sherry, and orange zest together in a mixing bowl. Cover and refrigerate. The mayonnaise can be prepared up to 2 days ahead.

2. Use a vegetable stripper to cut long strips of peel from the orange. Cut the orange peel into very thin julienne strips about 3 inches long. The julienned orange peel can be prepared a day ahead. Wrap in moistened paper towels and then tightly in plastic wrap. Cover and refrigerate.

3. To cook the shrimp, heat 2 tablespoons each of the butter and oil in a large heavy skillet over medium-high heat. When hot, add enough shrimp to fit comfortably in a single layer in pan. Sauté, turning once or twice, until the shrimp are curled and pink, about 3 to 4 minutes. Drain the shrimp on paper towels. Continue until all the shrimp are cooked, adding the remaining tablespoons of butter and oil in equal amounts as needed. The shrimp are served at room temperature, so they can be sautéed in advance and left at cool room temperature for 30 to 40 minutes.

4. To serve, place a bowl of the mayonnaise on a serving tray. Surround the bowl with a bed of lemon leaves or tea leaves. Arrange the shrimp around the mayonnaise. Sprinkle orange peel over the shrimp. *(continued)*

NOTE: If you prefer, the shrimp can be boiled rather than sautéed. I add crab boil to the water to enhance the flavor of the shrimp.

VARIATION: Scallops taste as good as shrimp with this mayonnaise, although they are not as colorful. Sprinkle the scallops with chopped fresh chives just before serving. If you are fortunate enough to have stone crabs in your local market, by all means try them with the mayonnaise.

Herbed Mayonnaise with Skewered Chicken and Red Peppers

Driving to work one day, I heard Julia Child giving directions on the radio for making homemade mayonnaise with cooked, rather than raw, egg yolks to reduce the risk from salmonella. At my cooking school, I created an herbed version based on her recipe. This method for making homemade mayonnaise is a basic for me now; this herbed variation is especially good with skewers of chicken and sweet red peppers.

Makes 36 portions

HERBED MAYONNAISE

(Makes 1½ cups)
Cooked Egg Mayonnaise (page 263)
1 tablespoon minced fresh chives
1 tablespoon minced fresh parsley
1 tablespoon minced fresh tarragon

3 tablespoons lemon juice
½ cup olive oil
¾ teaspoon salt
1 teaspoon coarsely ground black pepper
¼ teaspoon cayenne pepper
*1½ pounds boneless, skinless chicken breasts, cut into 1-inch cubes
     (about 36 pieces)*
*2 small sweet red peppers, stems, seeds, and membranes removed, cut
     into 1-inch squares*

146

6-inch wooden skewers, soaked for 15 to 30 minutes in water to
cover and drained

1. Prepare the mayonnaise as directed. Stir the fresh herbs into the mayonnaise and place into a serving bowl. The mayonnaise can be made a day ahead. Keep covered in the refrigerator.

2. Combine the lemon juice, oil, salt, and black and cayenne pepper in a nonaluminum shallow bowl or pan and mix well. Add the chicken and red peppers, cover, and refrigerate. Marinate, turning several times, 3 to 4 hours or overnight.

3. To assemble the skewers, place 1 piece of chicken and 1 square of red pepper on each skewer. The skewers can be prepared 3 to 4 hours ahead. Place on a large plate or tray, cover with plastic wrap, and refrigerate. Bring to room temperature 15 minutes before broiling.

4. When ready to cook the chicken, preheat the broiler and arrange the rack 5 inches from heat. Broil the skewers, turning once, until the chicken is tender, about 2 minutes per side. Watch carefully; overcooking will make the chicken tough. The skewers can be served warm or at room temperature.

5. To serve, place a bowl of the herbed mayonnaise on a serving platter. Arrange the pepper and chicken skewers around the bowl.

SHOPPING: This is one dish in which I always use fresh herbs. The dried ones simply do not provide enough flavor. Parsley is almost always available, but if chives and tarragon are not to be found, you can use chopped green onion tops for the chives, and basil in place of the tarragon. The taste will be slightly different, but still very compatible with the chicken.

Curried Apricot Mayonnaise with Smoked Turkey and Grapes

Apricot-and-curry-scented mayonnaise is a standard dressing for chicken salad at my house. One day, however, I discovered by chance that moist chunks of smoked turkey and juicy grapes were delicious dipped in the sauce, and that the combination makes a quick and easy appetizer.

Makes 8 to 10 servings

CURRIED APRICOT MAYONNAISE

(Makes about 1 cup)

1 cup mayonnaise (Hellmann's or Best Foods is preferred)
1 teaspoon curry powder
3 tablespoons apricot preserves

1½ pounds smoked turkey, cut into ¾-inch cubes
1 small bunch red seedless grapes
1 small bunch green seedless grapes

6-inch wooden skewers

1. To prepare the curried apricot mayonnaise, place all the ingredients in a mixing bowl. Mix well to blend. The mayonnaise can be made up to 2 days ahead. Cover and refrigerate.

2. Place 1 piece of turkey and 1 grape, either green or red, on 6-inch wooden skewers. The skewers can be prepared 1 to 2 hours ahead. Cover with plastic wrap and refrigerate.

3. To serve, place a bowl of the mayonnaise on a large serving platter. Arrange the skewers around the bowl, alternating the skewers with red grapes with the ones with green grapes.

Fruit and Vegetable Appetizers

In general, we tend to think of vegetables for soups and salads or as accompaniments to entrées, and of fruit for salads or desserts. However, as I worked on this book, I came to realize what a rich and healthy resource vegetables and fruits are for the hors d'oeuvre table. Each season brings to our markets a wealth of produce that can be turned into surprisingly imaginative appetizers.

Some of the most interesting hors d'oeuvres I have created can be found in this chapter. Baked vegetables, such as skewers of zucchini, yellow squash, and cherry tomatoes cooked on a bed of fragrant rosemary sprigs, or skewered new potatoes and red onions, are different and appealing. Vegetable pâtés, like the Avocado Pâté with Parsley and Pistachios or the Shiitake Mushroom Pâté, are as tantalizing as their meat and poultry counterparts. Appetizers made with fruit have a lighter, more refreshing taste. For a deliciously satisfying but light temptation, try Melon with Pernod and Mint or Golden Apple Half-Moons.

Guests love surprises, and fruit and vegetables used in novel ways as appetizers provide the unexpected taste that separates an ordinary party from a memorable one.

Peaches Wrapped in Prosciutto and Mint

Fresh peach wedges wrapped with a band of prosciutto and garnished with mint are an unusual and delicious alternative to traditional prosciutto-wrapped melon.

Makes 32 portions

4 large ripe but firm peaches
3 tablespoons lemon juice
4 ounces prosciutto, thinly sliced (see note)
32 fresh mint leaves
6-inch wooden skewers, optional
Sprigs of mint, for garnish

1. Drop the peaches in boiling water to cover for 15 to 30 seconds. Remove and peel off the skin with a sharp paring knife. Cut each peach into 8 wedges. Place the peach slices in a bowl and toss with the lemon juice.

2. Trim the prosciutto of any excess fat. Cut the prosciutto into 1-inch-wide strips that are long enough to wrap and overlap around the peach slices. Wrap each peach slice with a strip of prosciutto, forming a band around the center of the slice. Tuck a mint leaf under the prosciutto. Place the peaches on skewers, if desired. The peaches can be prepared an hour ahead. Cover loosely with plastic wrap and refrigerate.

3. To serve, arrange the peaches in a spoke pattern on a decorative serving plate. Garnish the center of the plate with several sprigs of mint.

SHOPPING: Buy paper-thin slices of lean prosciutto. The thinner the slices, the easier they are to wrap around the fruit.

Melon with Pernod and Mint

I first sampled this dish at the celebrated three-star restaurant L'Ambroisie in Paris. As is the custom in many French restaurants, the waiter brought us a plate of hors d'oeuvres to enjoy while we read the menu. The chef had prepared slices of chilled melon, faintly scented with Pernod, an anise-flavored liquor, and garnished with mint.

Makes 64 portions

¾ cup sugar
¾ cup fresh mint leaves, torn in half
¼ cup Pernod
2 large ripe cantaloupes, about 2 to 2½ pounds each
6-inch wooden skewers
5 sprigs of mint, for garnish

1. Combine 2 cups water and the sugar in a heavy medium saucepan and place over medium-high heat. Stir until the sugar is dissolved. Then bring to a boil and boil 5 minutes without stirring. Remove from the heat.

2. Place the torn mint leaves in a small glass mixing bowl and pour the warm sugar mixture over them. Let the mixture steep for 45 minutes. Then strain and discard the mint leaves. Stir in the Pernod.

3. Halve, cutting through the stem end, and seed the cantaloupes. Then cut each half lengthwise into 8 wedges. Peel the wedges. Cut the wedges in half horizontally. Each melon will yield 32 wedges. Place the peeled cantaloupe wedges in a shallow glass or ceramic (not aluminum) dish and pour the mint mixture over them. Cover with plastic wrap and refrigerate for at least 3 hours or overnight, turning the wedges several times to ensure even marinating.

4. When ready to serve, skewer the melon wedges on 6-inch wooden skewers or toothpicks. Arrange on a serving platter and garnish with a cluster of fresh mint sprigs.

SERVING: For a special presentation line a serving platter with large, smooth, dark green tea leaves available from a florist's shop. Arrange the skewered melon wedges on top. When using tea leaves, I cut the mint leaves for the garnish into julienne strips and sprinkle them over the melon.

VARIATION: Sometimes I use a combination of cantaloupe and honeydew melons for a nice color contrast. Pineapple cut into cubes is another alternative.

Caramel-Glazed Grapes

At the restaurant Guy Savoy in Paris, I fell in love with these grapes at first bite. The grapes, with their shiny caramel coating, are not overly sweet and make an unusual and refreshing appetizer.

Makes about 80 portions

2 cups sugar
1 pound dark seedless grapes, each grape separated from the clusters
    with about ¼ to ½ inch of stem left intact
Grape leaves, for garnish

1. Place the sugar and ⅔ cup water in a heavy medium-size saucepan over medium heat. Stir and swirl the pan until the sugar is dissolved. Then bring the mixture to a boil and boil without stirring until it caramelizes, turning a rich tea brown color, about 15 to 20 minutes. Remove the pan from the heat and place carefully in a large shallow pan filled half full with hot water. The hot water will help keep the caramel mixture from thickening too much.

2. Have a large platter or several smaller plates ready. Holding a grape by the stem, swirl the bottom half into the caramel, then lift it from the caramel and swirl off the excess. Place the grape so it sits upright on the platter. Repeat with the remaining grapes. The whole process of dipping the grapes should take only a few seconds. If the caramel starts to thicken, reheat it over low heat without stirring to thin, and replace it in the pan of hot water.

3. The grapes can be refrigerated or left at cool, dry room temperature, but they are best eaten within 2 hours. Arrange on a platter and garnish with grape leaves.

SERVING: Serve these grapes arranged in diagonal rows on a silver platter. They look great on the silver because the shiny caramel coating on the grapes reflects off the silver. Bunches of grape leaves tied with thin ribbons on either end of the platter make a lovely garnish.

The caramel grapes are an attractive garnish for wheels of cheeses such as Brie and Camembert.

VARIATION: On a second trip to Guy Savoy I tasted caramel-glazed cherries. The chef left the long sleek stems on bright red cherries which he had swirled in the caramel.

Golden Apple Half-Moons

The charm of these appetizers lies in their simplicity. Golden Delicious apple wedges are first topped with strips of chives. Then, the wedges are wrapped with narrow bands of thinly sliced ham that are coated lightly with honey-mustard mayonnaise.

Makes 72 portions

3 large Golden Delicious apples, unpeeled
Juice of 1 large lemon
Honey-Mustard Mayonnaise (page 264)
5 to 6 ounces baked ham, very thinly sliced and cut into
*   1-inch-wide strips*
2 large bunches thin chives, cut into 3-inch lengths

1. Stem, halve, and core the apples, then cut each half into 12 wedges. You will have 72 slices. Place in a bowl and toss with the lemon juice.

2. To assemble the half-moons, spread the mayonnaise on one side of each ham strip. Place 2 chive pieces on top of each apple slice, and wrap a ham strip, mayonnaise side down, around the middle of each slice. Press gently to adhere. The apples can be assembled 2 to 3 hours ahead. Cover and refrigerate.

3. To serve, arrange the apples in overlapping, diagonal rows on a serving tray.

SHOPPING: Sweet apples taste better than tart varieties for this preparation.

SERVING: These simple appetizers look striking on a dark tray (earthenware or lacquer, for example), but they would also be attractive on a silver platter.

Herbed Olives

Olives are by definition a fruit, so it seemed appropriate to include these herbed olives in this chapter. Pam Park Curry, a teacher at my cooking school, brought this appetizer to a potluck Christmas party at the school. Everyone was so crazy about the olives, a mixture of black and green varieties flavored with herbs and hot pepper flakes, that I asked if she would show me how to make them. The olives need several days to marinate, but once seasoned, they can be kept in the refrigerator for several weeks.

Makes about 4 cups

¾ pound Kalamata olives (about 1¼ cups), drained
¾ pound ripe California green olives (about 1¼ cups), drained
¾ pound black olives (about 1¼ cups), either Niçoise or Alphonso, drained
¼ cup red wine vinegar
1 cup extra-virgin olive oil
3½ teaspoons very finely chopped garlic
1 tablespoon dried oregano
1 tablespoon dried dill
½ teaspoon salt, or more to taste
½ teaspoon crushed red pepper flakes
¼ teaspoon coarsely ground black pepper

1. Place the olives in a medium glass or nonaluminum mixing bowl. In the bowl of a food processor fitted with the metal blade or in a blender, place the vinegar, olive oil, garlic, oregano, dill, salt, red pepper flakes, and black pepper. Process until the mixture is well blended, about 20 to 30 seconds. Pour over the olives and cover with plastic wrap. Marinate for at least 2 days, at cool room temperature or in the refrigerator, stirring occasionally. Taste, and if desired, add more salt.

2. Transfer the olives to a clean jar, cover, and refrigerate. Bring to room temperature before serving so the oil, which will have congealed, will liquify. The olives can be stored for 2 to 3 weeks.

3. To serve, arrange in a large glass or ceramic bowl.

Avocado Pâté with Parsley and Pistachios

One summer, during one of the hottest Julys I can recall, I hosted a Sunday buffet at our house. The weather was so hot and humid that even air conditioning turned to the coolest setting could barely dissipate the warmth. This is one of the appetizers I offered our friends on that evening. Light and airy in texture, but with a spicy and piquant taste, it was a perfect beginning to our meal.

Makes 10 to 12 servings

Nonstick vegetable cooking spray
4 ripe avocados, peeled and pitted
2 8-ounce packages cream cheese, softened
2 tablespoons minced shallots
2 teaspoons minced garlic
2 tablespoons lemon juice, plus more for brushing the pâté
2 teaspoons chili powder, or more to taste
½ teaspoon cumin
½ teaspoon salt
¼ teaspoon cayenne pepper
2 tablespoons chopped fresh parsley
1 tablespoon chopped unsalted pistachios
Flat-leaf spinach leaves, for garnish
½ cup pitted ripe olives, for garnish
8 to 10 ripe cherry tomatoes, for garnish
Tortilla chips

1. Line a 6-inch rectangular pâté or terrine mold with three layers of waxed paper cut so that the paper extends 5 inches over both of the long sides of the mold. Do not worry about lining the short ends of the mold with waxed paper. Coat the top sheet of waxed paper generously with nonstick vegetable cooking spray.

2. Place the avocados and cream cheese in the bowl of a food processor fitted with the metal blade. Process until the mixture is smooth and there are no lumps, about 1 to 2 minutes. Add the shallots, garlic, 2 tablespoons lemon juice, the 2 teaspoons chili powder, the cumin, salt, and cayenne pepper and process to blend, about 30 to 60 seconds more. Taste, and if you want a spicier flavor, stir in additional chili powder. Fill the mold with the avocado mixture and spread the top evenly with a spatula. Cover the top of the mold with plastic wrap and refrigerate for at least 6 hours or overnight, until firm.

3. To unmold the pâté, remove the plastic wrap and run a knife around the edge of the pâté to loosen it from the sides of the pan and from the waxed paper. Invert the pâté onto a large serving plate and peel off the waxed paper. The pâté can be unmolded 4 to 5 hours ahead and kept refrigerated. Brush the pâté lightly with lemon juice to avoid discoloring.

4. When ready to serve, mix the parsley and pistachios together and arrange the mixture in a center line along the top of the pâté. Tuck clusters of spinach leaves around the corners of the pâté and scatter the black olives and cherry tomatoes over and around them. Arrange tortilla chips along the sides of the pâté.

SHOPPING: Buy very ripe, soft avocados for this dish so that they can be pureed easily. Lightly salted tortilla chips taste best with the pâté.

NOTE: If the pâté discolors even after brushing it with lemon juice, use a knife to scrape off a thin outside layer; underneath, the pâté will still be bright green.

SERVING: The Corn and Red Pepper Relish (page 127) also makes a delicious garnish for this pâté. Use it in place of the parsley and pistachio topping. Serve extra relish in a bowl.

Shiitake Mushroom Pâté

Tom Johnson, a close friend and a gifted chef, helped me create this dish, a combination of sautéed shiitake mushrooms, garlic, and scallions mixed with herbs and cream cheese, for former Ohio governor Dick Celeste. The governor, along with a little assistance from me, prepared the pâté, which included all Ohio-grown products, as part of the opening-day festivities at the Ohio State Fair one year. This creamy robust pâté tastes delicious mounded on crisp toast points.

Makes 10 to 12 servings

4 tablespoons unsalted butter, at room temperature
12 ounces shiitake mushrooms, stems discarded, caps finely chopped
1½ teaspoons finely chopped garlic
¼ cup finely chopped scallions (white parts only)
⅓ cup chicken stock
Pinch of well-crumbled dried rosemary
4 ounces cream cheese, at room temperature
2 tablespoons finely minced fresh chives or green tops from the scallions
Pinch of freshly grated nutmeg
Pinch of cayenne pepper
Salt to taste
2 teaspoons chopped fresh chives or green tops of scallions, for garnish
Toast points or slices of French bread

1. Melt 2 tablespoons of the butter in a medium-size skillet over high heat. When hot, add the chopped shiitake mushrooms and sauté 2 to 3 minutes. Add the garlic and scallions and sauté 1 minute more. Add the chicken stock and rosemary, and cook over high heat until all the liquid has evaporated, 4 to 5 minutes. Let the mushroom mixture cool to room temperature.

2. Combine the cream cheese and the remaining 2 tablespoons butter in a mixing bowl. Stir to mix well. Add the mushroom mixture, minced chives, nutmeg, cayenne, and salt. Mix well. Fill a 1-to-2-cup ramekin or soufflé dish with the mixture. Cover with plastic wrap and refrigerate. The pâté can be made a day in advance.

3. When ready to serve, sprinkle the pâté with the chopped chives and place on a decorative platter. Serve with toast points or slices of French bread.

SHOPPING: I always make this pâté with fresh shiitake mushrooms, but if unavailable, you can substitute 4 ounces dried shiitake mushrooms. Soak in hot water to cover for 30 minutes. Drain and squeeze out excess moisture, and remove and discard the stems.

VARIATION: Substitute Belgian endive leaves for the bread.

Skewered Vegetables Baked with Rosemary

After finding a large bunch of rosemary sprigs in the refrigerator, left over from a class the evening before at my cooking school, my assistant, Emily Bell, and I decided to try baking vegetable skewers on beds of rosemary. We were delighted with the results. The rosemary lightly permeates the vegetables and imparts an aromatic scent to the dish.

Makes 8 to 10 servings

2 medium zucchini
2 medium yellow summer squash
About ⅓ cup extra-virgin olive oil
About 2 teaspoons dried rosemary
About 2 teaspoons dried thyme
Salt and freshly ground black pepper to taste
2 to 3 fresh bunches rosemary
Nonstick vegetable cooking spray
1 to 2 pints ripe but firm cherry tomatoes, stems removed

6-inch wooden skewers

1. Trim and discard the ends from the zucchini and summer squash. Cut the zucchini and summer squash into ¾-inch-thick slices and cut each slice in half. Set aside.

2. Place 1 piece each of zucchini and yellow squash on 6-inch wooden skew-

159

ers. Brush the skewered vegetables generously with the olive oil, then sprinkle lightly on all sides with about two thirds of the dried rosemary and dried thyme. Season generously with salt and pepper.

3. Spray two large heavy baking dishes with nonstick vegetable cooking spray. Cover the bottom of each baking dish with rosemary sprigs, reserving a few sprigs for garnish. Arrange the vegetable skewers on the beds of rosemary. The skewers can be prepared 2 to 3 hours ahead to this point. Cover and refrigerate.

4. Brush the cherry tomatoes with the olive oil, and sprinkle with remaining dried rosemary and dried thyme and with salt and pepper. Place in a bowl and leave at room temperature for up to 3 hours.

5. When ready to bake, preheat the oven to 375°F.

6. Bake the skewers of zucchini and summer squash 8 to 10 minutes. Remove from the oven and turn the skewers over. Add 1 cherry tomato to each skewer and bake another 8 to 10 minutes. Remove from the oven. Arrange the skewers on a serving dish and garnish with fresh rosemary sprigs. Serve warm.

SERVING: I serve these vegetable skewers as an appetizer with grilled dinners in the summertime.

Skewered New Potatoes and Red Onions

No matter how many of these I make, there never seem to be any leftovers!

Makes about 48 portions

1 to 2 large sweet red onions or Vidalia onions
48 small (1 inch in diameter) new potatoes, unpeeled
8 tablespoons unsalted butter, melted
About 2 teaspoons dried rosemary
About 2 teaspoons dried basil
Salt, preferably coarse, and freshly ground black pepper to taste
Nonstick vegetable cooking spray
Sprigs of rosemary and basil, for garnish
6-inch wooden skewers

1. Peel the onions and halve through the stem ends. Cut ¾-inch-thick slices from each half, then cut each slice into 3 wedges.

2. Skewer a wedge of onion on a 6-inch wooden skewer, then a potato, and then another wedge of onion. Continue until all the potatoes and onions are skewered. Brush the potatoes and onions generously with the melted butter. Sprinkle lightly with the herbs and then with salt and pepper.

3. Spray two large heavy baking pans very generously with nonstick vegetable cooking spray. Arrange the skewers in the pans. The skewers can be assembled 1 to 2 hours ahead and left at cool room temperature.

4. When ready to bake, preheat the oven to 375°F.

5. Bake 10 minutes and turn the skewers over. Continue baking another 20 minutes, or until the potatoes are tender when pierced with a knife. Remove and cool about 5 minutes.

6. To serve, arrange on a serving tray and garnish with clusters of fresh rosemary and basil.

SHOPPING: If small new potatoes are not available, use large new potatoes cut into 1-inch chunks. Since the flesh will be exposed, they will start to discolor, but when brushed generously with butter, they usually can remain uncovered at cool room temperature for about an hour.

Oriental Carrots

Soy sauce, rice vinegar, and peanut oil elevate the humble carrot to new status. The carrots, blanched until just tender and then marinated briefly, are light in taste and make a good pre-dinner appetizer.

Makes about 72 to 80 portions

1 pound carrots
4 tablespoons rice wine vinegar
6 tablespoons soy sauce
6 tablespoons peanut oil
4 teaspoons finely chopped peeled gingerroot
2 teaspoons minced garlic
¼ teaspoon hot chili oil
2 teaspoons sugar
6-inch wooden skewers
Several sprigs of flat-leaf parsley, for garnish
5 to 6 scallions, root ends and all but 2 inches of green stems cut off on a diagonal, for garnish

1. Peel the carrots and discard the stems. Starting at the stem end, cut the carrots into ⅜-inch diagonal slices.

2. Place 3 quarts of water in a large heavy saucepan over high heat. Bring to a boil and add the sliced carrots. Boil until the carrots are just tender, but not mushy, about 6 to 8 minutes. Drain well and pat dry with a clean kitchen towel. The carrots can be cooked a day ahead. Cool, cover, and refrigerate.

3. When ready to marinate the carrots, place them in a shallow nonaluminum dish. Combine the rice wine vinegar, soy sauce, peanut oil, ginger, garlic, chili oil, and sugar in a mixing bowl and whisk well to blend. Pour the marinade over the carrots. Marinate for 1 hour—no longer or the carrots will darken in color because of the marinade. Drain the carrots. The carrots can be prepared to this point a day ahead. Cover and refrigerate.

4. To serve, spear the carrots on 6-inch wooden skewers. Arrange the carrots on a serving plate. Garnish with sprigs of flat-leaf parsley and the scallions.

SERVING: I like to serve these carrots skewered, but if you do not have the time to do so, arrange the carrots on a serving plate and place the skewers in a small vase or jar.

Apple-and-Sausage-Stuffed Mushrooms

These mushrooms, mounded with a mixture of sautéed sausage, shallots, and diced apples mixed with cream cheese and honey mustard, are hearty and robust. They can be made completely in advance and are perfect to serve during the cold weather months.

Makes 24 portions

24 large mushrooms (1½ inches in diameter; about 1½ pounds)
7 tablespoons unsalted butter, plus more if needed
3 tablespoons vegetable oil, plus more if needed
Salt and freshly ground black pepper to taste
½ pound bulk pork sausage
½ cup chopped shallots
2 cups peeled, finely chopped tart apples (about 4 to 5 apples)
1 tablespoon sugar
4 ounces cream cheese
2 teaspoons honey mustard, or more to taste
2 tablespoons chopped fresh parsley, for garnish

1. Wipe any dirt or grit from the mushrooms with a clean, damp kitchen cloth. Cut out or twist off the stems and discard or save for another use. Carefully scrape out the cavities of the mushroom caps with a teaspoon. Heat 3 tablespoons each of the butter and vegetable oil in a large heavy skillet over medium-high heat. When hot, add enough of the mushrooms to fit comfortably in the pan, flesh side down, and sauté until golden, about 2 to 3 minutes. Turn and sauté on the other side until golden, another 2 to 3 minutes. Continue in this way until all mushrooms are sautéed. If necessary, add more butter and oil in equal amounts. Remove the mushrooms and sprinkle the cavities lightly with salt and pepper. Drain the mushroom caps, hollowed-out side down, on paper towels.

2. To prepare the filling, cook the sausage, breaking it into small pieces with a spoon, in a large heavy skillet over medium-high heat, stirring, until browned. Remove the sausage with a slotted spoon and drain on paper towels. Pour off any fat remaining in the skillet.

3. Add the remaining 4 tablespoons butter to the skillet and place over medium-high heat. Add the shallots and sauté 2 minutes. Add the chopped apples and sprinkle with the sugar. Sauté, stirring, for 3 to 4 minutes, until the apples are light golden. Add the cream cheese and honey mustard and stir and cook until the cheese has melted. Remove from the heat and stir in the sausage. Taste and season as desired with salt and pepper. Add more honey mustard if you want a tarter taste.

4. Mound the mixture into the mushroom caps and place on a greased baking sheet. The mushrooms can be prepared a day ahead to this point. Cover with plastic wrap and refrigerate.

5. When ready to serve, preheat the oven to 350°F.

6. Place the mushrooms, uncovered, on the center shelf of the oven and bake until hot, about 8 minutes. Remove and sprinkle with the parsley. Arrange on a serving plate. Serve hot.

Mushrooms Stuffed with Walnuts and St. André

Makes 24 portions

24 large mushrooms (1½ inches in diameter; about 1½ pounds)
3 tablespoons unsalted butter, plus more if needed
3 tablespoons vegetable oil, plus more if needed
Salt and freshly ground black pepper to taste
5 ounces St. André cheese, with rind (see note), cut into large
    chunks
4 tablespoons coarsely chopped walnuts
4 tablespoons dry unflavored bread crumbs
Generous pinch of cayenne pepper
2 tablespoons chopped fresh parsley, for garnish

1. Wipe any dirt and grit from the mushrooms with a clean damp kitchen cloth. Cut out or twist off the stems and discard or save for another use. Carefully scrape out the cavities of the mushroom caps with a teaspoon. Heat the butter and oil in a large heavy skillet over medium-high heat. When hot, add enough of the mushrooms to fit comfortably in the pan, flesh side down, and sauté until golden, about 2 to 3 minutes. Turn and sauté on the other side until golden, another 2 to 3 minutes. Continue in this way until all mushrooms are sautéed. If necessary, add more butter and oil in equal amounts. Remove the mushrooms and season the cavities lightly with salt and pepper. Drain the mushroom caps, hollowed-out side down, on paper towels.

2. To prepare the filling, place the chunks of cheese in the bowl of an electric mixer and beat on medium speed until smooth and creamy. Or beat the mixture by hand with a wooden spoon. Stir in the walnuts, bread crumbs, and cayenne pepper. Mound the filling into the mushrooms and place them on a greased baking sheet. The mushrooms can be prepared a day ahead to this point. Cover and refrigerate.

3. When ready to bake, preheat the oven to 350°F.

4. Bake the mushrooms, uncovered, until the cheese is bubbling, about 8 minutes. Remove and sprinkle with the parsley. Arrange on a serving plate. Serve hot.

SHOPPING: Brie or Camembert can be substituted; do not remove the rinds.

✳ Spicy Italian-
Sausage-Stuffed Mushrooms

Large, juicy sautéed mushroom caps mounded with a combination of hot Italian sausage and onions blended with cream cheese and basil make irresistible appetizers. I serve these savory morsels as an opener for Italian meals. As in the two preceding recipes, the mushrooms can be assembled ahead and baked when needed.

Makes 24 portions

24 large mushrooms (1½ inches in diameter; about 1½ pounds)
6 tablespoons olive oil, plus more if needed
Salt to taste
½ pound hot Italian bulk sausage
⅔ cup chopped onions
1 tablespoon dried basil
6 ounces cream cheese, broken into small pieces
Pinch of crushed red pepper flakes, optional
Fresh basil leaves, for garnish

1. Wipe any dirt and grit from the mushrooms with a clean damp kitchen cloth. Cut out or twist off the stems and discard or save for another use. Carefully scrape out the cavities of the mushrooms with a teaspoon. Heat the oil in a large heavy skillet over medium-high heat. When hot, add enough of the mushrooms to fit comfortably in the pan, flesh side down, and sauté until golden, about 2 to 3 minutes. Turn and sauté on the other side until golden, about 2 to 3 minutes more. Continue in this way until all the mushrooms are sautéed. If necessary, add more oil to the pan. Remove the mushrooms and season the cavities lightly with salt. Drain the mushroom caps, hollowed-out side down, on paper towels.

2. To prepare the filling, add the sausage to the skillet in which the mushrooms were sautéed. Cook over medium-high heat, breaking the sausage into small pieces with a spoon, until lightly browned, about 4 to 5 minutes. Add the onions and dried basil and sauté until the onions are softened, 2 to 3 minutes more. Add the cream cheese and stir until the cheese has melted completely and is well incorporated into the mixture. Taste and season with more salt, if needed. If you want a spicier taste, add the red pepper flakes. Drain the filling on paper towels.

3. Mound the filling into the mushroom caps. The mushrooms can be prepared up to a day in advance to this point. Cover and refrigerate.

3. When ready to bake, preheat the oven to 350°F.

4. Bake the mushrooms, uncovered, until hot, about 8 minutes. Remove and arrange on a serving tray. Garnish each mushroom with a basil leaf.

Cherry Tomatoes with a Summer Stuffing

Ricotta, fontina, and Parmesan cheeses flavored with fresh herbs and grated orange zest make a delicious filling for baked cherry tomatoes. Served hot from the oven, these delectable morsels seem to melt in your mouth.

Makes about 40 portions

8 ounces part-skim ricotta cheese
⅔ cup grated fontina, divided
¼ cup grated imported Parmesan cheese
¼ teaspoon crushed red pepper flakes
1 teaspoon grated orange zest
2 tablespoons chopped fresh basil
¾ tablespoon chopped fresh mint
1 generous teaspoon minced garlic
Salt and freshly ground black pepper to taste
2 pints cherry tomatoes, stems removed
Sprigs of basil and mint, for garnish

1. To prepare the filling, combine the ricotta, ⅓ cup of the fontina, and the Parmesan cheese in a mixing bowl. Add the red pepper flakes, orange zest, chopped basil and mint, and garlic. Mix well to blend. Season lightly with salt and black pepper. The filling can be made a day ahead. Cover and refrigerate.

(continued)

2. Cut a thin slice from the bottom end of each tomato. Scoop out the insides with a small spoon. Season the cavities generously with salt and pepper. Turn the tomatoes hollowed-out side down on paper towels and drain for 15 minutes.

3. Stuff the tomatoes with the cheese filling, mounding the tops, and sprinkle generously with the remaining fontina cheese. Place the tomatoes on a lightly greased baking sheet. The tomatoes can be prepared a day ahead. Cover and refrigerate.

4. When ready to bake, preheat the oven to 350°F. and adjust a rack in the center of the oven.

5. Bake the tomatoes until hot, about 5 to 7 minutes. Remove and arrange on a serving plate. Garnish the plate with a bouquet of basil and mint sprigs. Serve hot.

NOTE: Cutting a slice from the bottom rather than the stem end of the tomatoes makes the tomatoes sit flat on the tray and not wobble the way they usually do.

SERVING: If you have an attractive baking dish that can go from the oven to the table, serve the tomatoes in that and garnish with basil sprigs.

VARIATION: The Toasted Pine Nut Pesto (page 262) also makes a delicious filling for these tomatoes. Scoop out the tomatoes, fill with pesto, and sprinkle with grated Parmesan cheese. Place on a lightly greased baking sheet and bake in a 350°F. oven until hot, about 5 to 7 minutes. Transfer to a serving plate, and garnish the plate with basil sprigs.

Asparagus Wrapped in Smoked Salmon

Makes about 48 portions

48 thin asparagus spears (2½ to 3 pounds)
24 thin slices smoked salmon, about 5 inches by 2 inches (about 10
*   to 12 ounces)*
Cracked black pepper
1 tablespoon finely julienned lemon zest
1 to 2 tablespoons lemon juice
3 tablespoons extra-virgin olive oil
2 tablespoons julienned fresh mint leaves
Sprigs of mint, for garnish

1. To prepare the asparagus, cut off the tough, woody ends and discard. Trim the asparagus spears so they are all about the same length. In a large deep pan or skillet, bring enough water to cover the asparagus to a boil. Lightly salt the water, and add the asparagus. Simmer until just tender, about 3 minutes. Remove the asparagus, place in a colander, and place under cold running water to refresh. Drain and pat the asparagus dry. The asparagus can be cooked a day ahead. Cover and refrigerate.

2. Place the slices of smoked salmon on a work surface so that a long edge of each slice is in front of you. Cut the slices in half lengthwise so that you get two pieces approximately 2½ inches by 2 inches. Starting just below the tip of an asparagus spear, wrap a piece of smoked salmon tightly around the center of the stalk. Repeat with the remaining asparagus and salmon. Sprinkle with pepper. Arrange the asparagus spears in a spoke pattern on a nonmetallic serving tray. Sprinkle the spears with the lemon zest. Mix the lemon juice and olive oil together and drizzle over the asparagus. The asparagus stalks can be prepared 1½ to 2 hours in advance. Cover with plastic wrap and refrigerate.

3. To serve, sprinkle the julienned mint over the asparagus. Garnish the serving tray with mint sprigs.

SHOPPING: Thin asparagus spears are preferable to large, thick ones for this hors d'oeuvre. If you can only find the thicker ones, peel the stalks, starting just below the tips, before cooking.

Warm Artichoke Leaves
with Brie

I found a way to combine two of my favorite tastes, Brie and artichokes, in these easy-to-assemble appetizers.

Makes about 60 portions

2 large artichokes
10 to 12 ounces Brie, with rind, very well chilled
Dried thyme
Dried rosemary, well crumbled
Cayenne pepper

1. To cook the artichokes, bring a 3- to 4-quart saucepan of water to a boil. While the water is heating, cut the stems from the artichokes. Place each artichoke on its side and, with a sharp knife, cut off about an inch from the top. Use scissors to trim any sharp tips from the leaves. Place the artichokes in the boiling water, cover with a lid that is slightly ajar, and cook until the artichoke bases are tender when pierced with a knife, about 35 to 40 minutes. Drain the artichokes and cool. The artichokes can be cooked up to a day in advance. Cover with plastic wrap and refrigerate.

2. Remove the leaves from the artichokes and place them on two aluminum foil-lined baking sheets. Slice ⅛-inch-thick wedges from the Brie, making certain that each wedge has some of the rind, and trim the cheese slices to fit the bottom half of the artichoke leaves. Place a cheese slice on each leaf and sprinkle lightly with the dried thyme and dried rosemary. Sprinkle lightly with cayenne pepper. The artichoke leaves can be prepared 3 to 4 hours ahead to this point. Cover with plastic wrap and refrigerate. Bring to room temperature 30 minutes before baking.

3. When ready to bake the artichoke leaves, preheat the oven to 400°F.

4. Bake the leaves just until the cheese melts and leaves are warm, about 4 to 5 minutes. Watch carefully.

5. To serve, arrange the leaves on a platter in parallel diagonal rows. Serve warm.

VARIATION: Blue cheese is another good topping for artichoke leaves. Try Gorgonzola with a sprinkling of oregano instead of thyme and rosemary.

Cheese

I cannot imagine planning a party menu without cheese. People will always find their way to a tray of cheese, whether it's served as is, unadorned, or embellished with special touches. Creating the appetizers for this section was a joy, because the versatility of cheeses made it a pleasure to develop intriguing new recipes; but the task was also frustrating, because it was difficult to decide which of the many exceptional cheeses there are available to include.

Among the dishes served warm, there are pastry-wrapped and stuffed wheels of cheese, fondues, crisp wafers, bite-sized golden popovers, and creamy cheese squares. A terrine, a mousse, potted cheese, and cheese croutons are all offered at room temperature. Though bread, crackers, or toasts are the most common accompaniments to cheese, I find that apples, grapes, wedges of plum tomatoes, and tortilla chips all enhance the flavor of cheese as well.

Some of these preparations are real show-stoppers—perfect for an important party. Try the Baked Brie with Plums and Walnuts, Brie with Cranberry Chutney served on pine branches, or Sherried Cheddar Terrine garnished with bunches of grapes and apples wedges.

Many of the entries are especially appropriate for informal entertaining. Herb-Garlic Cheese Fondue, Rio Grande Fondue, and Saga Blue with Roasted Garlic are delectable offerings for casual get-togethers.

Baker's Brie

When Russell Baker, well-known author and columnist for *The New York Times*, came to Columbus, Ohio, to give a reading, I hosted a party in his honor. One of the appetizers I served was a baked wheel of Brie topped with a sauté of sun-dried tomatoes, shallots, garlic, and basil.

Makes 10 to 12 servings

1 6- to 8-ounce jar sun-dried tomatoes packed in oil
6 tablespoons chopped shallots
4 teaspoons finely chopped garlic
1 tablespoon chopped fresh basil or 1 teaspoon dried
½ cup chopped fresh parsley
Salt and freshly ground black pepper to taste
1 2.2-pound wheel of Brie, rind left on
1 loaf French bread, cut into ½-inch-thick slices
Sprigs of basil, for garnish

1. Drain ¼ cup oil from the jar of sun-dried tomatoes. Place the oil in a medium heavy skillet. Finely chop enough sun-dried tomatoes to make ½ cup. (Unused sun-dried tomatoes can be kept tightly covered in the jar and refrigerated for several weeks.)

2. Heat the oil in the skillet over medium-high heat. When hot, add the shallots and sauté, stirring, until softened, about 3 minutes. Add the garlic and sauté a minute more. Then add the ½ cup chopped tomatoes and the basil and stir and cook 2 minutes more. Remove from the heat and stir in the parsley. Taste and season with salt and pepper.

3. Brush the top and sides of the wheel of Brie lightly with a little more of the oil from the jar of tomatoes. Spread the cooked sun-dried tomato mixture on top of the cheese. Place a sheet of aluminum foil or parchment paper on a rimless baking sheet. Carefully transfer the Brie to the baking sheet. Refrigerate for at least 30 minutes or up to 5 hours before baking.

4. When ready to bake the Brie, preheat the oven to 350°F.

5. Arrange the slices of bread on a baking sheet and place in the oven until lightly toasted, about 5 minutes. Remove from the oven.

6. Place the Brie on the center oven shelf and bake until heated through, about 8 to 10 minutes. Watch carefully. Remove from the oven. Lift the Brie on the foil or parchment paper to a serving platter and trim away excess foil or paper. Surround with overlapping slices of the toasted bread. Garnish with sprigs of basil. Serve warm.

SHOPPING: If a 2.2-pound wheel of Brie is too large for your party, you can use a 1.1-pound wheel. Halve the topping and bake as for the larger Brie.

~~

Baked Brie with Plums and Walnuts

This is a glorious party dish that looks as if it takes far more time than the few minutes actually needed to assemble it. A wheel of Brie, scooped out to form a shell, is filled with thin slices of fresh plums and chopped walnuts and then baked and served with French bread.

Makes 10 to 12 servings

1 2.2-pound wheel of Brie, rind left on
*4 small ripe red plums, unpeeled, cut into ¼-inch-thick wedges
   (about 1½ cups)*
⅔ cup walnuts, coarsely chopped
2 tablespoons plum jam, heated until warm
Sprigs of sage, for garnish
1 loaf French bread, cut into ⅓-inch-thick slices

1. Use a sharp paring knife to make a cavity in the Brie. Insert the knife ½ inch in from the outside edge of the wheel and trace a ½-inch-deep circle in the top of the cheese. Then use the knife to gently loosen the top rind until it can be removed. With a teaspoon, scoop out enough of the soft Brie to form a cavity ½ inch deep. Save the top and the scooped-out Brie for another use.

2. Combine the sliced plums and walnuts in a mixing bowl. Mound the mixture in the Brie. Line an unrimmed baking sheet with aluminum foil or parchment

174

paper and transfer the Brie to the baking sheet. Refrigerate for 30 minutes before baking. The cheese can be prepared 2 to 3 hours ahead to this point. Keep covered and refrigerated.

3. When ready to bake the cheese, preheat the oven to 350°F.

4. Bake the Brie on the center shelf of the oven until the cheese is warm and just softened, about 8 to 10 minutes. Watch carefully. Remove and cool on the baking sheet for 3 to 4 minutes. Then brush the plums and walnuts with the plum jam.

5. To serve, lift the cheese on the foil or parchment paper to a serving dish. Cut the excess foil or paper away. Garnish the cheese with sage sprigs and surround with the sliced French bread.

SHOPPING: Although I think this recipe is more attractive when made with a large 2.2-pound wheel of Brie, you can use a small 1.1-pound cheese. Halve the filling and bake as directed for the larger wheel.

VARIATIONS: There are many possibilities for varying the filling for wheels of Brie. Try, for example, peaches and almonds tossed with 1 to 2 tablespoons lemon zest and brushed with peach or apricot jam; fresh apricots and pecans brushed with apricot jam; or halved seedless grapes (red or green or a combination) and walnuts brushed with red currant jam.

Baked Brie with Cranberry Chutney

This baked Brie topped with homemade cranberry chutney and served on a bed of long-needled pine has become one of my favorites for holiday entertaining. The chutney can be made four to five days in advance and then spread on the Brie just before baking.

Makes 10 to 12 servings

1 2.2.-pound wheel of Brie, rind left on
Cranberry Chutney (page 267)
Several small branches of long-needled pine, optional
1 loaf French bread, heated and cut into ⅓-inch-thick slices

1. Place a sheet of aluminum foil or parchment paper on a rimless baking sheet. Place the Brie in the center. Spread the cranberry chutney over the top of the cheese. Refrigerate for 30 minutes before baking. The Brie can be prepared 2 to 3 hours in advance. Keep covered and refrigerated.

2. When ready to bake, preheat the oven to 350°F.

3. Place the Brie on the center shelf of the oven and bake until heated through, about 8 to 10 minutes. Watch carefully.

4. Remove the Brie from oven. If desired, arrange small branches of long-needled pine on the serving tray. Lift the Brie on the foil or paper to the serving tray and trim away the excess foil or paper. Serve with a basket of the warm sliced French bread.

SHOPPING: If you wish to use a 1.1-pound wheel of Brie, halve the amount of chutney and bake as for larger wheel.

VARIATIONS: This chutney-topped cheese also tastes delicious on apple wedges. I use tart red apples and toss them in lemon juice to prevent discoloring, before arranging them on the pine branches.

If you want to serve Brie with another chutney topping at other times of the year, try the following:

Brush a 2.2-pound wheel of Brie with 1 tablespoon melted unsalted butter mixed with ½ teaspoon curry powder. Spread 8 ounces store-bought mango chutney over the top of the Brie and sprinkle with ¼ cup slivered almonds. Bake as directed above and serve with French bread or apple slices.

Brandied Brie with Dried Sour Cherries and Walnuts

Brie prepared this way is so delicious that I once packed a wheel, completely assembled with its dried cherry and walnut filling and wrapped in a brandy-soaked towel, in my briefcase and flew halfway across the country with it for a special party. It suffered no ill effects from the journey and was perfect when served hot from the oven.

Makes 6 to 8 servings

1 1.1-pound wheel of Brie, rind left on
¼ cup brandy
½ cup dried sour cherries
⅓ cup coarsely chopped toasted walnuts (page 268), plus 3 walnut halves for garnish
Sprigs of flat-leaf parsley, for garnish
1 loaf French bread, cut into ⅓-inch slices

1. Use a sharp paring knife to make a cavity in the Brie: Insert the knife ½ inch in from the outside edge of the wheel and trace a ½-inch-deep circle in the top of the cheese. Then use the knife to gently loosen the top rind until it can be removed. Set aside. With a teaspoon, scoop out enough of the soft Brie to form a cavity ½ inch deep. Trim the underside (the side with the cheese) of the "lid" so that it is flat. Save the scooped-out cheese for another use.

2. Prick the inside and outer sides of the cheese all over with the tines of a fork. Drizzle ½ tablespoon of the brandy over the cavity. Combine the dried sour cherries and chopped walnuts in a bowl and pack into the cheese. Place the lid on top and press it into place. Arrange the 3 walnut halves in the center of the lid.

3. Prick the lid well with the tines of a fork. Brush the top and sides of the Brie with more of the brandy. Then wrap the cheese in a clean kitchen towel and sprinkle the towel with the remaining brandy. Place the cheese in a plastic bag and tie tightly. Refrigerate for at least 24 hours or up to 3 days before baking.

4. When ready to bake the cheese, preheat the oven to 350°F.

5. Place the cheese on a baking sheet lined with aluminum foil or parchment paper. Bake on the center shelf of the oven until the cheese is warm and just softened, about 8 to 10 minutes. Watch carefully. Remove and cool on the baking sheet for 2 to 4 minutes.

(*continued*)

6. To serve, lift the cheese on the foil or paper to a serving tray. Cut the excess foil or paper away. Garnish the cheese with sprigs of flat-leaf parsley and arrange the slices of bread around the Brie.

SHOPPING: Dried sour cherries are becoming more readily available, but if you cannot find them in your area, see page 281 for mail order information.

Baked Camembert with Mushrooms and Scallions

A wheel of Camembert hollowed out and filled with sautéed mushrooms and scallions, then baked, makes an absolutely mouth-watering appetizer. Serve it hot on slices of French bread.

Makes 4 to 6 servings

2 tablespoons unsalted butter
4 ounces mushrooms, thinly sliced through the stems
1 teaspoon chopped garlic
2 tablespoons finely chopped scallions
Salt and freshly ground black pepper to taste
1 8-ounce wheel of Camembert (see note)
1½ tablespoons chopped fresh parsley or chives or a combination of
  both, for garnish
1 loaf French bread, cut into ⅓-inch slices

1. Heat the butter in a medium-size skillet over high heat until melted and hot. Add the mushrooms and sauté for 2 to 3 minutes. Add the garlic and scallions and sauté until all the liquid has evaporated, about 3 to 4 minutes more. Remove from the heat and let cool to room temperature. Season to taste with salt and pepper.

2. Use a sharp paring knife to make a cavity in the cheese. Insert the knife ½ inch in from the outside edge of the cheese and trace a ½-inch-deep circle in the
178

top of the cheese. Then use the knife to gently loosen the top rind until it can be removed. With a teaspoon, scoop out enough of the soft cheese to form a cavity ½ inch deep. Save the scooped-out cheese and the rind for another use.

3. Fill the cheese with the sautéed mushroom mixture. Place the Camembert on a baking sheet lined with aluminum foil or parchment paper. Chill at least 30 minutes. The cheese can be prepared 4 to 5 hours ahead. Cover and refrigerate.

4. When ready to bake the cheese, preheat the oven to 350°F.

5. Bake the cheese on the center shelf of the oven until warm and just softened, about 6 to 8 minutes. Watch carefully. Remove and cool for 3 to 4 minutes.

6. To serve, lift the cheese on the foil or parchment to a serving tray. Cut the excess foil or parchment away. Garnish the top of cheese with the chopped parsley and/or chives. Arrange the slices of French bread around the Camembert.

SHOPPING: If you want to use a larger wheel of cheese, substitute Brie, which is available in 1.1-pound (½ kilo) and 2.2-pound (1 kilo) sizes. For the 1.1-pound Brie, double the filling; for the 2.2-pound Brie, quadruple the filling. Camemberts are usually available in 8-ounce or smaller wheels. If you find larger ones, adjust the filling as for the Brie. The baking times for the larger wheels will be about 8 to 10 minutes, but watch carefully.

Honey-Mustard-Glazed Camembert

A wheel of Camembert spread with honey mustard and baked until warm makes a simple, but delectable, appetizer to spread on pear or apple wedges.

Makes 4 to 6 servings

1 to 2 tablespoons honey mustard
1 8-ounce wheel of Camembert (see note)
2 to 3 ripe pears or tart apples
1 tablespoon lemon juice
Several sprigs of watercress, for garnish

1. Using a spatula, spread enough honey mustard over the top and sides of the Camembert to coat it well. Line a baking sheet with aluminum foil or parchment paper. Place the cheese on the sheet and refrigerate for 30 minutes before baking. The cheese can be assembled 2 to 3 hours ahead. Keep covered and refrigerated.

2. When ready to bake the cheese, preheat the oven to 350°F.

3. Halve and core, but do not peel the pears or apples. Cut each pear or apple into ⅜-inch-thick wedges and toss in the lemon juice to prevent discoloring.

4. Bake the cheese on the center shelf of the oven until warm and just softened, about 6 to 8 minutes. Watch carefully. Remove and cool for 3 to 4 minutes.

5. To serve, lift the cheese on the foil or parchment paper to a serving tray. Trim away the excess foil or paper. Garnish the cheese with watercress and with the pear or apple wedges.

SHOPPING: You can substitute Brie for Camembert in this recipe if you like. See page 179 about the various sizes of Camembert and Brie available. If you use a larger wheel, simply increase the honey mustard so that you have enough to coat the top and sides of the cheese generously.

Gouda Baked in Pastry

My students tell me that their guests always assume they spent hours preparing this dish when, in fact, it can be assembled in a matter of minutes. The pastry encases a round of Gouda that has been coated lightly with honey mustard; a "cluster of grapes," made from pastry scraps, makes a striking but simple decoration on top of the cheese.

Makes 6 to 8 servings

1 sheet frozen puff pastry (from a 17¼-ounce package of 2 sheets pastry), defrosted
1 7-ounce round of Gouda cheese with caraway (about 3¾ inches in diameter)
1 tablespoon honey mustard
1 large egg, beaten
3 large apples, unpeeled, cored, seeded, and sliced into 16 thin wedges each (Granny Smith, Delicious, or Red Rome work well)

1. Roll out the puff pastry to a 14-inch square on a lightly floured surface. Cut out one 7½-inch circle and a one 4-inch circle.

2. Remove the wax coating from the cheese. Center the cheese on the 7½-inch circle. Spread the honey mustard over the top and down the sides of the cheese. Pull the circle of puff pastry up as far as it will go around the sides of the cheese and press with your fingers to make it adhere. Brush the sides of the pastry with the beaten egg. Brush the outer edge of the smaller circle with the beaten egg and place it, moistened side down, over the pastry-wrapped cheese. Press with your fingers to seal the two doughs together. Brush the top pastry circle and sides with the egg. Cut out decorations from the scraps of puff pastry to decorate the top of the cheese. Small ¾-inch circles and leaves arranged like a cluster of grapes make an attractive garnish. Brush the design with the egg. Refrigerate the cheese for at least 30 minutes to firm. Draped loosely with aluminum foil, it can be refrigerated for up to 4 hours.

3. When ready to bake, preheat the oven to 375°F.

4. Bake on an aluminum foil-lined and greased baking sheet for 30 minutes, or until the pastry is browned and the cheese is melted.

5. Transfer the cheese on the foil to a serving dish. Trim away the excess foil and arrange the apple wedges around the cheese.

VARIATION: Smoked Gouda can be substituted.

Apricot-Glazed Havarti in Phyllo

Havarti cheese, glazed lightly with apricot preserves, dusted with chopped walnuts, and wrapped in layers of phyllo leaves and baked makes a very tempting hors d'oeuvre. The cheese melts to a rich, creamy consistency and the phyllo sheets become crispy and flaky.

Makes 6 to 8 servings

4 sheets phyllo (14 x 18 inches)
6 tablespoons unsalted butter, melted, plus more if needed
3 tablespoons dry unseasoned bread crumbs
1 7-ounce round of Havarti cheese (see note)
3 tablespoons apricot preserves
¼ cup chopped toasted walnuts (page 268)
2 to 3 large tart apples
1 tablespoon lemon juice

1. Stack the phyllo sheets on a work surface and trim to a 13-inch square. Leave 1 sheet on the work surface and cover the others with a dampened kitchen towel so they do not dry out. Brush the phyllo sheet generously with the melted butter, and sprinkle 1 tablespoon of the bread crumbs over the sheet. Place a second sheet on top of the first and repeat the process. Repeat with the third and fourth sheets, but do not sprinkle the last sheet with bread crumbs.

2. Place the cheese in the center of the stacked phyllo sheets. Brush the top and sides with the apricot preserves, and sprinkle the chopped walnuts over the top.

3. Bring the four corners of the square together over the cheese and twist securely to enclose the cheese. Use your fingers to spread out the edges of the twisted leaves to form a kind of pouf. Brush the phyllo dough generously all over with the remaining melted butter. Place on a baking sheet lined with aluminum foil. The cheese can be assembled 4 to 5 hours in advance. Loosely wrap a dampened kitchen towel around the prepared cheese and refrigerate.

4. When ready to bake the cheese, preheat the oven to 350°F.

5. Bake the cheese until the phyllo dough is golden, about 18 to 22 minutes. If the dough seems to be browning too quickly, cover loosely with foil. While the cheese is baking, core the apples but do not peel. Cut into ½-inch-thick wedges and toss with the lemon juice.

182

6. Remove the baked cheese from the oven and let cool for 5 minutes. Then lift the cheese on the foil and place it on a serving tray. Trim away the excess foil. Garnish the cheese with the apple wedges.

SHOPPING: If a 7-ounce round of Havarti is unavailable, you can use a block of Havarti and cut it to make a square about 4 inches across and 1½ inches high.

~

Warm Chèvre with Plum Tomatoes

As an administrator at Amherst College, my husband has met many of the school's alumni. Among them is Prince Albert of Monaco, whom we had the pleasure of meeting on a visit to his principality. When he returned to Amherst the following year for his tenth reunion, we invited him to our home. I served this breaded and herbed chèvre, baked until warm and served with tomato "leaves." The cheese, seasoned with rosemary and thyme and spread on deep red wedges of tomato, is redolent of the south of France where Monaco is nestled and brought a smile to our guest's lips—and a request for more!

Makes 4 to 8 servings

8 ounces chèvre, at room temperature
¾ teaspoon dried thyme
½ teaspoon dried rosemary, crushed
3 tablespoons fresh bread crumbs
About 1 to 2 tablespoons olive oil
4 ripe large plum tomatoes (about 3½ ounces each)
Salt and coarsely ground black pepper to taste
Zest of 1 large thick-skinned lemon
Sprigs of rosemary and thyme, for garnish

1. Place the chèvre in a mixing bowl and add ½ teaspoon of the thyme and ¼ teaspoon of the rosemary. Mix well to blend. Using your hands, shape the

183

chèvre into a flat disc about 4 inches wide by 1 inch high. Place the chèvre in the center of a round or oval oven-to-table dish.

2. In a small bowl, combine the remaining ¼ teaspoon each thyme and rosemary with the fresh bread crumbs. Mix well. Brush the top and sides of the cheese lightly with olive oil. Pat the bread crumb mixture over the top and sides of cheese and drizzle the top of the cheese very lightly with more olive oil. The cheese can be prepared to this point up to a day in advance. Cover with plastic wrap and refrigerate.

3. When ready to bake the cheese, preheat the oven to 400°F.

4. Halve the tomatoes lengthwise and scoop out the seeds and membranes. Cut each half into 3 wedges. Set aside.

5. Bake the cheese until it just starts to melt, but still holds its shape, about 10 to 12 minutes. Remove from the oven. Arrange the tomato wedges, flesh side up, in a spoke pattern around the warm chèvre in the dish. Season the tomatoes generously with salt and pepper, and sprinkle with the lemon zest. Garnish the dish with clusters of fresh rosemary and thyme. To eat, spread the chèvre on the tomato wedges.

VARIATION: Add ¾ teaspoon dried basil to the thyme and rosemary: Mix ½ teaspoon into the cheese and use the remainder for the bread coating. Include fresh basil along with fresh thyme and rosemary sprigs as part of the garnish.

Herbed Chèvre Heart with Roasted Red Peppers

After I took a group to France for a week-long culinary extravaganza, the participants organized a potluck reunion party to reminisce about the trip. As a contribution, I brought this French-inspired chèvre heart surrounded by fresh herbs, roasted red peppers, Niçoise olives, and toasted French bread croutons.

Makes 25 servings

3 small loaves French bread, each about 14 inches long and 2½ to
   3 inches in diameter, cut into ⅓-inch slices
About ¾ cup plus 1 to 2 tablespoons of virgin olive oil
1¾ pounds chèvre, at room temperature
1 teaspoon dried basil
1 teaspoon dried rosemary, crushed
Sprigs of basil, for garnish
Sprigs of rosemary, for garnish
2 to 3 Roasted Red Peppers (page 269) or 1½ cups store-bought
   roasted red peppers, cut into 1-inch-wide strips, for garnish
½ cup Niçoise or Kalamata olives, for garnish

1. Preheat the oven to 350°F.

2. To prepare the croutons, brush the bread slices generously on both sides with olive oil. Place on baking sheets and bake until lightly golden and crispy, about 5 minutes per side. Remove and cool. The croutons can be made several hours ahead and kept, uncovered, at cool room temperature, or they can be made up to a day ahead and placed in an airtight container.

3. To prepare the chèvre heart, use a 1½-inch-deep heart-shaped mold about 8 inches across at the widest point and about 7½ inches long from the center indentation to the bottom tip. Line the mold with aluminum foil and then with parchment or a double thickness of waxed paper. Spread the softened chèvre evenly in the mold and smooth the top with a spatula. If you do not have a heart-shaped pan, draw a pattern with the same dimensions and use as a guide to shape the cheese into a heart about 1½ inches high. Refrigerate the cheese, covered with plastic wrap, to firm for at least 1 hour or up to 2 days.

4. When ready to serve, loosen the mold with a knife and unmold the heart onto

a serving tray. Remove the foil and paper and smooth the top and sides with a spatula. Sprinkle the dried basil and rosemary over the top of the cheese and drizzle with 1 to 2 tablespoons olive oil. Arrange half the fresh basil sprigs in a cluster around the top of the heart and the other half around the lower edge; arrange the rosemary sprigs in between the basil clusters. Garnish the tray with the roasted red peppers and olives. Place the croutons in a napkin-lined basket.

VARIATION: Although I always serve this dish at room temperature, you can also bake the heart on an aluminum foil-lined baking sheet for 10 to 12 minutes in a 350°F. preheated oven. Transfer the cheese on the foil to a serving tray and trim away the excess foil before adding the garnishes.

Chèvre Croutons Mélange

If you love chèvre, this appetizer is for you. At a cocktail party given at the Grand Hotel in Paris, waiters passed trays of bite-sized morsels of chèvre garnished every way imaginable. Some were coated with herbs, others with cracked black pepper. A few had been dusted with cumin or with paprika. Each platter was a visual feast and so inviting that I indulged every time the *garçons* came my way. For my version, I use small toasted French bread slices, spread them with chèvre, and choose simple garnishes as toppings. Arrange them on a tray lined with fresh grape leaves and black olives.

Makes 25 servings

*3 small loaves French bread, approximately 14 inches long and 2½
    to 3 inches in diameter, cut into ¼-inch slices*
About ¾ cup olive oil
1¾ to 2 pounds chèvre, preferably in a log shape

Assorted toppings (recipes follow)

1. To prepare the croutons, preheat the oven to 350°F.

2. Brush the bread slices generously on both sides with olive oil. Arrange on baking sheets and bake until light golden and crisp, about 4 to 5 minutes per side. Remove and cool. The croutons can be prepared several hours ahead and kept at cool room temperature, or they can be made up to a day in advance and placed in an airtight container.

3. When ready to serve, cut the chèvre into ¼-inch-thick slices and place on the croutons. (Dental floss works beautifully to slice the cheese.)

4. Choose all or a combination of the toppings to garnish the croutons. Arrange the croutons on large serving trays. Garnish the trays with lemon leaves or clusters of grape leaves and olives. The trays of croutons can be assembled 1 hour ahead and kept at cool room temperature.

HERB TOPPING

Dried thyme
Dried rosemary
Extra-virgin olive oil

Combine equal amounts of the herbs and sprinkle over the cheese. Drizzle lightly with olive oil.

(continued)

PINE NUT AND TOMATO TOPPING

½ cup toasted pine nuts (page 268)
½ cup sun-dried tomatoes packed in oil, drained and chopped

Combine the nuts and tomatoes. Place ½ teaspoonful on top of each crouton.

LEMON-PEPPER TOPPING

Coarsely ground or cracked black pepper
2 to 3 teaspoons very finely julienned lemon zest

Sprinkle the croutons with cracked pepper and garnish each one with 2 to 3 julienned pieces of lemon zest.

ROASTED RED PEPPER TOPPING

½ cup chopped roasted sweet red peppers, (page 269)
Basil leaves

Mound a teaspoon of chopped peppers on each crouton and garnish with a basil leaf.

BACON-APRICOT TOPPING

6 to 8 strips bacon, fried until crisp and crumbled
½ cup diced dried apricots

Combine the bacon and apricots and mound a teaspoonful on top of each crouton.

Roasted Red Pepper Cheese Mousse

Lee Porter, a talented cook from Amherst, Massachusetts, shared the recipe for this easy hors d'oeuvre with me. It is made simply by puréeing roasted red peppers, farmer cheese, and garlic until smooth. The mousse-like mixture is placed in a soufflé dish or ramekin to firm and then unmolded and served with toasted pita triangles.

Makes 50 to 60 portions

2 large sweet red peppers (1 pound), roasted (page 269)
11 ounces farmer cheese, broken into chunks (see note)
1 large clove garlic, peeled and sliced
1 teaspoon olive oil
⅛ teaspoon salt, or more to taste

Flat-leaf spinach leaves, for garnish
Toasted Pita Triangles (page 267), made from 3 or 4 pitas

1. To prepare the mousse, place the roasted red peppers, farmer cheese, and garlic in a bowl of a food processor fitted with the metal blade. Process until smooth, about 2 minutes. Add the olive oil and salt and process to blend, about 10 seconds more. Taste and, if desired, add more salt. Line a 2-cup container, such as a soufflé dish or small terrine, with plastic wrap. Fill with the mousse and spread it evenly with a spatula. Cover and refrigerate to firm. The mousse can be made up to 2 days ahead.

2. When ready to serve, arrange the spinach leaves on a serving plate. Unmold the mousse onto the leaves and discard the plastic wrap. Smooth the top and sides of the mousse with a spatula. Surround with the toasted pita triangles.

SHOPPING: Farmer cheese is a semisoft, snow-white cheese with a neutral flavor. I have seen some cheeses that are firm and pale yellow in color labeled farmer cheese; look for the soft white type.

SERVING: Sometimes I surround this mousse with basil clusters instead of using spinach. The pita toasts can be replaced with slices of French bread if desired.

Six-Layer Bombay Cheese

My assistant, Emily Bell, and I both like Indian food and have a real fondness for curries. We created this layered appetizer in which curry-flavored cheese is topped with chutney, coconut, nuts, scallions, and currants. Serve it with crisp crackers or tart apple slices.

Makes 6 to 8 servings

8 ounces cream cheese, at room temperature
4 ounces sharp Cheddar cheese, grated
½ teaspoon curry powder
⅓ cup mango chutney
2 tablespoons flaked coconut, preferably unsweetened
¼ cup toasted pecans or almonds (page 268)
1 tablespoon finely chopped scallions, including some of the green stems
1 to 1½ tablespoons currants
2 to 3 apples, cut into thin wedges
1 tablespoon lemon juice
Crackers, such as water biscuits

1. Combine the cream cheese, Cheddar, and curry powder in the bowl of an electric mixer and mix until well blended and smooth. Or beat by hand with a wooden spoon until smooth. Shape the mixture into a disc about 5½ inches in diameter and 1 inch high. Refrigerate to firm, about 45 minutes. The cheese can be made up to 2 days ahead, covered, and refrigerated.

2. To assemble, place the cheese on a serving tray. Spread the chutney on top. Sprinkle the coconut flakes, nuts, scallions, and currants over the chutney. The cheese can be prepared an hour ahead and kept at cool room temperature.

3. Toss the apple wedges with the lemon juice to prevent discoloration. To serve, arrange the crackers and apple wedges around the cheese.

Four-Star Potted Cheese

After many a party, I have found myself in a quandary trying to figure out what to do with the bits and pieces of cheese that are left. Elly Persing and Emily Bell, two of my inventive assistants, came up with a solution to this dilemma. They combined four different cheeses, blended them until they were smooth and creamy, and then packed the mixture in a lidded earthenware pot. The cheese spread will keep for four to five days in the refrigerator and can be served from its container.

Makes 6 to 8 servings

4 ounces Vermont white Cheddar, grated
4 ounces cream cheese, softened
5 to 6 ounces Brie, rind removed, cut into chunks
3 to 4 ounces Saga blue, rind removed, cut into chunks
Seedless grapes
1 loaf French bread, cut into ⅓-inch slices

1. Combine the cheeses in the bowl of an electric mixer and mix on medium speed until the mixture is smooth and of spreading consistency, about 2 to 3 minutes. Or beat by hand with a wooden spoon until smooth.

2. Pack the cheese into a 2-cup earthenware ramekin or crock. Smooth the top with a spatula. The cheese can be prepared 4 to 5 days ahead. Cover and refrigerate.

3. To serve, place the container with the cheese on a serving tray. Garnish the tray with bunches of grapes and slices of French bread.

Sherried Cheddar Terrine

Created by Adrienne Batlin, a talented caterer from Fort Wayne, Indiana, this appetizer pairs French Roquefort with a Cheddar from New England. The cheeses are creamed with a little butter (the Cheddar gets a splash of sherry as well) and layered with walnuts in a terrine. The terrine, which can be prepared several days ahead, makes a striking presentation garnished with bouquets of sage, clusters of red and green grapes, and wedges of Granny Smith apples.

Makes 12 to 14 servings

Nonstick vegetable cooking spray
1 pound Vermont Cheddar cheese, shredded
6 tablespoons unsalted butter, slightly softened, divided
2 tablespoons dry sherry, port, or brandy
8 ounces Roquefort or Stilton cheese
1½ cups coarsely chopped walnuts, divided
3 walnut halves, for garnish
Fresh sage leaves, for garnish
3 Granny Smith apples
1 to 2 tablespoons lemon juice
Several bunches red seedless grapes

1. Line a 4-cup terrine or loaf pan with 3 sheets of waxed paper so that paper extends over the long sides of the pan. Spray the top layer of paper with nonstick vegetable cooking spray. Or use an 8-inch cake pan: Line the bottom with a triple thickness of waxed paper cut to fit the pan. Spray the top sheet with nonstick spray.

2. Place the Cheddar cheese, 4 tablespoons of the butter, and the sherry in a mixing bowl and beat with an electric mixer or by hand with a wooden spoon until well blended and smooth. Set aside.

3. Combine the Roquefort cheese with the remaining 2 tablespoons butter and mix, using an electric mixer or a wooden spoon, until smooth.

4. Press half the Cheddar mixture into the prepared pan. Pat firmly but gently to make an even layer. Sprinkle half the chopped walnuts over this layer. Then add all of the Roquefort mixture, again pressing down firmly but gently to make an even layer. Top with the remaining walnuts, and make a final layer with the remaining cheddar mixture. Cover the terrine with plastic wrap and refrigerate overnight or up to 2 days.

5. To unmold, remove the plastic wrap. Run a knife around the sides of the pan to loosen. Invert the terrine onto a serving plate and remove the waxed paper. Arrange 3 walnut halves equidistant from each other down the center of the terrine. Surround with several sage leaves. The terrine can be unmolded several hours in advance and refrigerated. Bring to room temperature 30 minutes before serving.

6. To serve, core and halve the apples, but do not peel. Cut each half into 8 wedges and toss the wedges with the lemon juice to prevent discoloring. Arrange bunches of grapes and the apple wedges around the terrine.

Rio Grande Fondue

This Tex-Mex–style fondue, a creamy mixture of melted white Cheddar and spicy Monterey Jack cheese combined with sautéed onions, chilies, and red peppers, makes an addictive dipping sauce with a bowl of crisp tortilla chips. It is a perfect appetizer to serve at casual get-togethers.

Makes 8 to 10 servings

1½ tablespoons vegetable oil
¾ cup chopped onions
1 teaspoon finely chopped garlic
1 large roasted sweet red pepper (page 269), chopped
4 ounces canned mild green chilies, seeded and chopped
1½ tablespoons all-purpose flour
1 teaspoon chili powder
½ teaspoon cumin
½ teaspoon cayenne pepper
1 cup chicken stock
8 ounces white Cheddar, grated
4 ounces Monterey Jack cheese with jalapeño peppers, grated
½ cup sour cream
Tortilla chips

1. Heat the vegetable oil in a large heavy saucepan over medium-high heat. When hot, add the onions and sauté, stirring, until softened, about 3 to 4 minutes. Add the garlic, chopped red pepper, and chilies, and sauté and stir a minute more. Add the flour, chili powder, cumin, and cayenne pepper and stir and cook another 2 minutes. Add the stock and stir until the mixture thickens, about 2 to 3 minutes. Stir in both the cheeses, a few tablespoons at a time, making certain that each addition has melted completely before adding the next. When all the cheese has been incorporated, remove the saucepan from the heat. The fondue can be made a day ahead. Cool, cover, and refrigerate. Reheat, stirring, before serving.

2. When ready to serve, whisk the sour cream into the hot fondue. Transfer the fondue to a fondue pot or a chafing dish. Serve with tortilla chips.

VARIATION: Boiled or steamed shrimp go well with this fondue.

Herb-Garlic Cheese Fondue

This untraditional fondue, made by melting homemade or store-bought herb-garlic cheese in cream, is served with fresh steamed vegetables. It makes a striking presentation for a small or large party.

Makes 8 to 10 servings

2 cups heavy or whipping cream
10 to 12 ounces Herb-Garlic Cheese (page 264)
Salt and freshly ground black pepper to taste

2 teaspoons salt
1½ pounds small (1 inch in diameter) new potatoes, scrubbed but
*   unpeeled*
1 pound baby carrots, peeled
¼ pound snow peas, ends trimmed
½ pound asparagus, tough ends trimmed and discarded
Sprigs of flat-leaf parsley, for garnish
Sprigs of dill, for garnish
6-inch wooden skewers

1. To prepare the fondue, place the cream in a large heavy saucepan over medium-high heat. Break the cheese into chunks and add to the cream. Cover, stirring constantly, until the cheese has melted and the sauce has thickened so it coats the back of a spoon lightly, about 5 minutes. Taste and season with salt and pepper as desired. The fondue can be made 1 to 2 days ahead. Cover and refrigerate.

2. Bring 8 quarts of water to a boil in a large heavy pot and add the 2 teaspoons salt. Add the potatoes and cook until tender but not mushy, 12 to 20 minutes depending on the size of the potatoes. Remove with a slotted spoon and drain. Add the carrots to the pot and cook until tender but still firm, about 5 to 8 minutes. Remove with a slotted spoon and drain. Add the snow peas and cook just long enough to blanch, about 1 to 2 minutes. Remove with a slotted spoon, drain, and refresh under cold water. Add the asparagus spears and cook until just tender, about 3 to 4 minutes. Remove with a slotted spoon, drain, and refresh under cold water. The vegetables can be prepared 4 to 5 hours ahead. Pat vegetables dry and cover with plastic wrap and refrigerate. Bring to room temperature before serving.

3. To serve, reheat the fondue over medium heat, stirring constantly. Transfer to a fondue pot or chafing dish. If desired, reheat the vegetables in a microwave for a few seconds and serve them warm; however, they are fine at room temperature. Arrange the vegetables on a platter and garnish with sprigs of fresh herbs. Place 6-inch wooden skewers in a glass or small vase.

VARIATIONS: Any vegetable that can be dipped can be used with the fondue. Uncooked julienne strips of red and green peppers, blanched green beans, and blanched broccoli florets are all good alternatives.

Camembert Walnut Wafers

Serve these crisp, golden wafers as a pre-dinner appetizer with glasses of hearty red wine.

Makes about 40 wafers

8 tablespoons unsalted butter, at room temperature
8 ounces Camembert cheese, rind left on, cut into small chunks, at room temperature
1 cup all-purpose flour
⅛ teaspoon salt
About 20 walnut halves, halved lengthwise

1. Using an electric mixer on medium speed, cream the butter and Camembert together until the mixture is completely blended and smooth, about 1 to 2 minutes. Add the flour and salt and beat until thoroughly mixed, about 2 minutes.

2. Shape the cheese mixture into a log 2 inches in diameter by 10 inches long. Wrap in plastic wrap, and place in the freezer for 45 to 60 minutes to chill and firm. Then transfer to the refrigerator. The dough can be made ahead and refrigerated for up to 2 days. It can also be frozen up to 2 weeks. Wrap tightly in plastic wrap and then in aluminum foil. Defrost in the refrigerator before slicing and baking.

3. When ready to bake, preheat the oven to 450°F.

4. Cut the chilled log into ¼-inch-thick slices and place on two aluminum-foil-lined baking sheets. Place a walnut quarter in the center of each slice. Bake until crisp and lightly browned, about 10 minutes. Remove the crisps with a spatula and let cool on a cooling rack for 2 to 3 minutes. Place crisps on a serving plate or in a napkin-lined bowl and serve warm.

VARIATION: Brie can be substituted for the Camembert and pecan halves and almond slivers for the walnuts.

Smoked Cheddar Wafers

Like the preceding recipe for Camembert wafers, these smoked Cheddar rounds are thin and crispy and perfect before a special dinner.

Makes about 32 wafers

8 tablespoons unsalted butter, at room temperature
6 ounces smoked Cheddar cheese, rind left on, grated
1 cup all-purpose flour
¼ teaspoon cayenne pepper
⅛ teaspoon salt

1. Place the butter and cheese in a bowl and beat with an electric mixer until smooth. With the mixer on slow speed, gradually blend in the flour. Add the cayenne pepper and salt and mix until incorporated.

2. Shape the dough, which will be soft, into a log approximately 2 inches in diameter and 8 inches long. Wrap the log tightly in plastic wrap and then roll it on the counter several times to make the log compact. Put the log in the freezer to firm, about 45 to 60 minutes. Then transfer to the refrigerator. The dough can be made ahead and refrigerated for up to 2 days. It can also be frozen for up to 2 weeks. Wrap tightly in plastic wrap and then in aluminum foil. Defrost in the refrigerator before slicing and baking.

3. When ready to bake the crisps, preheat the oven to 400°F.

4. Cut the log into ¼-inch-thick slices, and place them 1 inch apart on an ungreased baking sheet. Bake until lightly golden, about 10 minutes. Watch carefully. Remove the crisps with a spatula and let cool on a cooling rack for 2 to 3 minutes.

5. Serve the crisps warm, on a serving tray or in a napkin-lined basket.

Gruyère and Rosemary Popovers

Made from a classic popover batter to which grated Gruyère and rosemary are added, then baked in mini-muffin tins, these delectable bite-sized pastries are glorious mounded in a napkin-lined basket and served piping hot.

Makes 24 popovers

Nonstick vegetable cooking spray
2 large eggs
½ cup plus 2 tablespoons milk
¼ teaspoon salt
⅛ teaspoon cayenne pepper
½ cup plus 2 tablespoons all-purpose flour
½ cup very finely grated Gruyère
¾ teaspoon dried rosemary, crushed

1. Preheat the oven to 375°F. Spray two mini-muffin tins with 12 molds, each 1¾ inches in diameter, with nonstick vegetable cooking spray.

2. Place the eggs in a mixing bowl and beat lightly. Whisk in the milk to blend. Combine the salt, cayenne pepper, flour, cheese, and rosemary in another mixing bowl. Gradually beat the liquids into the dry ingredients. Do not overbeat.

3. Spoon or ladle a scant tablespoon of batter into each mold. Bake on the center shelf of the oven for 18 minutes, until the popovers have risen and are a rich golden brown.

4. Remove from the oven and immediately remove the popovers from the molds. Mound in a napkin-lined basket and serve piping hot.

Saga Blue with Roasted Garlic

When whole heads of garlic are baked slowly in the oven, the cloves lose their pungent taste and become sweet and tender. In fact, baked garlic is so soft it can be easily spread on a slice of French bread, as in this recipe. To complement the sweet taste of the garlic, the croutons are topped with thin slices of creamy Saga blue cheese.

Makes 10 to 12 servings

6 heads garlic (*choose fresh, firm large heads without blemishes*)
2 tablespoons olive oil
½ teaspoon dried thyme
Freshly ground black pepper to taste
Several sprigs of thyme or watercress, for garnish
1½ pounds Saga blue cheese, cut into ¼-inch-thick slices
1 to 2 loaves French bread, heated and cut into ⅓-inch-thick slices

1. Preheat the oven to 350°F.

2. Remove, rubbing with your fingers, just the dry, paper-like outer skin from each head of garlic. Cut off and discard the pointed tips from the garlic heads.

3. Place the garlic in a medium-size heavy ovenproof skillet or baking pan. Drizzle the olive oil over garlic. Sprinkle with the thyme and black pepper. Place the pan on the center shelf of the oven and bake until the cloves expand and start to pull apart, and are tender when pierced with a knife, about 1¼ hours. Remove from the oven. Hold each garlic head with a kitchen towel and slice off the top of the head so that all the cloves are exposed.

4. Arrange a cluster of three heads of garlic at either end of a serving tray, and tuck sprigs of thyme or watercress around the garlic. Arrange overlapping slices of the Saga blue cheese in the middle. Serve the warm French bread in a basket. To eat, use a serving knife to scoop out a softened cooked garlic clove, and spread on a slice of bread. Top with a slice of the cheese.

Seafood

I still remember the first cocktail party I planned where I felt I could afford to serve fresh seafood. I bought six pounds of fresh shrimp, and cooked, shelled, and served them with a Creole dipping sauce to a group of sixteen. I had been certain that there would be enough leftovers for my husband and me to enjoy the day after the party—but at the end of the evening, the shrimp tray was empty! That scene has been repeated many times at our house, bearing out an axiom of cocktail party planning: People love seafood and will eat all that is offered!

Several of the seafood specialties in this chapter are served warm: Baked Shrimp with Garlic-Basil Butter and Shrimp with Tomato-Curry Sauce are both more exciting than the usual plates of cold, cooked shrimp offered with a traditional sauce. The warm French Bread Stuffed with Smoked Salmon and Leeks is one of the most unusual and elegant appetizers in this book.

Some of these recipes pair seafood with unexpected ingredients: Oysters and cooked fennel, scallops wrapped in prosciutto, and crab flavored with orange zest are all winning combinations. Smoked seafood is delicious, and is becoming more readily available in stores or through mail order companies. Smoked Trout and Walnut Pâté and Cherry Tomatoes Stuffed with Smoked Seafood are easily assembled dishes, which require no cooking.

Always buy the freshest and best seafood available. It may be costly, but is well worth the expense. The fresher the fish, the better the dish!

French Bread Stuffed with Smoked Salmon and Leeks

A loaf of partially sliced French bread filled with sautéed leeks and paper-thin slices of smoked salmon makes an unusual and elegant appetizer.

Makes 36 to 40 slices

1 loaf French bread, about 20 inches long and 2½ inches in diameter
6 tablespoons olive oil, or more as needed
6 tablespoons unsalted butter, or more as needed
2 cups chopped leeks (including 2 inches of the green leaves)
1 teaspoon dried dill
Salt and freshly ground black pepper to taste
10 to 12 ounces smoked salmon, thinly sliced
Sprigs of dill, for garnish

1. Slice the bread on the diagonal into ½-inch slices, cutting almost but not quite all the way through the loaf.

2. In a medium heavy skillet over medium heat, heat the olive oil and butter until the butter is melted. Stir to mix well. Generously brush the mixture over the top and sides of the loaf of bread and on each slice. You should have about ¼ cup of the mixture left in the skillet. If not, add an equal amount of additional oil and butter to make ¼ cup.

3. Heat the reserved oil and butter in the skillet over medium heat until hot. Add the chopped leeks and stir constantly until the leeks are softened, about 5 minutes. Add the dried dill and cook a minute more. Remove and season with salt and pepper. Stir to mix.

4. Place the loaf of bread on a baking sheet. Spoon some of the leek mixture between each slice of bread. The bread can be prepared an hour ahead to this point. Cover loosely with foil and keep at room temperature.

5. When ready to serve, preheat the oven to 350°F.

6. Bake the loaf, uncovered, on the center oven shelf until the bread is warm and the crust is crispy, about 5 minutes. Remove from the oven and insert 1 thin slice of the smoked salmon between each slice of bread. Return to the oven for 2 to 3 minutes, just to warm the salmon. Remove from the oven.

7. To serve, place the warm loaf on a long, narrow serving plate or wooden board. Garnish with fresh dill sprigs. Cut all the way through the loaf to separate the slices and serve each slice topped with salmon and leeks.

Toasted Mini-Bagels with Smoked Salmon and Lemon Yogurt Cheese

Bagels with cream cheese and lox are a tried-and-true favorite, and this new interpretation of that classic is equally good. Split mini-bagels, just the right size for hors d'oeuvre servings, are delicious toasted, then topped with slices of smoked salmon and lemon-scented yogurt cheese.

Makes 24 portions

½ cup Low-Fat Yogurt Cheese (page 265)
2 teaspoons lemon juice
12 mini-bagels
4 tablespoons unsalted butter, melted
4 ounces smoked salmon, thinly sliced
1 tablespoon grated lemon zest
Freshly ground black pepper to taste
Sprigs of dill, for garnish

1. Place the yogurt cheese in a mixing bowl and whisk in the lemon juice. The lemon yogurt cheese can be prepared up to 2 days ahead. Cover and refrigerate.

2. Preheat the oven to 300°F.

3. Slice the bagels in half and brush the cut sides generously with the melted butter. Arrange the bagels on a baking sheet and bake on the center oven shelf until light golden brown, about 8 minutes. Remove from the oven and cool slightly. The bagels can be toasted up to 3 hours ahead. Cool completely, then wrap tightly in aluminum foil and leave at cool room temperature.

4. When ready to serve, spread each mini-bagel with a ½ teaspoon of the yogurt cheese. Cover with slices of the smoked salmon and top with a small dollop of the yogurt cheese. Sprinkle the bagels with the lemon zest and season lightly with pepper. Garnish each bagel with a small sprig of dill.

Baked Shrimp with Garlic-Basil Butter

Nothing could be easier than shrimp baked with a generous coating of garlic-basil butter and served hot. This dish can be assembled in advance and then popped in the oven for a few minutes before serving.

Makes about 40 to 50 portions

GARLIC BUTTER

12 tablespoons (1½ sticks) unsalted butter, at room temperature
2 teaspoons finely chopped garlic
3 tablespoons finely chopped shallots
½ cup chopped fresh basil (see note)
¼ teaspoon salt, or to taste
Freshly ground black pepper to taste

2 pounds large (21/30 count) shrimp, shelled and deveined
Salt and freshly ground black pepper to taste
Sprigs of basil, for garnish
6-inch wooden skewers

1. To prepare the garlic butter, place all the ingredients in a mixing bowl and mix well to incorporate. Cover and refrigerate. The butter can be made 1 to 2 days ahead.

2. Using a little of the garlic-basil butter, grease a large oven-to-table dish. Spread the shrimp evenly in the dish. Salt and pepper the fish. Dot the remaining garlic butter evenly over the shrimp. The shrimp can be prepared to this point 3 to 4 hours ahead. Cover with plastic wrap and refrigerate. Bring to room temperature 15 minutes before cooking.

3. When ready to cook the shrimp, preheat the oven to 375°F.

4. Bake the shrimp, uncovered, on the center shelf of the oven until curled and pink, about 8 to 10 minutes. Remove from the oven and garnish with basil sprigs. Serve hot, along with a small glass filled with wooden skewers.

SHOPPING: If fresh basil is not available, use ½ cup chopped fresh parsley and 1½ teaspoons dried basil, and chop together.

VARIATION: Large sea scallops can be substituted for the shrimp.

Shrimp with
Tomato-Curry Sauce

Many years ago when I was a fledgling cook, I regularly made a dish from Simone Beck's *Simca's Cuisine* called Porc au Pili-Pili, in which pork is braised in a seductive tomato sauce seasoned with curry, basil, and hot peppers. The flavors of that sauce are so enticing that I tried a slightly different version as an accompaniment to shrimp. Now the seafood variation has become a popular appetizer at our house.

Makes about 40 to 50 portions

2 tablespoons olive oil
½ cup finely chopped leeks
½ cup coarsely grated peeled carrots
1½ teaspoons chopped garlic
½ teaspoon dried thyme
¼ teaspoon crushed red pepper flakes
2½ teaspoons curry powder
1 bay leaf, broken in half
3 cups chopped seeded ripe tomatoes (about 1½ pounds tomatoes) or
   drained and chopped canned plum tomatoes
1 cup chicken stock
Salt and freshly ground black pepper to taste
2 pounds large (21/30 count) shrimp, cooked, peeled, and deveined

1. To prepare the sauce, heat the olive oil in a large heavy skillet over medium-high heat. When hot, add the leeks and carrots and sauté, stirring, until softened, about 5 minutes. Add the garlic, thyme, red pepper flakes, curry powder, and bay leaf and cook and stir a minute more. Add the tomatoes and chicken stock and cook at a simmer until thickened, about 10 to 12 minutes. Remove from the heat and season to taste with salt and pepper. Remove the bay leaf. The sauce can be made 1 to 2 days ahead. Cool, cover, and refrigerate. Reheat, stirring, before serving.

2. To serve, place the hot sauce in a bowl in the center of a serving tray. Mound the shrimp, either chilled or at room temperature, around the bowl. To eat, dip the shrimp in the sauce or ladle sauce with a spoon over each shrimp.

Orange-and Lemon-Scented Crab Puffs

Accents of orange and lemon complement the crab in these warm seafood canapés. Grated Havarti cheese and a hint of cayenne pepper add another dimension of flavor.

Makes 28 puffs

¼ cup mayonnaise (Hellmann's or Best Foods is preferred)
½ cup packed grated Havarti cheese (see note)
½ cup packed crab meat, all bits of shell and cartilage removed (see note)
⅓ cup finely chopped scallions
⅛ teaspoon cayenne pepper
2 teaspoons lemon juice
¼ teaspoon grated lemon zest
½ teaspoon grated orange zest
Salt to taste
7 slices firm white sandwich bread
¼ cup chopped fresh chives or parsley, for garnish

1. Combine the mayonnaise, Havarti, crab meat, scallions, cayenne pepper, lemon juice, lemon zest, and orange zest in a mixing bowl. Mix well to blend. Taste, and add salt as needed. The crab mixture can be prepared a day ahead. Cover and refrigerate.

2. To prepare the bread, preheat the oven to 350°F.

3. Remove the crusts from the bread and save for another use. Cut each slice into 4 squares. Place the bread on baking sheets and bake for 5 minutes. Turn over and continue to bake until bread is lightly toasted on both sides, about 5 minutes more. Remove from the oven. The toasts can be prepared several hours ahead. Keep loosely covered with foil at cool room temperature.

4. When ready to bake the crab puffs, preheat the oven to 350°F.

5. Spread each toast with a generous ½ tablespoon of the crab mixture. Place on two baking sheets and bake until the topping is puffed and golden, about 10 to 12 minutes. Remove from the oven and sprinkle with the chives or parsley. Arrange on a serving tray and serve warm.

SHOPPING: For this recipe, buy plain Havarti cheese. The varieties with caraway seeds or dill do not combine well with the other flavors in the dish.

Fresh, canned, or frozen crab meat can be used for these puffs. If frozen is used, drain thoroughly and pat dry.

In place of white bread, pumpernickel can be used.

Prosciutto-Wrapped Scallops

Tossed in lemon juice, then wrapped in paper-thin slices of prosciutto, these succulent sea scallops are coated lightly with olive oil and a sprinkling of rosemary before being baked for just a few minutes.

Makes about 40 portions

2 pounds large sea scallops (about 40)
3 tablespoons lemon juice
8 ounces prosciutto, sliced paper-thin (see note)
3 to 4 tablespoons virgin olive oil
2 teaspoons dried rosemary, crushed
2 teaspoons grated lemon zest
Salt
6-inch wooden skewers (optional)

1. Remove and discard the small muscle found on the side of each scallop. Place the scallops in a nonaluminum mixing bowl, add the lemon juice, and toss to mix. Let marinate for 5 to 10 minutes.

2. Cut the prosciutto slices lengthwise into ¾-inch-wide strips long enough to just overlap when wrapped around the sides of the scallops. Wrap a prosciutto strip around each scallop and arrange on a broiler pan. Brush the tops and sides of the scallops with the olive oil, and sprinkle the tops with the crushed rosemary. The scallops can be prepared 1 to 2 hours ahead to this point. Cover with plastic wrap and refrigerate. Bring to room temperature 15 minutes before broiling.

(continued)

3. When ready to cook the scallops, preheat the broiler and arrange a rack 7 to 8 inches from the heat source.

4. Broil the scallops until opaque, about 3 minutes. Watch carefully, as overcooking will make them tough. Remove from the broiler and sprinkle the tops of the scallops with the lemon zest and lightly with salt. To serve, either skewer each scallop with a wooden skewer or simply arrange the scallops on a serving tray.

SHOPPING: Be certain that the prosciutto you buy is sliced into paper-thin see-through slices. If the slices are too thick, the flavor of the prosciutto tends to overpower the scallops.

Smoked Trout and Walnut Pâté

Smoked trout puréed with a little cream cheese or yogurt cheese and seasoned with walnut oil makes a delicious spread for apple wedges or slices of French bread. Very light and delicate in flavor, this is a good pre-dinner choice.

Makes 6 to 8 servings

8 ounces smoked trout

3 ounces cream cheese or nonfat Yogurt Cheese made from 6 ounces
   nonfat plain yogurt (page 265)

2 tablespoons walnut oil

Salt to taste

2 to 3 tablespoons chopped toasted walnuts (page 268)

Several sprigs of watercress, for garnish

3 to 4 large red Delicious apples, cored but unpeeled, cut into
   ¼-inch wedges and tossed with 1 tablespoon lemon juice to
   prevent discoloring; or

1 loaf French bread, cut into ¼-inch slices and lightly toasted in
   the oven

1. Remove and discard any skin from the smoked trout. Place the trout and cream cheese or yogurt cheese in the container of a food processor fitted with the metal blade. Process until the mixture is smooth, 30 to 60 seconds. Add the walnut oil and process several seconds more to blend. Taste and season with salt to taste. Transfer to a small earthenware or glass bowl. The pâté can be made a day ahead. Cover and refrigerate. Bring to room temperature 30 minutes before serving.

2. To serve, place the bowl of pâté on a serving tray. Sprinkle the chopped walnuts over the pâté and garnish the tray with watercress. Surround the pâté with the apple wedges or toasted French bread or both.

SHOPPING: The quality of the smoked trout will determine how good this dish is. Kendall Brook from Ducktrap Fish Farms (page 281) produces excellent smoked trout that is distributed in many parts of the country.

Cherry Tomatoes Stuffed with Smoked Seafood

Nothing could be simpler, quicker, or more sophisticated than these cherry tomatoes stuffed with smoked fish. Years ago, when I first started to entertain, a friend shared with me her favorite hors d'oeuvre recipe—cherry tomatoes split and filled with canned smoked oysters. When smoked fish products from New England began to appear in the marketplace, I devised this recipe using some of these special ingredients. Smoked trout, scallops, shrimp, mussels, or salmon—all taste delicious tucked into juicy cherry tomatoes.

Makes about 40 portions

2 to 3 pints (about 40) ripe cherry tomatoes, stems removed
½ pound smoked fish, such as smoked scallops, mussels, shrimp, oysters (page 281)
Several branches of lemon leaves, for garnish
Coarsely ground black pepper
1 cup Kalamata or other dark olives
1 tablespoon lemon zest cut into very fine julienne strips

1. Make a slit in each tomato starting at the bottom end and cutting not quite all the way to the stem end. Fill each tomato with some of the smoked fish: If using smoked trout, break or cut the fish into 1-inch pieces; large scallops and shrimp work best if cut into halves. The tomatoes can be filled, up to 3 hours in advance. Cover with plastic wrap and refrigerate. Bring to room temperature 30 minutes before serving.

2. To serve, arrange lemon leaf branches on a serving plate. Sprinkle the tomatoes lightly with pepper. Mound the tomatoes on the plate, leaving a border of lemon leaves around them. Arrange several clusters of the olives on the lemon leaves, then scatter the julienned lemon zest between the clusters of olives. Serve at room temperature.

Mussels with a Trio of Garnishes

These mussels, steamed in white wine and herbs, are served in their sleek, elegant black shells with three special garnishes. Curried orange mayonnaise, fresh tomato and cucumber salsa, and gremolata—a classic Italian combination of parsley, lemon zest, and garlic—complement the mussels superbly both in color and taste.

Makes about 24 portions

6 tablespoons unsalted butter
3 medium garlic cloves, peeled and thinly sliced
⅓ cup coarsely chopped shallots
1 large bay leaf
½ cup parsley sprigs
2 sprigs fresh thyme or 1 teaspoon dried
1½ cups dry white wine
2 pounds medium mussels (about 2 dozen), in the shells, scrubbed
  (see note)

Garnishes (recipes follow)

1. Melt the butter in a large 6- to 8-quart pot over medium-high heat. When hot, add the garlic and shallots and sauté, stirring, until softened, about 2 minutes. Add the herbs and wine and bring to a simmer. Add the mussels, with their hinged sides down. Cover and steam until the mussels are open, about 5 to 7 minutes. Remove and discard any mussels that have not opened.

2. Remove and discard the top half shell from each mussel, leaving the mussel in the bottom shell. Arrange the bowls of garnishes in the center of a serving tray and surround with the mussels. Or, spoon the garnishes over the mussels and arrange the mussels on a serving tray.

CURRIED ORANGE MAYONNAISE

(Makes about 1 cup)

1 cup mayonnaise (Hellmann's or Best Foods is preferred)
1 teaspoon curry powder
2 to 3 teaspoons orange juice
½ to 1 teaspoon grated orange zest

(continued)

1. Combine all the ingredients in a mixing bowl and whisk to blend. Transfer to a serving bowl. Cover and refrigerate. The sauce can be made a day ahead.

TOMATO CUCUMBER SALSA

(Makes about 1½ cups)

¾ pound (3 to 4) plum tomatoes, seeded and chopped
1 medium cucumber, peeled, seeded, and coarsely chopped
1 tablespoon lime juice
1 scant teaspoon salt
½ teaspoon finely chopped garlic

1. Combine all the ingredients in a mixing bowl and stir to mix. Transfer to a serving bowl. Cover and refrigerate. The salsa can be made a day ahead. Drain before serving if too much liquid has accumulated in the bowl.

GREMOLATA

(Makes about ¾ cup)

½ cup chopped fresh parsley
2 teaspoons finely chopped garlic
2 teaspoons grated lemon zest
¼ cup finely chopped scallions

1. Combine all the ingredients in a mixing bowl and stir to mix. The sauce can be made a day ahead. Transfer to a serving bowl and cover with a moistened, folded paper towel and then with plastic wrap. Refrigerate.

SHOPPING: When buying mussels, look for those with tightly closed shells. If a shell is open, place the mussel under cold running water, if it does not close, discard.

Broiled Oysters with Fennel and Lemon Cream

Makes 12 portions

1½ tablespoons unsalted butter
1 large fennel bulb, chopped
Salt and freshly ground black pepper to taste
½ cup heavy or whipping cream
¼ cup grated imported Parmesan cheese
1 teaspoon grated lemon zest
12 oysters in their shells
About 1 tablespoon dry unflavored bread crumbs
Rock salt for serving, optional

1. Melt the butter in a medium-size heavy skillet over medium-high heat. When hot, add the fennel and sauté, stirring, until it is tender and lightly browned, about 7 to 8 minutes. Remove from the heat. Lightly salt and pepper the fennel. The fennel can be sautéed a day ahead. Cool, cover, and refrigerate. Bring to room temperature 30 minutes before using.

2. Place the cream in a small saucepan over medium-high heat. When hot, gradually stir in the cheese, a little at a time, until it is melted and the sauce has thickened. Stir in the lemon zest and remove from the heat. The sauce can be made a day ahead. Cool, cover, and refrigerate. Reheat to warm before using.

3. When ready to assemble the oysters, preheat the broiler and arrange a rack about 4 to 5 inches from the heat.

4. Shuck the oysters. Save 12 of the nicest half-shells and rinse and dry them. Divide the fennel evenly among the oyster shells. Top each with an oyster. Season the oysters lightly with salt and pepper and top each one with about 2 teaspoons of the cream sauce. Sprinkle with the bread crumbs. Transfer the shells to a baking sheet with sides.

5. Broil until the sauce is hot, about 5 minutes. Watch carefully. Remove, and carefully transfer the oysters to a serving tray, lightly spread with rock salt if desired. Serve hot.

Great Party Entrées

For large gatherings, I love to serve what I call party entrées—that is, dishes that require the guests to use a small plate and fork. These special entrées have proven, more often than not, to be the most popular appetizer of the evening. I have seen guests surround a roast filet of beef and pile slices, along with relishes, atop French bread with such efficiency that a large platter was emptied in less than half an hour. And I have made what I considered to be enough glazed chicken wings to feed a host of teenagers only to see them disappear before a party was half over.

More substantial than typical appetizers, these party entrées are perfect for cocktail buffets, receptions, open houses, or other events where many guests are expected. The recipe yields are larger than those of other recipes in this book. And, since cooking in advance is crucial when hosting a large party, all these dishes can be partially or completely made in advance.

Among them are three unique savory cheesecakes: a smoked salmon cheesecake, a curried cheesecake, and one flavored with Mexican seasonings. Roast fillet of beef is offered with Roquefort sauce and walnuts, or with a Mediterranean olive relish. There are chicken wings and ribs, dishes people invariably adore. And for the chafing dish, I created a sausage-tomato ragoût, a chicken curry, and dill-scented veal balls.

Because many of these entrées are accompanied by colorful sauces or relishes, the dishes make striking presentations. A holiday baked ham arranged on pine branches, and served with three condiments, and Beaujolais-Glazed Chicken Wings mounded on fall maple leaves are just two examples.

Beaujolais-Glazed
Chicken Wings

Cut up so they are easy to eat, these wings are marinated in soy sauce, orange juice, and Beaujolais, then brushed with red currant jelly and roasted until rich mahogany brown in color. They can be made ahead and reheated at serving time so that there is no last-minute fuss.

Makes 36 to 40 servings

3 pounds chicken wings, wing tips removed and discarded, wings split at the joints into 2 pieces (have the butcher do this if you prefer)
1/3 cup soy sauce
1/3 cup orange juice
2/3 cup plus 2 tablespoons dry red wine, preferably Beaujolais
3 cloves garlic, peeled and mashed
2 tablespoons chopped peeled gingerroot
Nonstick vegetable cooking spray
6 tablespoons red currant jelly
2 tablespoons grated orange zest
Several branches of lemon leaves for garnish
1 tablespoon thin julienne strips of orange zest, for garnish

1. Place the split wings in a large shallow glass, ceramic, or other nonaluminum pan. Mix the soy sauce, orange juice, the 2/3 cup red wine, the garlic, and gingerroot together and pour over the chicken wings. Cover the pan with plastic wrap and refrigerate overnight, turning the wings several times in the marinade.

2. When ready to bake, preheat the oven to 375°F. Line a baking pan with aluminum foil. Coat a cooking rack with nonstick vegetable cooking spray, and place the rack in the baking pan.

3. Drain the chicken and arrange on the cooking rack. Roast for 45 minutes, turning the wings once. Remove the wings from the oven, but do not turn off the oven.

4. Combine the red currant jelly, the remaining 2 tablespoons red wine, and the grated orange zest in a small saucepan over medium heat. Stir until the jelly is melted. Brush the wings generously with the glaze and return to the oven for 10 minutes. Turn the wings and brush again with the glaze. Bake for another

10 minutes, or until the wings are a rich dark brown and shiny. Remove from the oven and cool 5 minutes. The wings can be baked up to a day ahead. Cool, cover, and refrigerate; reheat, uncovered, in a preheated 350°F. oven until hot, about 15 to 20 minutes.

5. To serve, place lemon branches on a serving plate. Arrange the wings in overlapping rows on top of the branches. Sprinkle the julienned orange zest over the wings. Serve warm.

$\mathcal{L}$*ime-Marmalade–Glazed Chicken Wings*

These chicken wings are among the most popular hors d'oeuvres at my house. They are marinated in tequila with seasonings of lime, cilantro, and pepper, and when they are cooked, the skin becomes a rich, dark shiny brown while the flesh beneath stays incredibly moist and tender.

Makes 36 to 40 servings

3 pounds chicken wings, wing tips removed and discarded, wings split at the joints into 2 pieces (have the butcher do this if you prefer)
½ cup tequila or gin
3 medium cloves garlic, peeled and mashed
¼ cup olive oil
½ cup chopped fresh cilantro
7 tablespoons lime marmalade, divided
4 tablespoons lime juice, divided
1 teaspoon grated lime zest, divided
1 teaspoon hot pepper sauce
1 teaspoon salt, or to taste
1 tablespoon coarsely ground black pepper
2 limes, cut into 6 wedges each, for garnish
Small bunch of cilantro, for garnish

1. Place the split chicken wings in a large glass, ceramic, or other nonaluminum shallow dish. Combine the tequila, garlic, olive oil, chopped cilantro, 3 tablespoons of the lime marmalade, 2 tablespoons of the lime juice, ½ teaspoon of the lime zest, the hot pepper sauce, salt and pepper, and mix well. Pour this marinade over the chicken. Cover with plastic wrap and marinate at least 6 hours or, preferably, overnight, turning the wings several times in the marinade.

2. When ready to bake, preheat the oven to 350°F.

3. Remove the chicken from the marinade, reserving marinade. Arrange the chicken in a large shallow roasting pan and bake on the center shelf of the oven for 30 minutes, turning several times.

4. While the chicken is baking, strain the marinade and pour into a medium saucepan. Place over high heat and reduce the marinade by half, until it has a thick syrupy consistency, about 5 minutes. Add the remaining 4 tablespoons lime marmalade, 2 tablespoons lime juice, and ½ teaspoon lime zest and cook and stir only until the marmalade is melted, about 1 minute more.

5. Remove the chicken wings from the oven and brush generously on all sides with the reduced marinade. Preheat the broiler and arrange the rack 5 to 6 inches from heat.

6. Place the pan of wings under the broiler and broil, turning several times, until the wings are crispy and just lightly charred. The wings can be cooked several hours ahead, covered loosely with foil, and kept at room temperature. Reheat in a preheated 350°F. oven until hot, about 15 minutes.

7. To serve, arrange the chicken wings on a serving platter and garnish with the lime wedges and clusters of cilantro. Serve warm.

Chicken Curry with Pita Pockets

Years ago, my husband and I attended a party on an exceptionally cold winter night. I still remember how imaginative the food was and how well it complemented the blustery weather outside. The hosts had arranged a large chafing dish filled with an aromatic chicken curry on a table and by its side was a napkin-lined basket filled with pita pockets and small bowls mounded with condiments such as raisins, cashews, chutney, and yogurt. The food was so good that the guests continually refilled their plates throughout the evening. This is my version of that dish.

Makes 64 portions

5 tablespoons vegetable oil, plus more if needed
3 pounds boneless, skinless chicken breasts, cut into ¾-inch cubes
2 cups thinly sliced onions
1 teaspoon ground cardamom
2 teaspoons ground turmeric
2 teaspoons ground ginger
2 teaspoons ground cumin
1 tablespoon chili powder
2 teaspoons paprika, preferably Hungarian
4 cups chicken stock
Salt and freshly ground black pepper to taste
1 3-inch cinnamon stick
4 bay leaves, broken in half
1¼ cups coarsely chopped drained canned tomatoes (about 14 ounces canned tomatoes)
2 tablespoons cornstarch
¼ cup chopped fresh cilantro
32 small 4-inch pita breads, split in half
Raisins
Mango chutney
Unsalted cashews
1 cup plain yogurt mixed with ½ teaspoon ground cumin

1. Heat 4 tablespoons of the oil in a large nonaluminum skillet over medium-high heat. When hot, add enough chicken cubes to make a single layer and sauté, turning, about 3 to 4 minutes. Remove and drain on paper towels. Continue until all chicken is cooked, adding more oil if necessary.

222

2. Add the onions to the pan, adding a little more oil if necessary, and sauté until just softened, about 2 to 3 minutes. Remove and drain on paper towels. Remove the skillet from the heat and set aside.

3. Mix the cardamom, turmeric, ginger, cumin, chili powder, and paprika together in a bowl. Place 1 tablespoon of the oil in the skillet and set over medium heat. When hot, add the spices and heat, stirring constantly, for about a minute. Add the stock and stir well to mix. Return the chicken and onions to the pan. Season well with salt and pepper. Add the cinnamon stick, bay leaves, and tomatoes. Bring the mixture to a simmer, lower the heat, and cook, uncovered, until the chicken is very tender, about 45 minutes. Remove the cinnamon stick and bay leaves and discard.

4. Mix the cornstarch with 2 tablespoons cold water. Add to the pan of chicken and cook, stirring well, until the mixture has thickened, about 3 to 4 minutes. Taste and add salt if needed. The curry can be made 1 to 2 days ahead to this point. Cool, cover, and refrigerate

5. When ready to serve, reheat the curry and stir in the cilantro. Meanwhile, wrap the pita halves in foil and heat in a 350°F. oven until warm, about 10 minutes. Serve the curry in a chafing dish or large bowl and the pitas in a napkin-lined basket. Place the raisins, chutney, cashews, and yogurt in small bowls and arrange around the chafing dish.

Turkey with Cranberry Applesauce

This deep red, chunky applesauce is less sweet than most because of the tart cranberries. It tastes delicious with sliced roasted or smoked turkey.

Makes 15 to 20 servings

CRANBERRY APPLESAUCE

(Makes 3 cups)
½ cup plus 2 tablespoons sugar
2½ pounds Golden Delicious apples (4 large apples) peeled, cored,
  and cut into ½-inch dice
1¼ cups cranberries
1 teaspoon finely grated peeled gingerroot
¼ teaspoon cinnamon
½ teaspoon grated lemon zest

1 whole roasted or smoked turkey breast, about 5 to 5½ pounds,
  sliced very thin
Several branches of lemon leaves or long-needled pine, for garnish
1 cup cranberries, for garnish
1 to 2 loaves French bread, cut into ¼-inch slices

1. To prepare the applesauce, combine the sugar and ½ cup plus 2 table-spoons water in a large heavy saucepan over medium-high heat. Stir until the sugar is dissolved. Add the apples, cover, and cook, stirring, frequently, for 5 minutes. Add the cranberries, cover, and cook until the apples are very soft and the cranberries have popped, about 15 to 20 minutes. Stir often to make certain the mixture does not stick or burn.

2. Use a potato masher or a wooden spoon and mash the apple mixture to a chunky consistency, stir in the ginger, cinnamon, and lemon zest and cook uncovered for 5 minutes. The applesauce can be made 2 to 3 days ahead. Cool, cover, and refrigerate. Reheat over medium heat, stirring, before serving.

3. To serve, place the warm cranberry applesauce in a bowl and place on a large serving tray. Arrange the turkey in overlapping slices on the tray. Make a border with the lemon leaves or pine. Sprinkle the cranberries in clusters over the greenery, and place the bread in a napkin-lined bowl or basket.

Roast Fillet of Beef with a Mediterranean Relish

Garlic-studded and thinly sliced fillet, served open-faced on bread and accompanied by an olive relish, can be done in advance. Talented Columbus caterer Kathy Lane, who developed this dish, routinely increases this recipe, roasting 4 to 5 fillets at a time, making it ideal for large gatherings.

Makes about 40 portions

1 3- to 3½-pound fillet of beef, trimmed of all excess fat
2 cloves garlic peeled and cut into thin slivers
Salt and freshly ground black pepper to taste
Virgin olive oil to rub on the meat

½ cup virgin olive oil
1½ tablespoons lemon juice, or more to taste
2 tablespoons capers, drained
1½ teaspoons minced garlic
2 tablespoons chopped shallots
½ cup Greek black olives or purple Alphonso olives, pitted and
*   coarsely chopped*
1 cup loosely packed fresh basil leaves, cut into thin julienne slices
¼ cup grated imported Parmesan cheese
Salt and freshly ground black pepper to taste
2 to 3 tablespoons chopped fresh chives or parsley, for garnish
1 large loaf French bread, cut into ⅜-inch-thick slices

1. Preheat the oven to 350°F.

2. With the tip of a sharp knife, cut slits all over the surface of the beef and insert the garlic slivers. Season the meat generously with salt and pepper and then rub with olive oil. Set the roast on a roasting rack in a shallow roasting pan just large enough to hold the meat comfortably. Roast until the meat is medium rare, about 145°F. on a meat thermometer, about 45 minutes.

3. Remove the roast from the oven and let cool to room temperature. The meat can be prepared a day ahead to this point. Cover and refrigerate. Bring to room temperature before serving.

4. To prepare the relish, whisk together the olive oil, lemon juice, capers, garlic, shallots, olives, basil, and Parmesan cheese. Taste and add salt and pepper as needed. Add more lemon juice if desired. The relish can be made a day ahead. Cover and refrigerate. Bring to room temperature before serving.

5. To serve, slice the filet into ⅜-inch-thick slices and arrange overlapping slices on a serving tray. Ladle some of the relish over the meat and garnish with the chives or parsley. Serve the extra relish in a small serving bowl. Place the bread in a napkin-lined basket by the side of the tray. To eat, place a slice of meat with some relish on a slice of bread.

SERVING: Garnish with sliced ripe plum tomatoes. If plum tomatoes are unavailable, arrange clusters of cherry tomatoes on the serving plate.

VARIATION: In place of fillet of beef, you can substitute 3 flank steaks, ¾ to 1 pound each. Combine ⅓ cup red wine vinegar; 1 cup plus 2 tablespoons olive oil; 2 large cloves garlic, peeled and minced; and ¼ teaspoon freshly ground black pepper and pour this marinade over the meat in a nonaluminum pan. Marinate in the refrigerator for 2 hours. Broil until just pink inside, 6 to 8 minutes per side.

Roast Fillet of Beef with Roquefort Sauce

I prepared this special fillet of beef one year for our annual Christmas party at La Belle Pomme Cooking School. The herb-coated meat, which is roasted and then sliced and sprinkled with chopped parsley and walnuts, is served with a warm Roquefort sauce. The fillet disappeared within minutes of being placed on the hors d'oeuvre table.

Makes about 40 portions

¾ pound Roquefort, crumbled
1½ cups whipping or heavy cream
1 3-pound fillet of beef, trimmed of all excess fat
3 tablespoons vegetable oil
1 teaspoon salt
2 teaspoons coarsely ground black pepper
2 teaspoons dried rosemary, crushed
2 teaspoons dried thyme, crushed
3 tablespoons coarsely chopped walnuts
3 tablespoons chopped fresh parsley
1 large loaf French bread, cut into ⅜-inch slices

1. To prepare the sauce, place the Roquefort and cream in a large, heavy saucepan over medium-high heat. Cook, stirring constantly, until the cheese melts. Then stir and cook until the cream has reduced slightly and the sauce thickens so it coats the back of a spoon. The sauce can be made up to 2 days ahead. Cool, cover, and refrigerate.

2. When ready to cook the roast, preheat the oven to 350°F.

3. Pat the meat dry. Heat the vegetable oil in a large heavy skillet over medium-high heat. When the oil is hot, brown the beef well on all sides. Remove from the skillet and cool slightly. Combine the salt, pepper, and herbs and rub all over the meat. Place the meat on a rack in a roasting pan and roast until a thermometer registers 140° to 145°F., for medium rare, about 45 minutes. Cool to room temperature. The roast can be prepared up to 2 days ahead, covered, and refrigerated. Bring to room temperature before serving.

4. To serve, cut the roast on the diagonal into ⅜-inch-thick slices. Arrange on a serving plate in overlapping slices. Sprinkle the meat with the chopped walnuts and parsley. Reheat the sauce, stirring, and place in a small chafing dish or bowl. Arrange the bread in a napkin-lined bowl. To serve, place a slice of meat on a piece of bread and nap the meat with warm sauce.

SERVING: Serve the meat on slices of French bread with the sauce.

VARIATION: In place of fillet of beef, you can substitute flank steaks, ¾ to 1 pound each, marinated and broiled as directed on page 226.

Lemon-Dill Veal Balls

These meatballs, unlike the usual Swedish or Italian ones so often served at cocktail parties, are made with veal and generously seasoned with lemon and dill to give them a light touch.

Makes about 36 veal balls

4 tablespoons vegetable oil, plus more if needed
1 cup finely chopped onions
1 teaspoon dried dill
¼ teaspoon dried thyme
1 pound ground veal
1 cup fresh bread crumbs
6½ teaspoons grated lemon zest, divided
4½ teaspoons lemon juice, divided
1 teaspoon salt, or more to taste
¼ teaspoon freshly ground black pepper, or more to taste
½ cup plus 3 tablespoons all-purpose flour
2 tablespoons unsalted butter
1½ cups chicken stock
3 tablespoons chopped fresh dill
Several sprigs of dill, for garnish
6-inch wooden skewers

1. To prepare the veal balls, heat 2 tablespoons of the oil in a medium skillet over medium-high heat. When hot, add the onions and cook, stirring constantly, until the onions are softened, about 3 to 4 minutes. Add the dried dill and dried thyme and stir and cook a minute more. Remove from the heat and cool.

2. Place the sautéed onions, veal, bread crumbs, 2½ teaspoons of the lemon zest, 2 teaspoons of the lemon juice, the salt, and pepper in a bowl and mix well to blend. Spread the ½ cup flour on a dinner plate. Shape the veal mixture into 1-inch balls and roll to coat lightly in the flour. You should get about 36 balls.

3. Heat the remaining 2 tablespoons oil in a heavy medium skillet over medium heat until hot. Sauté a veal ball, turning often, until brown on all sides. Taste for seasoning and, if necessary, sprinkle the remaining veal balls with more salt and pepper. Add enough veal balls to fit comfortably to the pan and cook, turning often, until browned. Remove and drain on paper towels. Repeat until all the veal balls are sautéed, adding additional oil if necessary.

4. To prepare the sauce, pour all the oil out of the skillet. Place the pan over medium heat and add the butter. When hot, add the remaining 3 tablespoons flour and stir constantly with a whisk, scraping up any brown particles in the pan into the flour, until mixture is a rich nut brown, about 6 to 8 minutes. Add the stock and whisk until the sauce thickens slightly, about 4 minutes. Stir in the remaining 2½ teaspoons lemon juice and 4 teaspoons lemon zest. Taste and add salt and pepper to taste. Stir in 1½ tablespoons of the chopped dill.

5. The veal balls and the sauce can be made up to 2 days ahead. Cool, cover each separately, and refrigerate. To reheat, place the veal balls and sauce in a large heavy skillet over medium heat. Cook, stirring, until hot, 4 to 5 minutes longer.

6. To serve, place the hot veal balls and sauce in a chafing dish. Sprinkle with remaining 1½ tablespoons chopped dill and garnish with sprigs of fresh dill. Serve with a glass or vase of 6-inch skewers.

NOTE: Fresh dill is necessary as the garnish to this dish. Dried dill sprinkled over the veal balls simply does not provide the same burst of flavor or color.

Baked Ham with Three Condiments

A baked ham, sliced and served on a tray lined with long-needled pine branches and accompanied by a trio of condiments—cranberry chutney, honey-mustard mayonnaise, and brandied fruit—is always found at our holiday open houses.

Makes 40 to 50 servings

1 whole baked ham, about 14 pounds (if possible, buy a honey-baked ham that is thinly sliced)

Condiments

Branches of long-needled pine and small pine cones, for garnish
Sliced pumpernickel, rye, and/or French bread

BRANDIED FRUIT

⅓ cup sugar
⅓ cup brandy or apricot brandy
½ cup dried apricots, diced
½ cup dark or golden raisins
½ cup dried sour cherries
½ cup pitted prunes, diced

Bring the sugar, ⅓ cup water, and the brandy to a simmer in a small saucepan over medium-high heat, stirring to make sure the sugar dissolves. Add the fruit and boil gently until the sauce thickens slightly and the fruits are glazed, about 5 minutes. Remove from the heat. Cool, cover, and refrigerate at least 6 hours or up to 2 days.

HONEY-MUSTARD MAYONNAISE (PAGE 264)

Prepare a double recipe. The mayonnaise can be made a day ahead, covered, and refrigerated.

CRANBERRY CHUTNEY (PAGE 267)

Prepare a double recipe. The chutney can be prepared 5 to 7 days ahead covered, and refrigerated.

230

1. To serve, arrange pine branches on a large serving tray or in a large shallow basket. Place the sliced ham on the pine. Tuck clusters of pine cones between the pine branches. If the tray or basket is large enough, arrange small bowls of the condiments on the pine branches. If not, place to the side. Place sliced bread in a napkin-lined bowl or basket.

Chinese Roast Pork with Red Currant Sauce

Roasted pork tenderloins, rubbed with a mixture of soy sauce, sherry, sugar, and cinnamon, are served with a red currant jelly sauce flavored with soy and sesame oil. The thinly sliced pork is arranged in overlapping rows around a bowl of the sauce and garnished with scallions.

Makes 12 to 16 servings

3 pork tenderloins, about 12 ounces each
1 tablespoon dry sherry
4 tablespoons soy sauce, divided
6 tablespoons sugar, divided
1½ teaspoons salt
¼ teaspoon cinnamon
6 tablespoons white vinegar
2 tablespoons prepared yellow mustard (see note)
1 tablespoon Oriental sesame oil
3 tablespoons red currant jelly
½ teaspoon cornstarch
2 teaspoons sesame seeds, toasted (page 269)
6 to 8 scallions, roots and all but 3 inches of the green stems
    cut off

(continued)

1. Trim any excess fat from the pork and halve the tenderloins lengthwise. Combine the sherry, 2 tablespoons of the soy sauce, 2 tablespoons of the sugar, the salt, and cinnamon in a small bowl and stir with a spoon to blend. Rub the split tenderloins all over with the sherry mixture. Place in a nonaluminum pan or dish and cover with plastic wrap. Marinate for 2 hours in the refrigerator, then bring to room temperature 30 minutes before roasting.

2. When ready to roast the pork, preheat the oven to 350°F.

3. Place the tenderloins so they are not touching on a rack in a roasting pan; you may need to use more than one rack and pan. Fill the pan(s) with about an inch of water, making sure the water does not touch the meat. Roast the meat for 30 to 35 minutes, or until a meat thermometer registers 170°F.

4. Remove the meat and let cool completely. Refrigerate, covered, overnight or up to 2 days.

5. To prepare the sauce, combine the remaining 4 tablespoons sugar, the vinegar, the remaining 2 tablespoons soy sauce, the mustard, sesame oil, jelly, and cornstarch in a small pan. Mix well with a whisk. Place over low heat and whisk just until mixture thickens slightly. Remove and cool completely. The sauce can be prepared a day ahead. Bring to room temperature an hour before serving.

6. To serve, use a sharp knife and with the blade held almost horizontally, cut the meat into thin diagonal slices. Stir the sesame seeds into the sauce, place the sauce in a bowl, and put on a serving tray. Arrange the meat in overlapping slices around the sauce. Garnish the platter with scallions.

SHOPPING: The regular ballpark variety of yellow mustard works better here than a more pungent Dijon-style one.

SERVING: To make scallion flowers, use a sharp knife and make 4 to 5 lengthwise slits in the white portion of each scallion. Place the scallions in a bowl of ice water for 5 minutes, or until the white portions curl. Remove and drain.

Honey-Mustard Spareribs

Talented chef Tom Johnson, a good friend, makes these Cincinnati-style ribs with baby-back ribs. Precooked and then coated with a home-made barbecue sauce flavored with honey, raspberry mustard, and soy sauce, they are small enough to be passed on a tray. I serve these ribs at very casual parties, with lots of extra napkins.

Makes about 48 ribs

3 large cloves garlic, peeled

1 2-inch piece of gingerroot, peeled and coarsely chopped

1 tablespoon Oriental chili paste with garlic (see note)

1 cup raspberry vinegar

1 cup honey

½ cup sweet salty Indonesian soy sauce or ½ cup light Chinese soy
    sauce mixed with 1 tablespoon dark molasses

½ cup raspberry mustard or Dijon-style mustard

1 cup olive oil

6 racks, about 1¼ pounds each, baby-back pork ribs with about 8
    ribs each

4 cups white vinegar

4 tablespoons dried marjoram

3 tablespoons salt

1. To prepare the sauce, place the garlic and ginger in a food processor fitted with the metal blade. Process until a paste is formed, about 15 seconds. Add the chili paste and process a few seconds more to combine. Add the raspberry vinegar, honey, soy sauce, and mustard. Process to blend. With the processor running, add the oil through the feed tube. Process until the sauce thickens slightly, about 10 to 15 seconds. Pour the sauce into a nonaluminum pan and bring to a simmer over medium heat. Simmer, stirring often, until sauce thickens, and has the consistency of a light syrup, about 15 minutes. Cool and transfer to a bowl. The sauce can be prepared up to 2 days in advance, covered, and refrigerated.

2. Fill two large stock pots with 4 quarts water each (or use one very large pot), divide the white vinegar between the pots, and bring to a simmer. Add half the marjoram and half the salt to each pot. Cut each rack of pork in half and add to the pots. Simmer until the ribs are tender, about 1½ to 2 hours. Do not overcool so the meat is falling off the bone. Remove and drain. The ribs can be prepared to this point a day ahead. Cool, cover, and refrigerate.

(continued)

3. To finish the ribs, preheat the oven to 400°F.

4. Line two baking sheets with aluminum foil and place cake or cooling racks on top. Place the ribs on the racks and brush liberally on both sides with the sauce. Bake until the ribs are set, glazed and hot, about 20 to 30 minutes.

5. To serve, cut the racks into individual portions of one to two ribs each and mound on a serving tray. Serve the remaining sauce on the side.

SHOPPING: Oriental chili paste, also known as chili sauce or chili paste with garlic, is a mixture of chilies, garlic, and oil. Since it is very potent, a little amount makes a dish very hot.

Sausage-Tomato Ragoût with Polenta Rounds

When I served this colorful, hearty ragoût in a chafing dish, accompanied by a plate of bright yellow Parmesan-flavored polenta rounds, for a Valentine cocktail party, it was an unqualified success. Both the stew and the polenta can be prepared ahead and reheated. The polenta is poured out on a work surface, and then cut into circles with a cookie cutter.

Makes about 48 portions

POLENTA ROUNDS

Makes 48 (rounds)

6 cups chicken stock
7 tablespoons olive oil
1 teaspoon salt, or to taste
Freshly ground black pepper to taste
2 cups yellow cornmeal
2 cups grated imported Parmesan cheese

RAGOÛT

2 pounds sweet Italian sausage, removed from casings, or bulk
   sausage
3 tablespoons olive oil
4 cups chopped onions (about 5 medium onions)
2 teaspoons chopped garlic
4 tablespoons all-purpose flour
2 teaspoons dried basil
¼ to ½ teaspoon crushed red pepper flakes, to taste
4 cups chicken stock
2 28-ounce cans Italian plum tomatoes, drained and coarsely
   chopped
3 tablespoons tomato paste
Salt and freshly ground black pepper to taste

1 cup freshly grated imported Parmesan cheese
Sprigs of basil, for garnish

(continued)

1. To prepare the polenta rounds, place 6 cups chicken stock in a large, heavy pot over medium-high heat. Add 4 tablespoons of the olive oil, the salt, and pepper. Bring the mixture to a boil and slowly add the cornmeal in a very fine stream, stirring constantly with a whisk. Then gradually stir in 2 cups Parmesan cheese. Simmer, stirring constantly with a wooden spoon, until the mixture pulls away from the sides of the pan, about 8 to 10 minutes. Remove from the heat, and immediately pour the polenta onto a clean work surface, and, using a spatula, spread into a circle about ⅜ inch thick. Let cool about 5 minutes.

2. With a 2-inch cookie cutter, cut rounds from the polenta. The scraps can be gathered and reshaped into a circle and more rounds cut out. You should get about 48 rounds. Transfer the rounds to a greased baking sheet. Let cool completely. The polenta rounds can be made 1 to 2 days ahead, covered with plastic wrap, and refrigerated. They can also be frozen. Cover with plastic wrap and then with aluminum foil. Defrost in the refrigerator before baking.

3. When ready to bake the polenta, preheat the oven to 350°F.

4. Brush the polenta rounds with the remaining 3 tablespoons olive oil. Bake until golden brown, about 15 to 20 minutes. Remove from the oven.

5. To prepare the ragoût, sauté the sausage meat in a large deep pot (preferably nonaluminum) over medium-high heat, stirring constantly, until browned, about 10 to 12 minutes. Use a wooden spoon to break the sausage into small pieces as it cooks. Drain on paper towels.

6. Pour off all the fat in the pan. Add 3 tablespoons olive oil and place over medium-high heat until hot. Add the onions and sauté, stirring constantly, until softened, about 4 minutes. Add the garlic and cook a minute more. Sprinkle the flour over the mixture and cook and stir 2 minutes more. Return the browned sausage meat to the pan. Add the dried basil, red pepper flakes, 4 cups chicken stock, tomatoes, and tomato paste. Stir well and bring to a simmer. Lower the heat and cook, uncovered, stirring often to prevent the flour from sticking to the bottom of the pan, about 30 to 40 minutes, or until the flavors of the ragoût are well developed. The ragoût can be made 1 to 2 days ahead. Cool, cover, and refrigerate. It can also be frozen for up to 2 weeks. Be sure to cover tightly before freezing. Defrost in the refrigerator before reheating.

7. To serve, ladle the warm ragoût into a chafing dish. Arrange the warm polenta rounds in overlapping rows on a serving tray, and sprinkle with a little of the Parmesan cheese. Garnish the tray with basil sprigs. Place the remaining Parmesan cheese in a bowl. Guests can place polenta rounds on individual plates, ladle ragoût over them, and sprinkle Parmesan cheese over the ragoût.

Curried Cheesecake
with Chutney

Made with light cream cheese and yogurt and spiced with curry powder, ginger, and cayenne pepper, this unique cheesecake is topped with chutney after baking. It is garnished attractively with fresh mint sprigs and apple wedges.

Makes 15 to 20 servings

Nonstick vegetable cooking spray
1 cup (about 4 ounces) sliced almonds, toasted and finely ground
2 tablespoons unsalted butter, melted
4 tablespoons all-purpose flour
½ teaspoon ground cardamom
½ teaspoon ground coriander
2 pounds light cream cheese, softened
1½ cups plain low-fat yogurt, drained in a fine-mesh sieve for 30 minutes
4 large eggs
1 tablespoon curry powder
½ teaspoon ground ginger
¼ teaspoon cayenne pepper
¼ teaspoon salt
⅔ cup currants, soaked to soften in 1 cup hot water for 15 minutes, drained, and patted dry
¾ cup mango chutney, Fruit Chutney (page 266), or Cranberry Chutney (page 267)
Bunch of fresh mint, for garnish
6 tart apples, cored, seeded, cut into ¼-inch wedges, and tossed in the juice of 1 large lemon

1. Preheat the oven to 350°F. Spray a 9-inch springform pan with nonstick vegetable cooking spray.

2. Combine the ground almonds, melted butter, flour, cardamom, and coriander. Mix well and pat onto the bottom of the pan. Place on the center shelf of the oven and bake to set, about 10 minutes. Remove from the oven, but leave the oven on.

3. Place the cream cheese in the bowl of an electric mixer and beat on medium speed until creamy, about 2 minutes. Add ½ cup of the yogurt and mix to blend, scraping down the sides of the bowl as necessary. Add the eggs, one at a time, and mix to blend. Add the spices and salt and mix 1 to 2 minutes more to blend. Remove 1½ cups of the cheesecake batter and place in a bowl. Stir in the currants.

4. Spread the currant mixture on the bottom of the springform pan with a spatula. Pour the remaining batter on top and spread evenly with a spatula. Bake until the cheesecake is firm, about 35 to 40 minutes. Remove from the oven and let sit for 5 minutes; leave the oven on. Then spread the remaining drained yogurt over the top of the cheesecake and bake for 15 minutes more. Remove from the oven and cool completely, then cover and refrigerate. The cheesecake can be made up to 2 days in advance.

5. To serve, remove the sides from the springform pan and place the cheesecake on a serving tray. Make a border on top of the cheesecake with the chutney. Surround the base of the cheesecake with mint sprigs, and arrange the apple wedges on the tray. To eat, spread a little cheesecake on the apple wedges.

Mexican Cheesecake

This piquant cheesecake with its ground tortilla chip crust is a favorite of mine to offer at large parties. For the filling, light cream cheese and yogurt cheese are blended with chili powder, cumin, and cayenne pepper. Although the fresh salsa is delicious, if you find yourself in a pinch for time you can use a store-bought chunky tomato salsa.

Makes 15 to 20 servings

Non-stick vegetable cooking spray
1 cup ground corn tortilla chips (processed to the consistency of
    coarse meal in a food processor)
2 tablespoons unsalted butter, melted
4 tablespoons all-purpose flour
1 pound light cream cheese
2 cups Low-Fat Yogurt Cheese, made from 32 ounces plain low-fat
    yogurt (page 265)
4 large eggs
1 teaspoon dried oregano, preferably Mexican oregano
1½ teaspoons cumin powder
½ teaspoon garlic powder
1 teaspoon chili powder
½ teaspoon freshly ground black pepper
¼ teaspoon cayenne pepper
¼ teaspoon salt

SALSA

2 cups seeded and chopped ripe tomatoes
2½ tablespoons seeded and chopped fresh jalapeño peppers
½ cup finely chopped scallions
2 tablespoons chopped fresh cilantro
4 teaspoons minced garlic
2 tablespoons lime juice
Generous pinch of cayenne pepper
Salt and freshly ground black pepper to taste
Blue corn or regular tortilla chips

1. Preheat the oven to 350°F. Spray a 9-inch springform pan with nonstick vegetable cooking spray.

2. Combine the ground tortilla chips, melted butter, and flour in the pan. Mix

239

well and pat onto the bottom of the pan. Place on center shelf of the oven and bake to set, about 10 minutes. Remove from the oven, but do not turn off the oven.

3. Place the cream cheese and yogurt cheese in the bowl of an electric mixer and beat on medium speed until smooth, about 2 minutes, scraping down the sides of the bowl if necessary. Add the eggs, one at a time, and mix to blend. Add the seasonings and mix 1 to 2 minutes more to blend.

4. Pour the filling into the prepared pan and spread evenly with a spatula. Bake on the center shelf of the oven until firm, about 35 to 40 minutes. Remove from the oven and cool completely. Cover and refrigerate. The cheesecake can be made up to 2 days in advance.

5. To prepare the salsa, combine all the ingredients in a bowl and mix well. The salsa can be made up to a day ahead. Drain well before using.

6. To serve, remove the sides from the springform pan and place the cheese-cake on a serving tray. Spread half the salsa over the top of the cheesecake and place the other half in a serving bowl. Garnish the cheesecake with tortilla chips. To serve, spread a little cheesecake and salsa on a tortilla chip.

VARIATION: Sometimes I add 4 tablespoons canned mild green chilies, drained and chopped, to the filling mixture.

Smoked Salmon Cheesecake with Dill Toasts

This savory cheesecake, flecked with smoked salmon, lemon zest, and grated Parmesan cheese, makes a showstopper appetizer served on lemon leaves with a garnish of dilled toast triangles. It can be served warm or chilled.

Makes 15 to 20 servings

Nonstick vegetable cooking spray
½ cup dried bread crumbs
~~1¼~~ ¼ cups grated imported Parmesan cheese, divided
3 tablespoons unsalted butter, melted
5 ounces smoked salmon   *½ c. parm.*
2 pounds cream cheese, at room temperature
4 large eggs
~~¾ cup chopped fresh chives or parsley, divided~~
~~2 teaspoons grated lemon zest~~
½ teaspoon salt
Freshly ground black pepper to taste
1 cup sour cream

1 TBSP. 3 ONIUN
1½ TBSP. BASIL PASTE

DILL TOASTS

22 slices very thin white bread
4½ tablespoons unsalted butter, melted
4½ tablespoons olive oil
1 tablespoon plus 1 teaspoon dried dill
Lemon leaves, for garnish
2 cucumbers, peeled and sliced, for garnish

1. Preheat the oven to 350°F. and arrange a rack on the middle shelf of the oven. Spray a 9-inch springform pan with nonstick vegetable cooking spray.

2. Place the bread crumbs and ¼ cup of the Parmesan cheese in the springform pan and toss to mix. Add the melted butter and mix to blend. Press the crumb mixture into the bottom of the pan. Set aside.

3. Chop the smoked salmon fine in a food processor fitted with the metal blade, or by hand. Set aside in a medium bowl.

4. In the bowl of an electric mixer, beat the cream cheese on medium speed until smooth, about 2 minutes. Beat in the remaining 1 cup Parmesan cheese and blend well. Add the eggs, one at a time, mixing well after each addition. Add ½ cup of the chives or parsley, the lemon zest, salt, and pepper and mix well. Gently fold in the sour cream.

5. Remove 2 cups of the cheesecake batter and add to the reserved smoked salmon. Blend thoroughly. Pour the remaining batter into the prepared pan and level with a spatula. Spoon the reserved smoked salmon mixture over the batter and gently level it with the spatula.

6. Place the cheesecake on the middle rack of the oven and bake 45 minutes. Turn the oven off and set the door ajar. Leave the cheesecake in the oven for 30 minutes, then remove and let cool 15 minutes. The cheesecake can be served warm at this point or it can be cooled to room temperature, covered, and refrigerated for up to 2 days. Bring to room temperature 30 minutes before serving.

7. To prepare the dill toasts, preheat the oven to 350°F.

8. Remove the crusts from the bread. Stack the slices of bread and cut diagonally into triangles. Combine the melted butter, oil, and dill in a bowl. Brush the triangles on both sides with the mixture and arrange on baking sheets. Bake until just golden, about 10 minutes. Remove. The toasts can be made 5 to 6 hours ahead. Leave at cool room temperature, covered loosely with foil.

9. To serve, place the cheesecake in the center of a large serving tray. Sprinkle the remaining ¼ cup chives or parsley over the top. Arrange lemon leaves around the cheesecake. Garnish with the dill toasts and clusters of cucumber slices. To serve, spread the cheesecake on the toasts.

SERVING: I have served this cheesecake both warm and cold. Although it is delicious both ways, the warm version seems to taste lighter.

Baked Salmon with Lime-Scented Yogurt Sauce

Baked salmon fillets sprinkled with fresh mint and parsley, then topped with sweet red onions and slices of lime, make an elegant and delicious dish for a special occasion. I serve the salmon with slices of pumpernickel and a light lime-flavored yogurt sauce.

Makes 10 to 12 servings

1 cup low-fat plain yogurt
2 teaspoons lime juice
1 teaspoon grated lime zest
Vegetable oil

2 salmon fillets, preferably Norwegian salmon, about 1½ pounds each
Salt and freshly ground black pepper to taste
1 cup plus 2 teaspoons chopped fresh mint
½ cup chopped fresh parsley
2 cups sweet red onions sliced paper-thin, divided
4 limes, thinly sliced
2 cucumbers, peeled and finely grated
Sprigs of mint and flat-leaf parsley, for garnish
1 to 2 packages sliced party pumpernickel bread or 1 large loaf of pumpernickel, cut into thin slices and then into quarters

1. To prepare the sauce, place the yogurt, lime juice, and lime zest in a mixing bowl and whisk well to blend. The sauce can be prepared a day ahead to this point. Cover and refrigerate.

2. Line a baking sheet with aluminum foil and oil well. Generously oil the skin of the salmon. Place the fish skin side down on the foil. Run your fingers over the flesh of the salmon; if you feel any bones, remove them with tweezers. Sprinkle salt and pepper over the fish.

3. Combine 1 cup of the chopped mint and the chopped parsley and spread the mixture over the salmon. Arrange 1 cup of the onion slices over the herbs. Then arrange the lime slices, slightly overlapping, over the onions. The fish can be prepared up to 2 hours ahead to this point. Cover and refrigerate.

(continued)

243

4. When ready to cook the salmon, preheat the oven to 450°F.

5. Bake the salmon on the center shelf of the oven until the flesh is opaque, about 14 minutes. Remove from the oven. Remove the lime slices and onions and scrape off the herb mixture.

6. To serve, combine the remaining 1 cup sliced onions with the grated cucumbers in a mixing bowl. Stir the remaining 2 teaspoons chopped mint into the yogurt sauce. Arrange the onion/cucumber mixture on a serving platter, place the salmon fillets on top. Garnish the fish with a cluster of mint and parsley sprigs. Serve with a basket or bowl of sliced pumpernickel and the yogurt lime sauce. To eat, put a slice of salmon on bread, top with onion/cucumber mixture and with a dollop of yogurt sauce.

Double-Crusted Spinach and Sausage Torta

This rich pizza, stuffed with Italian sausage, spinach, three cheeses, and tomato sauce, is always popular; there are never any leftovers.

Makes 8 to 10 servings

1 recipe Pizza Dough (page 96; prepare through Step 2, then proceed as directed below)

1 pound sweet Italian bulk sausage
¾ cup chopped red onions
2 teaspoons minced garlic
¼ teaspoon crushed red pepper flakes
1 10-ounce package frozen chopped spinach, defrosted and squeezed dry in a clean kitchen towel
½ cup part-skim ricotta cheese
¼ cup plus 3 tablespoons grated imported Parmesan cheese
¼ teaspoon salt
⅛ teaspoon freshly ground black pepper
12 ounces whole-milk or part-skim mozzarella cheese, shredded
1¾ cups pizza sauce
1 egg, beaten
Flat-leaf spinach leaves, for garnish

1. Punch down the pizza dough and shape into a round. Pinch off a third of the dough and set aside. Roll out the larger piece on a floured surface to a 13- to 14-inch round. Fit the dough into a greased 9-inch springform pan so that the dough hangs slightly over the rim of the pan. Place the pan, plus the extra dough, in the refrigerator while you prepare the filling.

2. In a large heavy skillet over medium-high heat, sauté the sausage, breaking it into small pieces with a spoon, until it is lightly browned. Add the onions, garlic, and red pepper flakes and sauté, stirring, until the onions are softened, about 2 to 3 minutes. Remove the mixture from the pan and drain on paper towels. Transfer to a mixing bowl. Add the spinach, ricotta, the ¼ cup Parmesan cheese, the salt, and pepper and mix well. Cool slightly.

3. Spread half of this mixture in the dough-lined pan. Sprinkle a third of the mozzarella and 1 tablespoon of the remaining Parmesan over the filling. Spread half the pizza sauce over the cheese. Repeat the process, then sprinkle the remaining mozzarella and the remaining 1 tablespoon Parmesan over the final layer of pizza sauce.

4. Roll out the remaining pizza dough on a floured surface to a 10-inch round. Place over the filling in pan. Brush the edges of the round with the beaten egg. Fold the overhanging dough up over the top and pinch the edges of the dough together. Crimp to form a decorative edge. Cut two 2-inch slits in the top of the dough. The torta can be prepared up to a day ahead to this point. Cover with plastic wrap and refrigerate. Bring to room temperature 40 minutes before baking.

5. When ready to bake, preheat the oven to 450°F.

6. Bake the torta on the center shelf of the oven for 15 minutes. Cover loosely with aluminum foil and bake 25 minutes more, or until the crust is slightly browned. Remove and cool 10 minutes. Remove the sides of the pan. Place the torta on a bed of spinach leaves on a serving tray. Cut the torta into wedges and serve warm.

NOTE: Cut-outs (leaves, hearts, etc.) made from dough scraps can be used as decorations on top of the torta. Moisten the cut-outs with a little beaten egg to help them adhere.

Nuts, Sweet and Savory

Nuts are, undoubtedly, the easiest type of appetizer to prepare. They are delicious offered plain or simply roasted, but they can be combined with other ingredients for fancier presentations. They can be made in advance, so last-minute cooking is never necessary. And, most important of all, nuts know no season; they are available year-round!

Savory nuts make perfect finger food to accompany pre-dinner drinks. Sweetened nuts are the ideal light confection for cocktail buffets or receptions where people have sampled an array of hors d'oeuvres and welcome a sweet nibble.

Among the savory choices in this chapter are some unique offerings: roasted pecans flavored with curry and plum sauce, walnut halves stuffed with blue cheese, and smoked almonds seasoned with garlic. Orange-Glazed Pecans, chocolate-dipped walnuts stuffed with coffee-scented marzipan, and exotic Moroccan Almonds are all irresistible sweet confections.

Prepared nuts also make thoughtful gifts. As a guest you could take any of these nuts as a token of appreciation for a host or hostess. On occasion, I have even given departing guests a small package of homemade savory or sweet nuts as a little remembrance of a special party.

Orange-Glazed Pecans

I serve these spiced orange pecans every year at holiday parties.

Makes 2 cups

Nonstick vegetable cooking spray
1½ teaspoons grated orange zest
3 tablespoons orange juice
½ cup sugar
½ teaspoon powdered cinnamon
Generous pinch of ground cloves
Several generous gratings of fresh nutmeg
2 cups pecan halves (about 8 ounces)

1. Line a baking sheet with aluminum foil and generously spray with nonstick vegetable cooking spray.

2. Combine the orange zest, orange juice, sugar, and spices in a medium-size heavy saucepan over medium-high heat. Stir just until the sugar is dissolved, and then bring to a boil without stirring. Add the pecans, a handful at a time, stirring constantly. Then continue to cook and stir until the pecans are coated with the syrup, about 2 to 3 minutes.

3. Remove the pan from the heat and stir 2 to 3 minutes more. Then spread the pecans on the prepared baking sheet. Use two forks to separate the pecans so they are not stuck together. Let cool. Rather than having a shiny coating, the pecans will have a light opaque glaze. Store in an airtight container for up to 3 weeks.

Honeyed Walnuts

My friend Nancy Roehrs is a wonderful cook who is always surprising me with some delicious new dish such as these vanilla-and-honey-flavored walnuts. You will need a candy thermometer to prepare these nuts.

Makes 3 cups

Nonstick vegetable cooking spray
1½ cups sugar
¼ cup honey
3 cups walnut halves (about 12 ounces)
½ teaspoon vanilla

1. Line a baking sheet with aluminum foil and spray generously with nonstick vegetable cooking spray.

2. Combine the sugar, ½ cup water, and the honey in a heavy medium saucepan and cook over low heat, stirring only until the sugar dissolves. Swirl the pan occasionally. Increase the heat to medium high and boil without stirring until a candy thermometer registers 240°F. (soft-ball stage). Remove the pan from the heat.

3. Add the walnuts and vanilla to the pan and stir vigorously with a spoon until the syrup is thick and cream colored, about 5 minutes. Turn the mixture out onto the cookie sheet. Separate the walnuts using two forks. Cool completely. The walnuts can be stored in an airtight container for up to 3 weeks.

VARIATION: Substitute unsalted pecans, almonds, or cashews in place of the walnuts.

Almond Coffee Walnuts

A talented cook from Provence, Marie Claire Vallois, shared with me her recipe for walnut halves filled with coffee-flavored marzipan. My addiction to chocolate led me to dip the stuffed halves into melted chocolate as a final touch.

Makes 36 stuffed walnuts

⅔ cup almond paste (about 6 ounces)
2 tablespoons coffee-flavored liqueur
1 teaspoon instant espresso powder
72 walnut halves
8 ounces semisweet chocolate, chopped

1. Mix the almond paste, coffee liqueur, and espresso powder in a small bowl until smooth. Spread ½ teaspoon of this mixture on the flat side of a walnut half, top with a second walnut half, and gently squeeze together. Repeat with the remaining walnuts and filling.

2. Line a large baking sheet with waxed paper. Melt the chocolate in the top of a double boiler over barely simmering water, stirring until smooth. Remove the top pan from the heat. Dip one end of each stuffed walnut halfway into the chocolate and swirl, allowing excess chocolate to drip back into pan. Set on prepared sheet. Refrigerate the walnuts until the chocolate is set, about 30 minutes. The walnuts can be covered tightly with plastic wrap and refrigerated for up to 1 week.

Moroccan Almonds

Moroccan cuisine, known for its enticing combinations of both sweet and savory flavors, was the inspiration for these almonds.

Makes about 2 cups

Nonstick vegetable cooking spray
¼ cup sugar
1 teaspoon ground coriander
½ teaspoon ground cloves
2 teaspoons powdered cinnamon
1 egg white
1½ teaspoons grated orange zest
2 cups whole unblanched almonds (about 8 ounces)

1. Preheat the oven to 275°F. Line a rimmed baking sheet with aluminum foil and spray generously with nonstick vegetable cooking spray.

2. Combine the sugar, coriander, cloves, and cinnamon in a bowl and stir to mix.

3. Place the egg white in a mixing bowl and whisk until frothy. Add the sugar mixture and whisk again. Stir in the orange zest. Add the almonds and stir until all the nuts are well coated.

4. Transfer the nuts to the prepared baking sheet and spread them evenly. Bake on the center shelf of the oven for 40 minutes, stirring every 10 minutes. Remove and cool for 1 hour. The nuts can be stored in an airtight container for up to 3 weeks.

Lemon-Spiced Pecans

Flavored with lemon and aromatic spices, these crispy, sweet pecans are addictive.

Makes about 4 cups

Nonstick vegetable cooking spray
½ cup sugar
½ teaspoon salt
⅛ cup (2 tablespoons) grated lemon zest (see note)
1 teaspoon freshly grated nutmeg
½ teaspoon powdered cinnamon
2 egg whites
2 teaspoons lemon juice
1 pound pecan halves (about 4 cups)

1. Preheat the oven to 250°F.

2. Line two rimmed baking sheets with aluminum foil and spray generously with nonstick vegetable cooking spray. Combine the sugar, salt, lemon zest, nutmeg, and cinnamon in a large shallow bowl and mix well. Set aside.

3. Place the egg whites and lemon juice in a large bowl and mix with a whisk until foamy, 30 to 60 seconds. Add the pecans and stir to coat well. Pour about one quarter of the nuts into a large fine-meshed strainer and shake to remove excess egg whites. Repeat with remaining nuts.

4. Spread the pecans on a sheet of aluminum foil or parchment paper. Sprinkle the sugar mixture over the nuts. Toss gently to coat nuts well with the mixture.

5. Spread the nuts on the prepared baking sheets. Bake in the center of the oven until light golden and dry, about 35 to 45 minutes. After 20 minutes, reverse the trays front to back and top to bottom so that the nuts cook evenly. Watch carefully to avoid overbrowning.

6. Remove from the oven and cool. The pecans can be stored in an airtight container at room temperature for 2 to 3 weeks.

SHOPPING: Buy thick-skinned lemons for easier grating. For 2 tablespoons grated zest, you will need about 4 lemons. Although 2 tablespoons lemon zest is a large amount, do not skimp on this ingredient. It gives the strong lemony flavor to these nuts.

Curried Pecans with Plum Sauce

These curried pecans are especially easy to prepare, and can be stored up to three weeks in an airtight container.

Makes about 7 cups

1½ pounds pecan halves (about 6 cups)
5 tablespoons unsalted butter
5 tablespoons vegetable oil
3 tablespoons light brown sugar
3 tablespoons curry powder
1½ tablespoons ground ginger
¾ teaspoon salt
3 tablespoons plum sauce (see note)
1 cup raisins

1. Preheat the oven to 350°F. Line two rimmed baking sheets with aluminum foil.

2. Spread the pecans on the prepared baking sheets and bake on the center oven shelf for 10 minutes, stirring several times. Do not let the nuts brown. Remove the nuts from the oven, but leave the oven on.

3. Melt the butter with the oil in a large heavy skillet over medium heat until hot. Add the brown sugar, curry powder, ginger, and salt and stir well to blend. Add the nuts to the skillet and stir until well coated with the sugar mixture. Add the plum sauce and raisins and mix well. Remove from the heat.

4. Spread the nuts on the baking sheets and bake for 10 minutes, stirring several times. Remove and cool 1 hour. The pecans can be stored in an airtight container for up to 3 weeks.

SHOPPING: Plum sauce is available at Oriental grocery stores and some supermarkets.

Roasted Parmesan Pecans

These savory nuts take only a few minutes to prepare and bake. Pecan halves are coated with a mixture of honey mustard and melted butter seasoned with hot pepper sauce, then covered with Parmesan cheese and baked until golden.

Makes 2 cups

Nonstick vegetable cooking spray
¼ cup honey mustard
3 tablespoons unsalted butter, melted
½ teaspoon salt
½ teaspoon hot pepper sauce
2 cups pecan halves (about 8 ounces)
¾ cup grated imported Parmesan cheese

1. Preheat the oven to 250°F. Line a rimmed baking sheet with aluminum foil and spray generously with nonstick vegetable cooking spray.

2. Place the honey mustard in a medium mixing bowl and whisk in the melted butter. Add the salt and hot pepper sauce and mix to blend well. Add the pecans to the mixture and mix to coat well. Spread the Parmesan cheese on a plate and toss a few pecans at a time in the cheese, being sure to coat well on all sides. Transfer the pecans to the prepared baking sheet.

3. Bake the pecans on the center shelf of the oven for 15 minutes. Stir the nuts and bake about 8 to 12 minutes more. The nuts should be just golden, not brown, on both sides. Remove and cool to room temperature. The pecans can be stored in an airtight container for up to 3 weeks.

✳ Rock Run Pecans

My assistant, Emily Bell, has a pantry filled with make-ahead treats for impromptu entertaining. These roasted pecans flavored with celery salt, onion powder, and garlic powder are always on her shelf, ready for unexpected guests who stop by her house, called Rock Run.

Makes 2½ cups

Nonstick vegetable cooking spray
3 tablespoons unsalted butter
1½ teaspoons Worcestershire sauce
½ teaspoon celery salt
¼ teaspoon onion powder
¼ teaspoon garlic powder
2½ cups pecan halves (about 10 ounces)

1. Preheat the oven to 275°F. Line a rimmed baking sheet with aluminum foil and spray with nonstick vegetable cooking spray.

2. Melt the butter in a large heavy skillet over medium-high heat. When hot, add the Worcestershire sauce and seasonings. Stir to blend, then remove from the heat. Add the pecans and toss and stir to coat the pecans well with the seasoning mixture.

3. Scrape the pecans and any seasoning mixture remaining in the pan onto the prepared baking sheet, and spread evenly. Bake on the center shelf of the oven for 30 minutes, stirring every 10 minutes. Remove and cool for 1 hour. The pecans can be stored in an airtight container for up to 3 weeks.

Smoked Garlic Almonds

These lightly smoked nuts can easily become addictive. They are perfect to offer as pre-dinner nibbles.

Makes about 3 cups

Nonstick vegetable cooking spray
1 egg white
1 teaspoon liquid smoke
2 teaspoons garlic powder
2 teaspoons celery salt
¼ teaspoon salt
3 cups whole unblanched almonds (about 12 ounces)

1. Preheat the oven to 275°F. Line a rimmed baking sheet with aluminum foil and spray the foil with vegetable cooking spray.

2. Whisk the egg white until frothy in a large mixing bowl. Add the liquid smoke and seasonings and whisk until blended. Add the almonds and toss and stir until well coated.

3. Spread the almonds evenly on the prepared baking sheet. Bake on the center shelf of the oven for 40 minutes, stirring every 10 minutes. Remove and cool for 1 hour. The almonds can be stored in an airtight container for up to 3 weeks.

Blue-Cheese-Stuffed Walnuts

Sara Evans, one of my students and a dedicated cook, created these superb stuffed walnuts.

Makes 36 walnuts

2 ounces cream cheese, softened
2 ounces blue cheese, softened (see note)
1½ tablespoons chopped fresh chives
Salt and freshly ground black pepper to taste
72 walnut halves, toasted (page 268)

1. Combine the cream cheese, blue cheese, and chives or parsley in a mixing bowl and stir well to blend. Season with salt and pepper to taste. Chill until firm, about 30 to 40 minutes.

2. Spread ½ teaspoon of the filling on the flat side of a walnut half and top with another half. Continue with the remaining filling and walnuts. Place the walnuts on a serving plate, cover, and refrigerate. The walnuts can be prepared a day ahead.

SHOPPING: I use Saga blue because it is so smooth. I buy a 3-to-4-ounce wedge of the cheese, trim off and discard the rind, and weigh out 2 ounces for the filling. If using blue cheese without a rind, use only 2 ounces.

Fruit and Nut Mixes

Remember the standard "party mix" of cashews and raisins? Now, with so many unusual dried fruits (sour cherries, cranberries, papaya), nuts, and seeds available, the possibilities are endless. Here are some of my favorite combinations. The third combination is the creation of my friend Linda Schulman.

For each mix, toss the ingredients together in a bowl, and store in an airtight container for up to 3 weeks. For directions on toasting nuts, see page 268.

FRUIT AND NUT MIX #1

1 part toasted pecan halves
1 part toasted slivered almonds
2 parts dried sour cherries or raisins (see note)

FRUIT AND NUT MIX #2

5 parts roasted slivered almonds
1 part finely diced dried apricots
1 part golden raisins
1 part currants
1 part dried sour cherries (see note)
1 part flaked sweetened coconut

FRUIT AND NUT MIX #3

2 parts tamari sunflower seeds (see note)
2 parts tamari almonds (see note)
2 parts sesame sticks (oat bran or Cajun-flavored ones are
   particularly good)
2 parts unsalted roasted peanuts
1 part hot pumpkin seeds (see note)
1 part raisins

SHOPPING: Dried sour cherries are available in specialty food stores or in health food stores, or see page 281 for mail order information. They are moist and tart and taste delicious with toasted nuts. Tamari sunflower seeds and tamari almonds and hot pumpkin seeds are available in most health food stores.

Basics

Quick Tomato Sauce

Makes about 1½ cups

2 tablespoons olive oil
¾ cup chopped onions
1 teaspoon chopped garlic
1 28-ounce can Italian-style tomatoes, drained and coarsely chopped
1 teaspoon dried basil
Pinch of sugar
½ teaspoon salt, or more to taste

1. Heat the olive oil in a large heavy skillet over medium-high heat. Add the onion and garlic and sauté, stirring for 2 to 3 minutes. Add the tomatoes, dried basil, sugar, and salt. Reduce the heat to medium and cook, stirring often, until the mixture is thick and most of the liquid has evaporated, about 15 minutes.

2. Purée the sauce in a food processor, blender, or food mill. Taste and add salt if needed.

3. The sauce can be refrigerated for up to 2 days, or it can be frozen for 3 weeks. Thaw in the refrigerator before reheating.

Toasted Pine Nut Pesto

½ cup pine nuts
1 cup packed fresh basil leaves (see note)
1 clove garlic, peeled
⅓ cup olive oil
½ cup grated imported Parmesan cheese
Salt and freshly ground black pepper to taste

1. To toast the pine nuts, place them in a heavy medium-size skillet over medium-high heat. Cook, shaking the pan back and forth, until the nuts are golden on all sides, about 5 minutes. Remove from the pan and cool.

2. Place the nuts, basil leaves, garlic, olive oil, Parmesan cheese, and salt and pepper in the bowl of a food processor fitted with the metal blade or in a blender. Process until well puréed, about 15 to 30 seconds. The pesto can be covered with plastic wrap and refrigerated for up to a day; it will lose some of the bright green color, but will taste fine. You can also freeze pesto: Place the pesto in a freezer container and cover with a thin layer of olive oil. Cover tightly. Pour off the olive oil after defrosting.

VARIATION: If fresh basil is not available, substitute 1 cup chopped fresh parsley plus 1 tablespoon dried basil, chopped together.

Cooked Egg Mayonnaise

Makes about 1½ cups

2 tablespoons all-purpose flour
1 large egg, beaten
2 hard-cooked egg yolks, well crumbled
1 tablespoon lemon juice
½ teaspoon Dijon or stone-ground mustard
½ teaspoon salt, or more to taste
Generous pinch cayenne pepper
¾ cup corn or vegetable oil
¾ cup olive oil

1. Place the flour and ½ cup water in a small heavy saucepan over medium heat and stir to blend. Cook, stirring, until thickened and just boiling. Stir in the whole egg and cook 30 to 60 seconds, stirring constantly. Add the cooked yolks and mix well. Remove from the heat.

2. Transfer the mixture to the container of a food processor fitted with a metal blade and add the lemon juice, mustard, salt, and cayenne pepper. Process for several seconds. Then, with the machine running, slowly add the oil in a very thin stream. When all the oil is incorporated, process several seconds more to blend. Taste and add more salt if needed. The mayonnaise can be covered and refrigerated for 1 to 2 days.

Honey-Mustard Mayonnaise

⅔ cup mayonnaise (*Hellmann's or Best Foods is preferred*)
2 teaspoons honey mustard
4 teaspoons minced scallions

1. Combine the mayonnaise, honey mustard, and scallions and mix well to blend. The honey-mustard mayonnaise can be covered and refrigerated for 1 to 2 days.

Herb-Garlic Cheese

Makes about 12 ounces or 1¼ to 1½ cups

12 ounces light (*Neufchatel*) cream cheese, softened
3 tablespoons sour cream
2 medium cloves garlic, peeled and put through a garlic press or minced
¾ teaspoon dried dill
½ teaspoon dried thyme
1½ tablespoons finely chopped fresh parsley
1½ tablespoons chopped fresh chives
Generous 1 teaspoon garlic salt
Freshly ground black pepper to taste

1. Place the cream cheese and sour cream in a bowl. Add the garlic, herbs, garlic salt, and a little black pepper, and mix well to blend. The cheese can be refrigerated for 2 to 3 days.

Low-Fat Yogurt Cheese

Low-fat plain yogurt can be turned into yogurt cheese simply by draining the yogurt in a strainer in the refrigerator overnight. When the yogurt is drained, the volume is reduced by half.

Makes about ½ cup

8 ounces low-fat plain yogurt (buy yogurt that does not contain gelatin)

1. Place a fine-meshed sieve over a bowl, put the yogurt in the sieve, and place in the refrigerator for 12 hours. The water, almost half the amount of yogurt, will drain off, leaving a solid mass of yogurt cheese. The cheese can be covered and refrigerated for up to 2 days.

NOTE: A yogurt cheese funnel is inexpensive and a good investment if you plan to make cheese frequently from yogurt. The cheesemaker consists of a circular, mesh-lined piece of plastic that can be folded and snapped into a cone shape for draining the yogurt. Yogurt cheese funnels are available at many cookware shops.

Fruit Chutney

Makes about 4½ cups

1 garlic clove, peeled and minced
1 medium onion, peeled and finely chopped
2 cups cider vinegar
1 tablespoon ground ginger
½ tablespoon salt
½ teaspoon cinnamon
¼ teaspoon crushed red pepper flakes
2 teaspoons grated orange zest
½ pound Bartlett pears
½ pound Granny Smith apples
½ pound cranberries, stems removed
½ cup currants
3 cups packed light brown sugar

1. Place the garlic, onion, cider vinegar, ½ cup water, the ginger, salt, cinnamon, red pepper flakes, and orange zest in a large heavy saucepan over medium-high heat. Stir well to mix. Bring the mixture to a boil, lower the heat, and cook at a simmer for 15 minutes.

2. While the spice mixture is cooking, core, but do not peel, the pears and apples. Cut into ½-inch dice.

3. Add the diced fruit, cranberries, currants, and brown sugar into the spice mixture, and stir well until the sugar is dissolved. Simmer for about 1 hour, until the mixture has thickened slightly and fruits are tender and glazed. Remove from the heat and let cool to room temperature. The chutney will thicken as it cools. The chutney can be covered and refrigerated for 5 days. Bring to room temperature before serving.

Cranberry Chutney

⅔ cup granulated sugar
1⅓ cups cranberries
4 teaspoons cider vinegar
⅓ cup dark raisins
¼ cup coarsely chopped walnuts
2 teaspoons light brown sugar
¼ teaspoon ground ginger
½ teaspoon chopped garlic

1. Combine ⅔ cup water and the granulated sugar in a heavy 3-quart saucepan over medium-high heat. Stir to dissolve the sugar, then bring to a boil without stirring. Add the cranberries, vinegar, raisins, walnuts, brown sugar, ginger, and garlic. Boil very slowly, stirring occasionally, until fairly thick, about 5 minutes.

2. Allow the chutney to cool to room temperature, then cover and refrigerate. The chutney keeps for 5 days in the refrigerator.

Toasted Pita Triangles

1 6-inch pita bread
Olive oil for brushing the pita

1. Preheat the oven to 350°F.

2. Cut the pita in half horizontally so you get two rounds. Brush each round lightly on both sides with olive oil. Stack the rounds and cut into 8 wedges so you have a total of 16 wedges. Place on a baking sheet and bake until crisp and a light golden color, about 10 minutes. Remove and cool. The pita triangles can be stored in an airtight container for up to 3 days.

NOTE: Rather than a knife, use a pair of sharp scissors to cut the pita.

Toasted Nuts and Seeds

ALMONDS

1. Preheat the oven to 350°F.

2. Spread the almonds—blanched whole, slivered, or sliced—on a rimmed baking sheet. Bake on the center shelf of the oven until golden, 8 to 10 minutes, stirring once or twice. Watch carefully and stir once or twice.

3. Remove from the oven and transfer the nuts to a work surface to cool.

WALNUTS

1. Preheat the oven to 350°F.

2. Spread the walnuts on a rimmed baking sheet. Bake on the center shelf of the oven for about 8 minutes, stirring once or twice. Watch carefully and stir once or twice.

3. Remove from the oven and transfer the nuts to a work surface to cool.

PECANS

1. Preheat the oven to 350°F.

2. Spread the pecans on a rimmed baking sheet. Bake on the center shelf of the oven just until lightly browned, 5 to 8 minutes. Watch carefully and stir once or twice.

3. Remove from the oven and transfer the nuts to a work surface to cool.

PINE NUTS

1. Preheat the oven to 350°F.

2. Spread the pine nuts on a rimmed baking sheet. Bake on the center shelf of the oven until lightly browned, about 5 minutes. Pine nuts toast quickly and burn easily, so watch very carefully.

3. Remove from the oven and transfer the nuts to a work surface to cool.

1. Preheat the oven to 350°F.

2. Spread the sesame seeds on a rimmed baking sheet. Bake on the center shelf of the oven until golden, 10 to 12 minutes, stirring several times. Watch carefully and stir several times.

3. Remove from the oven and transfer the nuts to a work surface to cool.

Roasted Red Peppers

To roast peppers, place them directly on a gas or electric burner or on a baking sheet under the broiler. Roast, turning occasionally until the peppers are blackened and charred on all sides. Wrap the peppers in damp paper towels and put them in a plastic bag and seal the bag. Allow the peppers to steam in the plastic bag for 10 to 15 minutes. Then remove the black charred outside skin from the peppers with a sharp paring knife; you may need to run the peppers under cold water to remove all the charred skin. Using a paring knife, remove seeds and stems. The peppers can be placed in a jar or bowl, covered with olive oil, and then covered and refrigerated up to 3 days. Drain the peppers and pat dry before using.

Menus and Party Planning

As a cooking teacher and food writer, I get frequent requests for help with menu planning. People routinely call me at home, stop me at the market, or even drop me a line to ask for advice about menus, especially party menus. A menu is not only a listing of what will be offered—it is a planning scheme, a creative manipulation of recipe, presentation, and event.

I love the challenge of thinking of new formats for serving food, and as I developed the recipes for this book, I looked forward to writing a section on how to create menus with them. I kept four goals in mind: I always considered the time it would take to prepare each dish and tried to choose appetizers for each type of party that could be prepared ahead, over a period of several days. Next, I looked for variety; for instance, if there were dishes rich in butter or cheese, I balanced those with lighter offerings of vegetables and fruit. Perhaps most important of all, I assessed the taste and texture of each hors d'oeuvre and considered how it would work together with others in a menu. Finally, I tried to keep presentation in mind, so that the dishes would be enticing in both taste and appearance.

You will find here menus for many occasions: celebrations for each season, ideas for holiday entertaining, and thoughts for some unique get-togethers, such as a wine and cheese sampler or a cocktail pizza party.

These are among my favorite menus, but the appetizers in this book should inspire you to create your own special parties as well.

Herb-Garlic Cheese Fondue
(page 195)

Watercress Tartlets
(page 77)

Tempura-Fried Scallions
with Far East Dipping Sauce
(page 134)

Smoked Salmon Cheesecake
with Dill Toasts
(page 241)

Orange-Glazed Pecans
(page 249)

White Wine or Kirs

Baked Salmon
with Lime-Scented Yogurt Sauce
(page 243)

Summer Garden Tomato
and Eggplant Relish
(page 125)

Peaches Wrapped in Prosciutto
and Mint
(page 151)

Pesto Tartlets
(page 64)

Herbed Olives
(page 155)

Red and White Wines

Spring

Much of this colorful menu can be prepared ahead: The fondue and its vegetables, the cheesecake, and the nuts can be completely cooked in advance. The tartlets are best if baked just before serving (the shells can be pre-baked and the filling ready), but, if necessary, they can be baked ahead and reheated with only a slight loss of crispness in the dough. The scallions can be fried beforehand and kept warm in a low oven up to 45 minutes.

I always mound the vegetables for the fondue in a large wicker basket lined with herbs or lemon leaves. The rose-hued cheesecake also looks striking on a bed of lemon leaves.

Summer

The relish, the peaches, and the olives are all make-ahead dishes. The crusts for the tartlets can be pre-baked and the filling readied so that a quick baking is all that is needed before serving, but, if necessary, the tarts can be completely baked ahead and reheated at serving time with only a slight loss of crispness in the crusts. The salmon can be completely assembled ahead, then baked and served either warm or at room temperature.

Fall

For this menu, I serve Curried Apricot Mayonnaise with large cooked shrimp and broccoli florets (blanched for 3 to 4 minutes in lightly salted boiling water and refreshed under cold running water to set their bright green color). The chicken wings, which can be cooked ahead and reheated, look especially festive on a bed of fall yellow and orange maple leaves. The potted cheese, served with grapes and apple wedges in place of bread, and the nuts can be made ahead. The mushroom crostini can also be assembled and baked ahead.

Beaujolais-Glazed Chicken Wings
(page 219)

Four-Star Potted Cheese
(page 191)
with grapes and apples

Curried Apricot Mayonnaise
(page 148)
with shrimp and broccoli florets

Wild Mushroom Crostini
(page 33)

Roasted Parmesan Pecans
(page 255)

Beaujolais and Apple Cider

Winter

The polenta tartlets can be made days ahead and frozen and then defrosted and cooked at serving time. The tomato sauce can be prepared ahead and reheated and the shrimp cooked in advance as well. Garnish the red pepper mousse, which can be made two days ahead, with some Niçoise or Kalamata olives. Have on hand plenty of the garlic almonds, which can be made weeks in advance, since they always disappear quickly!

Cheese-Filled Polenta Tartlets
(page 91)

Roasted Red Pepper Cheese Mousse
(page 189)

Shrimp with Tomato-Curry Sauce
(page 207)

Smoked Garlic Almonds
(page 257)

Wine and Beer

Creole Dipping Sauce
with Green and Wax Beans
(page 136)

Asparagus and Fontina Pizzettes
(page 112)

Melon with Pernod and Mint
(page 152)

Baked Salmon
with Lime-Scented Yogurt Sauce
(page 243)

Corn and Red Pepper Relish
with Spicy Tortilla Chips
(page 127)

Wine and Mineral Water

Sensible Savories: Reduced-Calories Cocktail Party

The list of my friends who are counting calories and/or cholesterol increases with each year that passes, so more and more frequently I am reducing butter and fat in my recipes. Here is a menu of lighter but delicious appetizers that my guests love and never think of as diet cuisine. The Creole sauce and beans, the relish, and the melon can be prepared in advance. The pizzettes, which can be assembled ahead, need only 5 minutes baking time. The salmon can be served at room temperature or warm.

Skewered Vegetables Baked
with Rosemary
(page 159)

Shiitake Mushroom Pâté
(page 158)

Oriental Carrots
(page 162)

Potato and Chive Pizzettes
(page 107)

Roasted Red Pepper Sauce
with Summer Green Beans
(page 132)

Wine and Mineral Water

Simply Vegetarian

Among my guests, there seems to be a growing number of vegetarians. This menu includes recipes made with no meat, poultry, or fish. Substitute margarine and vegetable stock for the butter and chicken stock in the mushroom pâté. The Roasted Pepper Sauce is made with mayonnaise and contains eggs, but if eggs are taboo for your guests, substitute the Roasted Red Pepper Salsa (page 129) made with red peppers, oil, and herbs. The pâté, the carrots, and the red pepper sauce or the salsa can be made ahead. The vegetable skewers and the pizzettes can be assembled in advance and baked at serving time.

Appetizers That Travel Well

Many of my cooking students belong to gourmet clubs and often ask for recipes that will travel well. Each appetizer in the following menu can be prepared ahead in your own kitchen and then packed and carried to another location. Use fresh pineapple cubes (about 1- to 1½-inch chunks) from two pineapples in place of the melon in the Melon with Pernod and Mint recipe. Mound the cubes in scooped-out pineapple shells and garnish with mint at serving time. The chicken wings can be reheated or served at room temperature. Spread the salsa on the Mexican Cheesecake just before serving. The delicious nuts are easy to pack.

Hors d'Oeuvres Provençal

Over the past few years, I have spent summer vacations in the south of France and have fallen in love with the breathtaking landscapes, the ever-present dappled sunlight, and, most especially, the sensual food. Here is a menu redolent of the tastes of this special part of the world. The melon, the fillet and its relish, the red pepper sauce, and the beans can all be made ahead. The palmiers and the chèvre with the tomatoes can be assembled completely ahead and need only to be baked at serving time.

Mexican Cheesecake
(*page 239*)

Roasted Red Pepper Sauce
with Summer Green Beans
(*page 132*)

Pineapple with Pernod and Mint
in Pineapple Shells
(*page 152*)

Lime-Marmalade-Glazed Chicken
Wings
(*page 220*)

Smoked Garlic Almonds
(*page 257*)

Wine or Beer

Melon with Pernod and Mint
(*page 152*)

Provençal Palmiers
(*page 59*)

Warm Chèvre with Plum Tomatoes
(*page 183*)

Roast Fillet of Beef
with a Mediterranean Relish
(*page 225*)

Roasted Red Pepper Sauce
with Summer Green Beans
(*page 132*)

Côtes de Provence, Bandol,
and Pastis

Corn and Red Pepper Relish
with Spicy Tortilla Chips
(*page 127*)

Baked Ham
with Honey-Mustard Mayonnaise
(*page 230*)
and sourdough or rye bread

Beaujolais-Glazed Chicken Wings
(*page 218*)

Four-Star Potted Cheese
(*page 191*)
with grapes and apples

Beer, Wine, and Cider

~

Baker's Brie
(*page 173*)

Herb-Garlic Cheese Fondue
(*page 195*)
with fresh vegetables

Chèvre Croutons Mélange
(*page 187*)

Camembert Walnut Wafers
(*page 197*)

Sherried Cheddar Terrine
(*page 192*)

Full-Bodied Red Wines

~

A Winning Tailgate

I grew up in the South, with parents who loved to tailgate before football games in the Southeastern Conference, and I have spent a good deal of my life in the Midwest, where pregame festivities are a fall weekend ritual before Big Ten matches. This menu will be a hit no matter where you live! The Corn and Red Pepper Relish, the potted cheese (served with grapes and apples), and the honey-mustard mayonnaise can be prepared ahead. Buy a sliced baked ham and good sourdough or rye bread and serve with a bowl of the mayonnaise. The chicken wings can be baked ahead and served at room temperature.

A Wine and Cheese Sampler

Cheeses prepared in special ways and offered with robust red wines make wonderful hors d'oeuvres for a party. The Sherried Cheddar Terrine can be made two days ahead; since there are walnuts in the Camembert wafers, substitute whole unblanched toasted almonds for the walnuts in the terrine. The dough for the Camembert wafers can be made ahead, frozen, and baked when needed. The baked Brie and the fondue, with accompanying fresh vegetables, can be prepared ahead and the Brie and fondue heated when needed. The chèvre croutons can be assembled an hour ahead.

The Pizza Party

This inventive and imaginative party menu features exclusively bite-sized pizzas, or pizzettes. I use the same pizza dough recipe for all the crusts and prepare a variety of toppings. The pizza rounds can be cut out and prebaked, then refrigerated or frozen, and many of the toppings can be made at least a day ahead. Since the pizzettes can be assembled in advance and take only 5 minutes to bake, you can easily keep hot batches coming from the oven during a party.

Potato and Chive Pizzettes
(page 107)

Spicy Tomato and Brie Pizzettes
(page 100)

Roasted Red Pepper
and Shrimp Pizzettes
(page 111)

Smoked Cheddar
and Onion Pizzettes
(page 115)

Asparagus and Fontina Pizzettes
(page 112)

Chianti and Pinot Grigio

The Casual Get-Together

The dishes in this menu are earthy and unpretentious—the kind I love to serve when friends come over to see a special game on TV or to watch election night returns. The mussels and their garnishes can be prepared well in advance. The roasted red pepper mousse and the olives are two more make-ahead appetizers. The delicious Santa Monica Pizzas can be assembled ahead and need only to be baked a short time before serving.

Santa Monica Pizzas
(page 119)

Roasted Red Pepper Cheese Mousse
(page 189)

Mussels with a Trio of Garnishes
(page 213)

Herbed Olives
(page 155)

Wine and Beer

Chèvre, Hazelnut, and Mint Tartlets
(page 72)

Toasted Sesame Mayonnaise
with Asparagus Spears
(page 133)

French Bread Stuffed
with Smoked Salmon and Leeks
(page 203)

Shiitake Mushroom Pâté
(page 158)
with Belgian endive leaves

Caramel-Glazed Grapes
(page 153)
and/or Lemon-Spiced Pecans
(page 253)

Champagne or a Full Bar

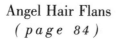

Angel Hair Flans
(page 84)

Herbed Chèvre Heart
with Roasted Red Peppers
(page 185)

Prosciutto-Wrapped Scallops
(page 209)

Creole Dipping Sauce
(page 136)
with winter crudités

Almond Coffee Walnuts
(page 251)

Champagne

A Sophisticated Soirée

There are always special occasions when a very chic, elegant fête is expected. This is one of my favorite menus for such an event. The mushroom pâté can be prepared a day ahead, as can the sesame mayonnaise and the asparagus. The French bread stuffed with smoked salmon can be assembled several hours ahead and heated when needed. The tartlets, always best assembled and baked at serving time (the tart shells can be prebaked and the filling readied ahead), can be baked ahead and reheated if necessary. The pecans can be made days ahead, and the caramel grapes are a special treat to be made the day of the party if time permits.

A Valentine Fête

A party given on Valentine's Day can be a very special event. The following menu is one that works particularly well. The Almond Coffee Walnuts, which are dipped in chocolate, can be prepared a week ahead, the flans and the Creole dip 3 days ahead, and the chèvre heart 2 days in advance. The scallops can be assembled a few hours before they are broiled. For winter crudités for the Creole dip, I often use julienned carrots, red peppers, and fennel, and lightly blanched broccoli and cauliflower florets.

July Fourth Picnic

This is an al fresco menu I like to serve for large Fourth of July celebrations. The pâté, summer relish, and red pepper salsa can be made a day ahead. The turnovers can be prepared in advance, frozen, and then defrosted when needed and the pecans roasted weeks ahead. The ribs can be precooked the day before and quickly baked when needed; they are good hot or at room temperature. Serve a bowl of fresh strawberries and blueberries garnished with mint along with the pecans as a sweet finale.

Avocado Pâté with Parsley
and Pistachios
(*page 156*)

Chicken Barbecue Turnovers
(*page 43*)

Roasted Red Pepper Salsa
(*page 129*)
with Summer Green Beans
(*page 132*)

Honey-Mustard Spareribs
(*page 233*)

Summer Garden Tomato and
Eggplant Relish
(*page 125*)

Orange-Glazed Pecans
(*page 249*)
and fresh fruit

Beer and Wine

Thanksgiving Open House

This is a menu that is manageable even after you have cooked a big Thanksgiving meal, perfect for a party on Friday or Saturday night of the long holiday weekend. The Cranberry Chutney can be made several days ahead; I make a large amount for Thanksgiving dinner and save some for the Brie. The curried mayonnaise can be put together two days in advance, and you can roast extra turkey on Thanksgiving or buy good smoked turkey. The Oriental Carrots look striking on a bed of Napa cabbage leaves. The walnuts can be made several weeks ahead. The biscuit dough is quickly mixed, and the biscuits need only a few minutes to bake.

Baked Brie with Cranberry Chutney
(*page 176*)

Curried Apricot Mayonnaise
with Sliced Roast or Smoked Turkey
and Grapes
(*page 148*)
and Buttermilk Biscuits
(*page 20*)

Oriental Carrots
(*page 162*)
on Napa cabbage leaves

Honeyed Walnuts
(*page 250*)

Full Bar

Cherry Tomatoes with
Toasted Pine Nut Pesto
(*p a g e   2 6 2*)

Mushroom and Leek Pinwheels
(*p a g e   5 6*)

Baked Ham with Three Condiments
(*p a g e   2 3 0*)

Roast Fillet of Beef
with Roquefort Sauce
(*p a g e   2 2 7*)

Roasted Red Pepper Salsa
(*p a g e   1 2 9*)
with Summer Green Beans
(*p a g e   1 3 2*)

Orange-Glazed Pecans
(*p a g e   2 4 9*)

Full Bar and/or Champagne

Holiday Buffet

Although there is no more hectic time of the year than the weeks preceding the winter holidays, it is my favorite season to entertain. Many of the dishes in this menu can be completely or partially prepared ahead so that everything is not left to the last minute. The pinwheels can be assembled ahead and frozen, then baked when needed. The pecans can be roasted several weeks ahead. The pesto can be prepared in advance and frozen. The beef can be cooked the day before, as can the red pepper salsa and the blanched green beans. I buy sliced baked ham and make the condiments to serve with it ahead.

Smoked Salmon Cheesecake
with Dill Toasts
(*p a g e   2 4 1*)

Shiitake Mushroom Pâté
(*p a g e   1 5 8*)
with blanched snowpeas and Belgian
endive leaves

Cheddar and Scallion Turnovers
(*p a g e   4 7*)

Confetti Angel Hair Flans
(*p a g e   8 6*)

Moroccan Almonds
(*p a g e   2 5 2*)

Champagne

New Year's Eve Celebration

We traditionally welcome in the New Year at our house with a small group of good friends and always try to serve a special menu. This is one of our favorites. The nuts can be made several weeks ahead, the flans and the cheesecake several days in advance, the cheese squares prepared and frozen, and the pâté made a day ahead.

Mail Order Sources

Kendall Brook ✓
Ducktrap Fish Farms
Lincolnville, ME 04849
207-763-3960
High-quality, vacuum-packed smoked trout and smoked salmon

Boyajian
33 Belmont Street
Cambridge, MA 02138
617-876-6677
Smoked seafood

American Spoon Foods
P.O. Box 566 or
1688 Clarion Avenue
Petoskey, MI 49770
1-800-222-5886
Dried cherries and other fruits as well as preserves

L'Esprit de Campagne ✓
P.O. Box 3130
Winchester, VA 22601
703-722-4224
Dried sour cherries

Index

cherry, stuffed with smoked seafood, 212

cherry, with summer stuffing, 167–168

corn muffins du Midi, 25

crostini with bacon and basil, 29–30

and cucumber salsa, 214

-curry sauce, with shrimp, 207

dill salsa with toasted pita triangles, 131

and eggplant galette, 121–122

fresh, and polenta tarts, 88–89

and Italian sausage tartlets, 68–69

and leek crostini, 35

and olive pizzettes, 105–106

and pine nut topping, 188

Provençal palmiers, 59–60

salsa, 239–240

Santa Fe scones with smoked chicken and, 17–18

Santa Monica pizzas, 119

sauce, quick, 261

-sausage ragoût with polenta rounds, 235–236

skewered vegetables baked with rosemary, 159–160

Sonoran pizzas, 117–118

summer garden, and eggplant relish, with pita toasts, 125–126

toast tartlets with chèvre, walnuts and, 90–91

warm chèvre with, 183–184

Toppings, 27, 187–188

bacon-apricot, 188

herb, 187

lemon-pepper, 188

pine nut and tomato, 188

roasted red pepper, 188

Triangles:

asparagus and prosciutto, 54–55

curried beef, 52–53

toasted pita, 267

Turkey, smoked:

buttermilk biscuits with cranberry butter and, 20–21

and grapes, with curried apricot mayonnaise, 148

Turkey with cranberry applesauce, 224

Turnovers, 41–47

Black Forest ham and spiced cranberry, 45–46

Cheddar and scallion, 47

chicken barbecue, 43–44

Veal balls, lemon-dill, 228–229

Vegetable(s):

acorn squash dip, 139–140

appetizers, 149, 158–170

artichoke leaves with Brie, 170

carrots, Oriental, 162

corn and red pepper relish, 127–128

Creole dipping sauce with green and wax beans, 136–137

cucumber tomato salsa, 214

eggplant and tomato galette, 121–122

endive and ham tartlets, 81–82

leek and smoked Cheddar flans, 87–88

onion, red, and Brie pizzettes, 114

onion and smoked Cheddar pizzettes, 115–116

onion tartlets, 66–67

potato and chive pizzettes, 107–108

potatoes with Neal's dill dip, 138

primavera pizzettes, 104

skewered, baked with rosemary, 159–160

skewered new potatoes and red onions, 161

spinach and sausage torta, 245–246

spinach–blue cheese mini-calzones, 48–49

tempura-fried scallions with Far East dipping sauce, 134–135

see also Asparagus; Mushroom; Red pepper, roasted; Tomato

Wafers:

Camembert walnut, 197

smoked Cheddar, 198

Walnut(s):

almond coffee, 251

baked Brie with plums and, 174–175

blue-cheese-stuffed, 258

brandied Brie with dried sour cherries and, 177–178

and Camembert phyllo bundles, 51

Camembert wafers, 197

galette, 120

honeyed, 250

mushrooms stuffed with St. André and, 165

scones with blue cheese, 19

sherried Cheddar terrine, 192–193

and smoked trout pâté, 211

toast tartlets with chèvre, tomatoes and, 90–91

Watercress tartlets, 77–78

Wild mushroom crostini, 33–34

Yogurt:

cheese, lemon, 205

cheese, low-fat, 265

sauce, lime-scented, 243–244